Archibald Lamont

Bright Celestials: The Chinaman at home and abroad

Archibald Lamont

Bright Celestials: The Chinaman at home and abroad

ISBN/EAN: 9783337198114

Printed in Europe, USA, Canada, Australia, Japan

Cover: Foto ©Andreas Hilbeck / pixelio.de

More available books at **www.hansebooks.com**

BRIGHT CELESTIALS

BRIGHT CELESTIALS

The Chinaman at Home and Abroad

BY

JOHN COMING CHINAMAN

LONDON
T. FISHER UNWIN
PATERNOSTER SQUARE
1894

PREFACE.

'BRIGHT CELESTIALS' is a story of Chinese life at Home and Abroad in relation to Christian Missionary enterprise. Its unique characteristic is that it is written from the Chinese point of view. Such questions as those of Opium, Chinese Emigration, Secret Societies, the Social Evil, the Christian Missionary problem and Chinese anti-foreign feeling are dealt with in relation to Western influence and Christianity.

For the facts, in addition to those observed by myself in the East, I am indebted to my Chinese friend, Mr. Teck Soon of Singapore. To that gentleman are also largely due the idea and structure of the story; and in thanking him for his invaluable help, I take the opportunity of gladly acknowledging his co-operation.

My thanks are also due to my friend, Mr. James A. Melville, of Edinburgh, for literary advice and aid in preparing the manuscript for the press.

'Bright Celestials' is intended as a tribute to the claims of Old and New China on Western thought and sympathy. If it helps to create an interest in Chinese matters among the British reading public, it will have fulfilled the chief purpose of its production.

JOHN COMING CHINAMAN.

CONTENTS.

CHAP.		PAGE
I.	BLACK ROCK	1
II.	THE WINE PARTY	8
III.	A PERIOD OF REFLECTION	22
IV.	FROM OLD TO NEW	32
V.	THE GRADUATE'S FUNERAL	43
VI.	THE COACHING DAYS	54
VII.	EVEN WAY	69
VIII.	SALISBURY	78
IX.	ARRESTED DEVELOPMENT	90
X.	TURNABOUT	106
XI.	TRANSITION	115
XII.	THE COOLY	129

CHAP.		PAGE
XIII.	PROTECTION	143
XIV.	HOME RULE	155
XV.	THE SOCIETY MAN	172
XVI.	FROM NEW TO OLD	186
XVII.	THE ODD CHRISTIAN	204
XVIII.	THE SOCIAL CANCER	218
XIX.	REDEMPTION	236
XX.	RESPONSIBILITY	254
XXI.	HOMEWARD BOUND	274
XXII.	THE OLD AND NEW COVENANT	284

BRIGHT CELESTIALS.

CHAPTER I.

BLACK ROCK.

THE China Sea—the sea of sickness and typhoons—lashes lustily the shores of Fokien province. Rocky promontories offer a grand and effectual resistance to the incessant attacks of dashing foam, and lend protection to the creeks and bays in which Fokien Celestials prosecute their calling as fishermen. The Fokiens are the plodding Saxons, in contrast with the Cantonese, who are the adventurous Danes of Southern China. Pirates also there are among the Fokiens; but piracy is the distinctive boast of the Cantonese. And although not so foolhardy as their brethren of Canton province, the Fokien people are equally brave, yet with a method in their bravery. They are the most successful of all the Chinese emigrants. They are a people who do and dare, and their watchwords are 'Order and Enterprise.'

At the head of one of the Fokien bays is a serpentine creek, and at the head of this creek stands the town of Black Rock. Hither the reader's eye must turn meanwhile, for here begins our tale.

It is a low-roofed house — none of your perpendicular tenements such as abound in the cities and towns of the Western world. It is a literal *house*, modest as to dimensions and inhabitants, and situated at the south-east side—people call it the back part—of the town.

Close by the entrance is a narrow pathway, the parading place, for generations past, of hardy sons of toil, whose industry, if you have respect to the burdens on their shoulders, would gladden the heart of a Carlyle. From earliest dawn till long after sunset there hurry along this narrow pathway Celestial citizens, whose title to such citizenship would seem to consist in the amount of diligence with which each burden-bearer, his two loads on a pole, constantly, and as if unconscious of the calculation, performs the double task of keeping these loads in even poise and himself in motion.

The typical one-man-between-two-loads has scarcely passed when not a transformation but a transposition scene arrests attention. The phenomenon is one-load-between-two-men. The bearers labour beneath the burden, as their bent forms and half-running speed clearly show. But their hearts are stout and brave; and they pass on—not however before there is time to discern that the freight is as bulky as it is heavy. It is a stout black-coloured live pig, of a size one often reads about, but seldom sees. It is enshrouded in a basket—if such description be permitted to the few strips of wicker-work interwoven as a single piece of mechanism whereby the front and hind legs of the prisoner pass down into a liberty that is vitiated by the hard and fast bondage of the rest of its body. This contrivance is indeed more cage than basket — the whole pig is visible to the naked eye of the beholder. In such glaring suspense the living freight quickly passes in music out of sight.

That sound has scarcely died away when onward comes a second pig, here also borne aloft by two men on the orthodox bamboo pole, but—alas for the inequalities of fortune in the lives of pigs as in the lives of men!— unlike his more fortunate predecessor, he is without the luxury of a merciful prison-basket. With head and feet turned upwards towards the skies; with legs fore and aft tightly bound by the rope that hangs from the bamboo; with back dangerously near to brushing the ground beneath him, he is borne along, quarrelling ineffectually with the inconvenience of his position, but so far as we know, thinking little of the early destiny of death that is to reward all his sufferings.

Other pigs also, including sows, with their numerous brood careering at will in the road and out of it, await in blissful ignorance their respective times of trial, imprisonment, and death—an order of things that will continue so long as man fulfils the dual condition of ruling creation and eating pork.

The neglected Chinese dog deserves notice here Like the pig, he has his day, if he has never had his regular meal. Chinese virtue is exercised otherwise than in feeding dogs. Hence it is that this pathway is a realistic Plato's cave, resembling that classic spot most of all in the picture of this forlorn dog that is more shadow than substance. His ugly sores and scabs, which serve as poor substitutes for decent hair, place him at a disadvantage when compared with the least lucky English dog, whose coat of hair the worst fortune usually leaves intact. Such are the conspicuous blemishes of the Chinese dog, more sinned against than sinning. A slim framework of bones, with nose turned downwards — his tyrant Chinese master dares not deprive him of this direction of his quest which is his sole prerogative—he seeks a morsel, and more if that were possible, in the casual rubbish-heap, thereby informing the world that he too has a right to live.

There are other and more eminent actors and sufferers in the scene of this pathway. A woman trying to walk as best she can by means of and yet despite her feet—crushed by a relentless custom that claims to confer on the Chinawoman the double benefit of beautifying her person, and checkmating her inborn and perverse tendency to gad after the men— passes along, leaning on her staff. Close behind her in single file are her two little ones, children in their years and stature, but old men in their faces. The supreme worth and dignity of humankind warrant much more than a casual look at this woman and her boys. But Browning has wisely said, or in words to the same effect :—

> 'Leave now for pigs and dogs
> Man has for ever.'

Upward progress in the town of Black Rock, the fountain-head of this story, is made by a passage over dead men's bones. On the other side of the pathway is a graveyard. The patch of ground is a gentle slope, dotted frequently with the tombs of ancestors recent and remote, tombs of earth and stone, which, shaped in horse-shoe Omega fashion and neatly ornamented, speak to Celestials of Doom. As to the mystery of Death—Confucius would call it the mystery of Life—whether Death ends all, or means to sleep, perchance to dream, the materialism of China has not yet reached its scientific stage in its treatment of the theme. The 'superstitions' of China, like those of the remaining two-thirds of humanity, die hard. Hence these tombs, the marks of sedulous attention paid by each successive generation to its dead. These are the unutterable groanings, too deep for a nation's choicest words or time-honoured institutions. They act the part of Banquo's ghost, stepping in betimes to mock and irritate the self-styled scientist, who, poor fool, imagines that he has solved all mystery when he has repeated his creed of dissolution, and reduced mankind to dust and ashes. The filial Chinaman, mourning for his fathers, like Rachel for her children, refuses to be comforted.

Running through these haunts of dead men, to meet at a well on the rough roadside, is a stream of living water, called by a truth-loving community 'Corpses' Juice Well,' known for several generations past to be the best drinking water in the town. It is praised for the health-giving qualities which it possesses as a remedy for the opium-smoking disease.

Near to this well—streaming from it—are the heroes of the Flowery Land. Here meet together the dying-living and the living-dead.

It is the afternoon of a day in the mid-autumn of the year 1867. Seated at the table of Lin Ming Kuang, Literary Graduate, is a company of representative men, worthy citizens of Black Rock. They take a keen interest in local affairs, including the viands on the table. But their conversation shows that they are no less interested in the wider concerns of their lives as Celestials and as men.

The women of the household are not in this scene. They are behind it. They prepare the dishes for this festival which mine host, the graduate, has commanded should be held to-day. The time-honoured custom of a mid-autumn festival adds strength and dignity to the injunctions of the head of the family, whose word in well-regulated Chinese families excites the envy of Western husbands, since it is absolute law.

Although the company of invited guests is not a large one, the women behind are kept busy. Victuals of rice, pork, fowl, frogs (which a sprinkling of pepper greatly improves), sea-slugs, and other dainties, dressed up in different bowls, hospitably overladen, and cone-shaped as the degree of solidity will permit, are being brought from behind by men-servants for the guests in the front room. In this way is brought to its triumphant stage the work of these industrious women who remain in the back part of the house, their privileged and peculiar place. And when at intervals a lull takes place in the conversations of Ming Kuang and his guests, the subdued sound of voices behind is quite audible. The hostess has her own little group of female guests, helping her to execute the special tasks of the day on behalf of the lords of creation in front.

Such a hard and fast barrier as that which exists between the sexes appertains to the Chinese in common with other Oriental races. Chinese propriety demands that woman should be kept out of sight. Parliament, platform, and pulpit are *a fortiori* out of the question in

China. On our side are the Western Societies for the promulgation of Woman's Rights, on their side the Chinese rigorous restrictions on women: these are the two opposite extremities of the rope in the world' social tug-of-war.

CHAPTER II.

THE WINE PARTY.

OUR host, Lin Ming Kuang, is a scholar—according to the Chinese style of reckoning—a graduate of the first degree. He is between forty and fifty years of age, of middle height, and—if he may be described after the fashion of a detective proclamation—with the small beginnings of a whisker. His bearing is dignified beyond the average dignity of a Chinaman, and, with deliberation be it said, beyond the average dignity of a graduate. Propriety in actions, which means dignity in attitude, is the ideal quality of the Chinese people; and where is such a quality to be found if it be not found in their scholars? Our host is the typical embodiment of what ought to be expected of a Chinese scholar. He is the quintessence of those excellences that cast a halo round every educated Chinaman in the eyes of his fellow-countrymen. But, like Socrates, Ming Kuang is not prepossessing in appearance, although his large, penetrative eye redeems him from ugliness. The unusually large upper lip that seems to dispute the existence of the lower one, the long, straight, sharp, angular nose sloping normally downwards, and the large massive forehead, are some of the more pronounced features of a face which distinctly bears the marks of decision of character. But the "pale cast of thought" modifying these marks of decision is necessary to Ming Kuang's keenly chiselled face. Unless he is encouraging his polite guests to lift their chop-sticks or beckoning them to drink wine, his look is one of sadness bordering on gloom. The best Western parallel is the Agnostic, who, so often susceptible to fits of mental depression, due rather to temperament than to philosophy, has theoretically satisfied himself, having weighed all his earlier thoughts and hopes of God and heaven in the balance of his wisdom, that these have been found wanting. Not different is the impression given by the features of Ming Kuang seated at the head of his table.

The guests at this afternoon wine-party—for such is the festival technically called—are four in number. These four, with their host and croupier (one of Ming Kuang's relatives), make the modest number of six at table. On the left side of the host (the side of honour) are the two brothers Wu, both graduates, but much younger than their host, who has begun to be venerable in their eyes. Both these young men have already studied hard, and yet, as they themselves acknowledge —though only to such a man as their friend Ming Kuang—they have still much to learn. Opposite, at the right side of the host, are the other two guests. The one next to the host is Pun Kwi, a man well advanced in middle life. He is a retired merchant, who has spent more than twenty years in Canton, and who has just returned to spend the remainder of his days in his native town of Black Rock. The fourth guest is the Head-man of one of the wards of Black Rock. He acts as the champion of his fellow-townsmen in presenting their rights and demands to the civil and military authorities. Like his host and the other guests, he too is 'had in reputation' among the people. His position as Head-man has heavy responsibility as well as honour. He is one of the 'commoners' in the complicated Chinese governmental system. And according to the measure of trust which his fellow-townsmen repose in him as the mouthpiece of Democracy, he is powerful with the Emperor's Executive Government, including the district mandarin. And the trust of his constituency this Head-man enjoys to no mean extent. Freighted, however, as he is with the heavy duties and responsibilities of his ward, he can drink wine and be sociable like his neighbours. That a Chinaman who is a ruler takes time to dine is a lesson, moreover, which foreign ambassadors in Chinese territory have learned much to their profit. According to report, ambassadors from the West, untutored in this important respect, have come to the East and been made wise. Diligent in clinging to the truth that 'a little learning is a dangerous thing,' these apt pupils have so thoroughly excelled their tutors as to make dining their sole occupation. It is a case of Specialisation of Function. This age is an age of concentration, without which no one can expect to rise either to fortune or to fame.

The company are already well through their meal. First, the croupier served the wine in small cups for the guests, then for the host, and lastly for himself, and between the various dishes he has repeated the task. From the successive bowls brought by the servant and placed by the croupier in the centre of the table, the guests have taken morsels by means of their chopsticks, the host encouraging them from time to time.

The usual almond tea has been served. The indispensable bowl of hot water has been placed on the table, and here each one for himself washes his chop-sticks and spoon. Then at a given signal it is announced that drinking wine must cease. It is not that the host grudges the wine, for he encourages his guests to make the best use of their short time. 'We shall now fill our cups and eat our rice'—in this way he warns himself and his guests that their 'revels now are ended.'

The hard and fast Chinese custom forbids wine after rice. To violate this custom in ordinary instances is a mark of gross impiety. It would mean for a Chinaman disloyalty to his filial obligations. As a sign that the last dish has come, duck boiled in salted cabbage has been placed on the table, surrounded by the usual smaller dishes of salted onion, cucumber and pork, accompaniments for the rice. The conservative salt of Chinese custom (to say nothing of the particular quality of Chinese wine) does much to preserve this people from drunkenness, which accordingly is not and cannot be their national vice.

So far, the conversation has been measured and general. But now the spirit of reserve that prevailed when they first sat down to table loses its spell over them, and they become more lively.

'That foreign teacher came to our town yesterday, and is still here, I suppose,' remarked the elder brother Wu. There was nothing but politeness in the statement itself; but the tone in which it was uttered did not bespeak Scholar Wu's deep affection for the foreigner.

'Which of the foreign teachers do you mean?' asked Ming Kuang, whose interest was excited by the remark. 'I can recognise three of them now,' he continued, not waiting for an answer to his question. 'One of them has thick whiskers, and is always reading or writing while he sits in his chair. He takes notes of everything that is said to him. A poor shopkeeper not far from here, a worshipper of God in the foreigners' Ceremony-Hall, told me that when that teacher gets out of his chair at the end of his journey, before eating rice, he copies out from his smaller book, which he carries in his hand, all that he has noted down in the interval. The book into which he copies all his notes is a very large one, and is encased in a tin box made for the purpose. He is very laborious. No one wishing to be high in our august Emperor's court could work harder. Then, again, I can recognise two other foreign teachers, who come this way at intervals. The last time they were here they were together. The one is tall and quiet; the other is a stout man who speaks to everybody. From what I have seen and heard of him, I believe he is deeply versed in our manners and customs. These two men are younger than the teacher who carries the big book. I should like to know if the foreign teacher here just now is one of these, Wu, and if so, which of them he is.'

'I think it must be the man with the book,' replied Wu. 'He seemed to me to be a middle-aged man, although it was difficult for me to see much of him. A scholar is compelled to starve his curiosity when he is in the midst of a crowd. But these barbarians seem all of them to be very like each other. Old and young alike have whiskers. It is very strange. There can be no reverence or decorum among such a set of people.'

At this point the Head-man broke in on the conversation to say that the foreigner who had just come to

Black Rock was the same one that a year ago had been stoned and otherwise ill-treated by their fellow-townsmen for preaching foreign doctrine. It was, of course, only a few fellows of the baser sort who had used such violence towards the foreigner; but the rest of the community did not think it right to prevent such violence, as all alike were suspicious of the foreigner's doctrine. It sounded well enough, but it was clear that it tended to make men despise their ancestral tablets.

'O yes, I remember,' said Ming Kuang. 'He is the most elderly of the foreign teachers. It was he whom the people stoned, and he is the man who carries the big book. My opinion is that the people ought not to have stoned him until they first heard clearly what he had to say on behalf of himself and his doctrine. He is very courageous to come back again to our place. I am told that if he did not come back again he would consider himself unfaithful to his duty.'

'Well, teacher,' said the Head-man, 'I do not think that even the least polite of our people will ill-treat him again. Yesterday, the district warder, who is responsible to me for burials, showed to me by clear proof that that foreign teacher's heart is good.'

'Why?' sceptically asked the elder Wu.

'Yes,' ventured the younger Wu, who had remained silent till now. 'It is not easy for us to believe that any foreigner's heart can be good. These red-haired foreigners have already disturbed the peace of our Empire in many ways.'

'As to what red-haired foreigners usually are,' rejoined the Head-man, 'I dare not with my slight words speak emphatically in the presence of such distinguished scholars as are here.'

'You unduly honour us,' interjected the host. 'Give us the benefit of your weighty opinion, good friend. What do you think of the foreign teacher?'

'Venerable teacher, I shall tell you simply what I know, and you can do the thinking,' responded the Head-man. 'Well, the district warder but a few hours ago told me that a wayside traveller, an opium-devil, whose relatives live far away from this town, became seriously ill last night at an inn and died. The inn is close to the foreigners' Ceremony Hall. Not knowing what to do with the corpse, the innkeeper got it removed out to one of those tablet shrines for people without posterity, leaving it lying on the top of some straw there. That place is just opposite to the room occupied by the foreign teacher. This morning the foreign teacher's heart was moved to pity at the sight of the corpse; and sending for the warder, requested him to bury the corpse, promising at the same time to pay for the coffin and the expenses of burial. The expenses, amounting to three dollars three hundred cash, the foreigner has duly paid, showing by such an act that his heart is well disposed, and that he deserves happiness.'

'That sounds well, good friend,' said the elder Wu, still in a suspicious vein. 'But all foreigners have an eye to business. In this way he tries to avoid another stoning, that he may thus get a free hand to propagate his harmful teaching.'

'Teacher Wu is suspicious of even the best acts of foreigners,' slowly remarked the host, with a quiet, deliberate smile. 'My worthy friend Kwi, who has spent so many years at Canton, where foreigners abound, can speak weighty words on this subject.'

'Venerable teacher,' replied the merchant, 'I am unworthy of such an honour as that of giving my unimportant opinion. But such as it is I give it. To do the foreigners justice, they are very exact and proper in their commercial transactions with people. They don't seem to think it desirable, however, to make merit. Like merchants among ourselves, of course, they make all the money they can. But their words are always straight, and they fulfil their promises.'

'While you were in Canton, Kwi,' asked the host, 'did you hear the foreigner preach the doctrine just as the teacher does who is here in Black Rock just now?"

'Yes, once or twice. But I never went very near the spot where the preacher stood.'

'What is your opinion of the foreigner's doctrine?' asked Ming Kuang, following up his previous question.

'Alas! teacher, my words are slight. I think that their doctrine is good. They tell us to reverence and obey our parents; and they further tell us to reverence and obey the Heavenly Father. This latter doctrine is, however, not very plain to me.'

'Ay, good friend, that's it,' interrupted the elder Wu. 'And because it is not plain you don't know how it leads those who follow it into treacherous snares.'

'I could not help noticing,' continued Pun Kwi, 'that the many foreigners in Canton City despise the red-haired teacher, who seems to be of the same nation and language as themselves. There is little or no friendship between the foreign teacher and the other foreigners whose work it is to trade.'

'Do you think that there can be two sets of foreigners?' asked the younger Wu.

'That must be so, I think,' responded Pun Kwi.

'I venture to think,' said Ming Kuang, as a judge would sum up evidence, 'that this foreign teacher who carries the big book is not ignorant of what our ancient sages have taught us. One of our own townsmen, who professes belief in the foreigners' teaching, told me, however, that what we have learned from our sages is not enough, and that the Supreme Being has sent foreigners here to teach us further. "That we must be saved," is what the foreigner strongly emphasises. I have asked the friend of the foreigners what is meant by being "saved," and the answer I have invariably received is that to be saved means to get into heaven after death. This of course sounds pleasant enough. But what astonishes me is that a scholarly man like that foreign teacher with the big book should not only believe this himself, but also be so anxious as he seems to teach our countrymen the same thing.'

'After what our venerable host has said about the foreign teacher's being a scholar,' said the elder Wu, 'I dare not argue on the point of that foreign teacher's capabilities. But I should point out to my good friends here that the doctrine of Buddha, which came from India to China many centuries ago, is believed by the common people among us to this day. But we who have studied our sages and exercised our minds know quite well that what Buddha has taught us about happiness after death and the tortures of hell is not worthy of our serious thought.'

'It is the worship of Jesus Christ that the foreigners proclaim in these parts,' said the Head-man.

'Yes, it is very mysterious,' said the host. 'These men seem to vary at times between the worship of Jesus Christ and the worship of the Supreme Being.

That friend of the foreigner to whom I have already alluded told me the other day that Jesus Christ who lived in this world two thousand years ago was the Son of the Supreme Being, and that He rose from the dead, and is living now. That is rather a heavy demand to make on one's belief, is it not?'

'If we cannot believe it, venerable teacher,' said the elder Wu, 'we must conclude that it is not true.'

'To come to such a conclusion seems, in a way, right enough,' replied the host. 'But this foreign teacher seems to know all that we know, and more. He speaks very boldly about men's bad hearts and wrong actions, and about their need for repentance and reformation. And he speaks about a time of judgment after death. That he can speak so boldly is a great mystery to me.'

Readers not knowing the language of which the foregoing is a modified translation may congratulate themselves. The criticisms passed upon all foreigners alike by these Celestials were cruelly candid and unreserved. The merciful summary here given of the remarks of Lin Ming Kuang and his guests establishes it as an axiom that the Chinese dinner does not overshadow all other topics. It is very remarkable but quite accountable. Things Chinese are always arranged in inverse order.

Tea has already been served. The large ornamented pipes and the small cigarettes (an importation by Pun Kwi from Hong-Kong) are now being operated upon by the host and his guests.

By a gradual process the conversations between these friends became more strictly private in their character. The host entered into a quiet talk with the merchant. The subject was one lying close to the Chinese heart. As for Chinese duty, it stretches back into the past in filial piety, and the worship of ancestors. Chinese duty is retrospective. But Chinese happiness is prospective. A Chinaman is possessed of the germs of such happiness when he has the good fortune to have male children.

Both Ming Kuang and Pun Kwi are heads of families only in name. Both are childless. Yet when they sympathise with each other on their luckless fortune, both of them seem equally anxious to speak and to exchange thoughts on this very subject. Despondent people are not usually talkative in the direction in which lies the dark cloud of their despondency. But circumstances alter cases. By peculiar coincidence bright expectations have found a lodgment in the breasts of these two men, and their darkest cloud has for them its silver lining. For, within a few weeks' time, these heads of families hope to be heads of families indeed. They exchange congratulations, each one rejoicing in his neighbour's good prospect.

'Teacher,' said Pun Kwi, 'it is my earnest hope that there may be safely born to you a son who will one day not only bear his father's name, but inherit also his illustrious attainments.'

'I thank you, good friend,' replied Ming Kuang. 'You unduly honour me in referring to my attainments. It is true that men honour me as a scholar. But neither I nor other scholars of much greater distinction than myself can actually come up to the honours and expectations of those who remain outside the portals of learning. If scholarship has made me different from the common people, such a difference merely consists in this—that I know more definitely and feel more sorrowfully than they do that Life's mystery is great. All the same, good friend, your congratulating me on my contemplated happiness is most welcome, and I should be selfish indeed were I to deny equally warm congratulations to you, whose home will, I trust, be brightened before many weeks are over by a son filial and virtuous as yourself.'

'Alas, teacher, not for my virtues, but for my want of them!'

'Say not so, friend Kwi. Were it only for the many kind acts you have done on behalf of your friends, and on behalf of me in particular, praise of your virtues would be well merited.'

'If you refer, teacher, to the recent dispute I had with the oil merchant, and which I entrusted to your wise management to arrange with the mandarin,—well, teacher, you brought it to a successful issue for me, and therefore the honours of the case and my deep gratitude belong to you.'

'You paid me handsomely for my work, Kwi! That matter, and other matters which you entrusted me to manage for you, have helped to keep away poverty from a poor scholar, whose lasting gratitude you have thereby earned.'

With such deferential words these two friends gladdened each other's heart. It was Pun Kwi's turn to speak.

'Teacher, each of us in his own heart hopes for himself that a son will be born to him.'

'That is so, friend.'

'But both of us may be disappointed. We cannot be sure of our sons till they are born.'

'No mistake! Again, Kwi, you speak the truth.'

'Teacher, I now speak with less boldness. Suppose yours is the male and mine the female offspring.'

'Or contrariwise.'

'Exactly so.'

'And for that matter both of us may be destined to misfortune. Neither of us may have male offspring at all.'

'Let us hope against such an unhappy contingency, friend Kwi. You are not usually given to take such a dull view of the future as that. Such a remark as you have made is much more native to my dull humour than to your light-heartedness.'

'Well, teacher, leave the worst view of the case out of account. Assume for a moment that a son and a daughter will be born to us——'

Pun Kwi had scarcely finished stating the hypothesis when the host raised his voice suddenly and with decision.

'Servant,' he shouted, 'bring the wine and cups here.' Teacher Wu, and you other friends, we are going to disturb your conversation; but you will please favour us for a moment with your attention.'

The servant wondered at such an unusual request for wine at that moment, but he silently obeyed. Then, amid the modest protests of Pun Kwi, who, although he had virtually suggested the agreement, kept maintaining that he was in no way worthy to be connected with a family of such distinction as that of the scholar Ming Kuang; and amid the reciprocating protests of Ming Kuang, saying many modest things about himself, these two friends pledged their unborn children to each other. The other guests and the wine were the witnesses to a contract which consisted, first, in the assumption that to the one of these two friends should be born a son and to the other a daughter; and second, in the consequent betrothal, according to unwritten though popular Chinese usage, of the two unborn lovers to each other. The day of ratifying or cancelling the agreement would come when the birth of the second child should take place. The agreement was problematical.

CHAPTER III.

A PERIOD OF REFLECTION.

FOR the graduate and the merchant the weeks of anxiety alternating between hope and fear had passed. To the graduate, the brightest dawn had come when a male child was born to him. A fortnight later, Pun Kwi, although no less a parent than Ming Kuang, had to reconcile himself to his cloudier fortune in the birth of a baby girl. To contrast the parental emotions of these two men would be a work of supererogation. The value of Eve's daughters is sacrificed on the altar of Chinese national instinct. To bear the family name, to preserve the family tablets, and, in fine, to fulfil a parent's hopes, are duties that are held to properly belong to the male child. And although the conservation of the family cannot give woman an unimportant place—this consideration the Chinese themselves do not quite overlook—it is the characteristic backward look of the Chinese people that belittles woman in their eyes. As soon as China looks forward her daughters will become great. But Black Rock, meanwhile, is a part not of ideal but of actual China.

It is now the spring of 1868, about the time of the Feast of Tombs. Ming Kuang sits in his house, with the same thoughtful look as ever—the look that befits him so well. His friend Pun Kwi is with him. Their previous agreement as to their children's betrothal has now been ratified. Naturally enough, this recently established relationship brings these two men often together, and leavens much of their serious talk.

'I had thought,' said Ming Kuang, 'that, my best hopes having been realised in the birth of a son to me, the cup of my happiness should be full, and that I should now be in perfect tranquillity of mind. But whereas I looked for sunshine, the sky is still cloudy. The same old feelings of unrest possess me. The proverb is doubtless true: "Spring weather has a step-mother's face."'

'Had your hopes of having a son not been fulfilled, you would be much less happy than you are,' suggested Pun Kwi.

'That is true; but although a large supply is taken away from the ocean of my unhappiness, an ocean still remains. Believe me, Pun Kwi, I do not now think that ten sons could remove the burden of my mind's dull care. I have come to think that the more we advance in years, the more do we seem to become as children in need of their fathers than as fathers in need of their children.'

Pun Kwi's mind was less speculative than practical. He could not follow the lofty flights of Ming Kuang's imagination.

But it was Ming Kuang's habit oftentimes to speak as though he were speaking to himself. He continued: 'The birth of my son has not brought me what I felt I had a right to expect.'

Pun Kwi looked uneasily at his friend. He declared

that next to the happiness which he himself would have had, had he been fortunate enough to get a son, was the happiness which he had in his daughter's betrothal. And if the solemn agreement which they had just ratified might be still more explicitly drawn out, then he was willing, Pun Kwi declared, to make it more advantageous to Ming Kuang. Ming Kuang laughed. That a merchant should misunderstand metaphysic was not to be wondered at. Ming Kuang, who subsequently tried to explain the true meaning of his reflections, was thinking of no less comprehensive a subject than that of the Chinese Empire—its relation to foreign powers, and the imminent consequences which these relations seemed to Ming Kuang to have for his own personal hopes and aspirations. The mighty heart of all China seemed to beat in this one man's breast.

'My good friend Kwi,' he went on to say, 'it is a matter of considerable doubt whether we shall live to see our children, having passed through the trials and ailments of childhood, reach marriageable age. And even if we are spared to witness that time, we may be the witnesses of serious changes in our country. For, as our sages tell us, "The periods of fulness and of decay come in rotation." I am suspicious that the foreigners, about whom you know so much, are destined to set our country's hopes adrift from their moorings. Foreigners in our country are getting more numerous every year. They have already filled our land with opium, and only a few years ago their armies of soldiers and great explosive machines kept invading our coasts and attacking our walled cities and forts. You and I, Kwi, are not yet what people would call old men; yet, the changes to our country within these few recent years of our lives are for their greatness unknown to any previous period of the present dynasty. What the changes in the coming years may be I tremble to think!'

Pun Kwi had not taught himself to look at foreigners in such a light. When in Canton, he had in his business transactions become acquainted with a goodly number of foreigners. These he had always found to be polite and deferential. What the foreigners seemed to wish was a good market for their merchandise, and in return to strike a good bargain in buying up Chinese produce, which foreigners in their own land valued highly.

'China confers many benefits on other countries, and this the foreigners themselves well know,' said Pun Kwi. 'Those foreigners whom I have met seem grateful for our favours.'

'Do you know much about Hong Kong?' asked Ming Kuang. 'I have been to that place several times. One must pass through Hong Kong on the way to or from Canton. But I am not deeply acquainted with the place. It belongs, as you know, to the great English Kingdom, having been given as a favour by the Emperor to the Queen of that people.'

Ming Kuang acquiesced in Pun Kwi's interpretation of the history of the cession of Hong Kong.

'Yes,' said the graduate. 'The English people are making diligent use of their advantage. Has it not occurred to you, Kwi, that before many more generations are over, other parts of our Empire may be occupied by foreigners; and that, as in Hong Kong now, our graves may be desecrated, the Fung-Shuy harmony outraged, and the whole fabric of our most cherished customs seriously impaired, and perhaps altogether destroyed? What, then, Kwi, of the hopes that are bound up for us in our children and children's children? Not fulness but decay—such is the dispassionate prospect. Within these few months past, especially since our last mid-autumn festival, I have been led to look more closely and also more comprehensively at the future of our nation, and this contemplation has had a most depressing effect upon me. The conversation that I had three weeks ago with the foreign Teacher Bruce, who writes the big book, has simply added to my perplexity—although I had previously hoped that he would put matters before me in a more hopeful light. He is a benevolent and sociable man; but his doctrine—doctrine, as you know, Kwi, ought to be everything to a scholar.'

Pun Kwi ventured to ask Ming Kuang's opinion of the doctrine which seemed to trouble him.

'Teacher Bruce is of opinion that the great majority of our scholars feel too secure in our sages' precepts. We do nothing else, he says, than chew the cud of our own attainments. Teacher Bruce commended me for my curiosity to know his doctrine, while he added that Chinese graduates think it unscholarly to listen to the words of a foreigner. Teacher Bruce greatly admires our sages, while he finds fault with us scholars for keeping our minds closed to the sages of other kingdoms. He referred to a class of scholars among Western nations who were disciples of a wonderful man—Hegel is his name, if I remember rightly. These disciples of Hegel, said Teacher Bruce, are just like us. He said (but with great modesty and politeness) that

Hegel's followers are very proud and arrogant, inasmuch as they say of every one who does not think exactly as they themselves do, that he does not understand anything, Chinese scholars, Teacher Bruce further explained, keep, like the followers of Hegel, within a set form of thinking; and to deviate a hairbreadth from these forms is gross impiety in their eyes. Speaking thus, Teacher Bruce condemned us all by accusing us of being proud and self-contained. He said that there were many deep truths that we Chinese had not yet got possession of, and we must remain in this condition till we learned better manners. This foreign teaching begins by telling us that we are ignorant, and that our thoughts and practices must be changed. Teacher Bruce inwardly hopes and confidently predicts that China will soon undergo a great change. I myself suspect the truth of his words. To me this suspicion has more and more become an inward dread. I did not of course tell the foreigner all I thought and feared.'

'Will the change which you suspect mean more opium and gunpowder than we have yet had?' asked Pun Kwi, whose mind was most at home when moving among concrete things.

After a pause, the philosopher and scholar courteously manifested some reverential respect for Pun Kwi's feelings and his materialism.

"Doubtless gunpowder and opium will be included among the causes, or at anyrate in the process of the disruption and dismemberment of our Middle Kingdom. Thus will perish, as it seems to me, all the fondly cherished hopes concerning the duties which our children owe to us. I wish I could think life to be simply a dream—and if it were a dream,' said Ming Kuang, half correcting himself, 'it would be rather an unpleasant one.'

Pun Kwi remained silent. His mind, however, was not inactive. At that moment he did not give Ming Kuang the benefit of his reflections. Pun Kwi was beginning to regretfully feel that there was a want of community of interest between his friend and himself. At that moment Pun Kwi was thinking that it would be rather an inconvenient matter if the three thousand six hundred dollars, that represented his hard savings during all the years he had been in Canton, belonged merely to the shadowy stuff of dreamland. He was too polite to argue the point.

Gathering up the threads of his previous remarks, Ming Kuang conceded that the great English Kingdom had done much for China in connection with the Taiping rebellions. The Ever-Victorious Army had, during successive periods, been under the direction of English foreigners, whose tact and skill had led to the complete overthrow of the rebels. Nevertheless, for the Chinese Imperial Government to crush Taiping rebellions under the patronage of such allies seemed to Ming Kuang to be 'dropping out of the frying-pan into the fire.' During these recent years, so eventful because so changeful, by a mixture of force, threatening, and persuasion, foreigners had got the thin end of their destructive wedge into the solid block of Chinese life and institutious. When and how would this work end? Opium, hostile armaments, and the foreign missionaries' doctrine seemed to constantly militate against the welfare of China. As for the last mentioned of these hostile forces, it was difficult, said Ming Kuang, to unreservedly condemn it, owing to the bland persuasiveness with which it was being propagated. And again there was the personal character of Teacher Bruce. For months had Ming Kuang tried ineffectually to make up his mind as to the worth of Teacher Bruce's doctrine. That Teacher Bruce himself was a good man was beyond all dispute. But now, thought Ming Kuang, it was the duty of one who would be a patriot as well as a scholar to set aside all such personal considerations. Whether the foreign teacher himself admitted it or not, his doctrine would do harm to China. It would upset all Chinese calculations as to the contemplated happiness to parents to be derived from sons and grandsons. And it would subvert the whole of Chinese morality.

The graduate had often in eloquent terms instructed his friends, Pun Kwi among them, as to the supreme importance of filial piety. If filial piety were to lose its place in China, he had said, China would immediately crumble and decay. There was a time, thousands of years back, in the remote annals of the Middle Kingdom, when the child was the almost exclusive property of the mother, and the mother was the wife, not of one man, but of the tribe or clan. But sweeter manners and purer laws had come in time to China, and had brought with them China's life and glory. Fatherhood with its grand ideas of purity and self-restraint, had come to be written as with an iron pen on the Chinese mind.

In such bright colours Ming Kuang had painted Chinese moral law. Ming Kuang's intensity was that of no ordinary man, much less was it that of an ordinary Chinaman.

Had the faith which Teacher Bruce preached performed no other function than that of an enemy, it would still have remained for Ming Kuang to admit that that faith, in stirring up opposition within his soul, was making him a stronger and better moralist than he had ever been before. This admission he did not make. Not that he was ungenerous — he was all unconscious of the debt he owed to the real source of his criticism.

The vast difference in the constitution of their minds prevented these two friends from protracted discussion But they were not so far left to themselves as to make this difference palpable. They filled their pipes and smoked.

The smoke of peace made Ming Kuang more playful and humane; and in spite of relentless logic he seemed happy in his enquiries after the welfare of his betrothed daughter-in-law. She had been named Min Niang. Her parents had received many presents from friends on her account; and in turn they had put themselves to expense in the matter of festivities beyond the amount of expense usually lavished by parents when a baby girl is born. She was the first—perhaps she might be the only—child; and their national custom permitted the parents, now almost in their old age, to make the occasion ostentatious. The birth of their daughter, if it did not mean the promise of a son or sons yet to be born, meant, at all events, that the ancestral home had not been left quite desolate. There was no alternative to owning girls when boys did not exist.

As for the betrothed husband—Tek Chiu was the name given to him—he was thriving wonderfully. His fond mother, a pale, slim woman between thirty and forty, but looking much older than her years, brought out the boy for Pun Kwi's inspection. Wakened from his sleep by being brought to the front room, he made it plain by unrepressed screaming and without medical inspection that his lungs were good; and scared—as was natural enough—by the first look at a father-in-law, whose presence completed the discomfort of the situation, he persevered in his yells. Pun Kwi vainly attempted to take his daughter's place, and bewitch the boy with pleasant smiles and sweet words. Baffled in his attempts, he contented himself with saying pleasing things to the parents, who, protesting against the compliments, were grateful for them beyond measure.

CHAPTER IV.

FROM OLD TO NEW.

TEK CHIU and Min Niang spent the first seven years of their life in friendship. Their playful, sweet harmony was doubtless disturbed now and then by the momentary jealousies of children. But they were not yet wise enough either to make or to sustain a quarrel.

Circumstances, however, for which neither Tek Chiu nor Min Niang were responsible, conspired all at once to produce a change. Pun Kwi, tired of doing nothing, suddenly bethought himself to go back with his wife and daughter to Canton, and he suited the action to the thought. There he worked at his old occupation as a merchant. The business was much less lucrative than it had been for him in former times; but as he did not run any considerable risks, he found that he was able, after a period of five comparatively uneventful years, to return to Black Rock with a net loss on his previous savings of five hundred dollars. In this way five years were added to Pun Kwi's trading experience, and five hundred dollars were subtracted from his capital. But Pun Kwi, having moved in the company of philosophers, never lost heart. Failing health urged to go back to Black Rock, this time saying his last farewell to Canton. He knew that he would never return there. Black Rock was his home. There in his native soil he would find a grave.

After a quick passage, he is once more gazing upon familiar Black Rock faces. It is now thirteen years since Ming Kuang declared that he had closed his mind against the foreigners' teaching. The graduate's son and the merchant's daughter have now almost passed through the golden gates of childhood. Within the charmed circle of these thirteen peaceful years, two generations—the old and the new—have been mutually unconscious of their differences.

But almost every rule has its exception. Black Rock, a town so immovable and in harmony with its own name, is not quite what it was. Dr Bruce no longer journeyed in that region. A graveyard within a distance of seventy miles from the Black Rock that the missionary had loved, a small patch of ground neatly railed in by four stout iron bars, a stone of European make—there lie the mortal remains of George Bruce, preacher and scholar. Some Black Rock people who still speak of him make no attempt to conceal the tears that fill their eyes as they recount his deeds and words. Black Rock voices soften at the mention of Teacher Bruce, and the scolding, harsh tones so conspicuous in the Black Rock dialect of the Chinese language, are subject to a process of modification that is quite amazing.

And now, in the spring of 1881, while birds are singing, and when all Nature begins to understand that she possesses a new lease of life, Lin Ming Kuang's wife, the mother of an only son, lies dying. The scourge of cholera, so often known to be wielded by the hand of the Destroyer in that region of China, has found out a victim. The disease works with terrible rapidity on the weak system of the sufferer, whose languishing and pain have been doubly increased by the hundred and one appliances dignified with the title of medical treatment. The graduate's wife will not die without doctor's aid. The grief-stricken husband must needs have this one consolation not usually denied to relatives of dying friends.

It is now early dawn, the grey light of morning peering into the sick-room. Fifteen hours of suffering and anxiety have passed. Gradually Ming Kuang has brought himself to suspect that his wife's life is ebbing fast. The best-approved physicians of Black Rock have done their best with their enchantments, and have ceased to prolong their professional efforts. They now make it their duty to comfort Ming Kuang, and assure him that impending death is his wife's destiny. The pendulum of the Chinese mind hangs unevenly biassed, to oscillate much more towards the side of necessity and fate than towards the side of responsibility and freedom. Every man sooner or later yields to destiny, but a Chinaman yields sooner than anybody else. With unspeakable grudging, Ming Kuang yields to the stern decree. His suppressed emotion, while concealing itself, prohibits at the same time that feeling of stolid indifference which men with large heads and small hearts are wont to possess in times of deepest trial.

Pun Kwi, who has been waiting anxiously for news as to the patient's condition, urgently requests the graduate to allow the foreign doctor to see the sufferer. But Ming Kuang only darkens at the suggestion. 'She is past all hope now,' he mournfully utters.

Dr Gordon is the medical missionary, whose hospital is in the City of Even Way. He had arrived at the Mission Chapel on the previous night. He was simply passing through Black Rock at the time. While Pun Kwi was urging Ming Kuang to call the foreigner, Dr Gordon was strapping up his bed-clothes and giving instructions to his burden-bearers to proceed westward on the journey. The chair-bearers were late in arriving. Black Rock chair-bearers are known to be sound sleepers, and on that morning these functionaries were sustaining their reputation.

Pun Kwi eventually prevailed with his friend to allow Dr Gordon to be summoned simply to pass his opinion on the patient's condition. Ming Kuang knew everything already, but in the hour of his direst calamity a man is not needlessly obstinate.

Pun Kwi met Dr Gordon starting on his journey, at the entrance to the chapel. The conservative chair-bearers were still out of harness, partaking of refreshment at the chapel gate, on the pathway leading from the town. Dr Gordon was surveying the sky. He had a small felt hat on his head, while he held a large sun-hat at his side. The empty chair stood waiting for its occupant. A sturdy burden-bearer had gone off before him with the baggage, that consisted of a bundle of bed-clothes, a string of cash, a medicine-chest, and a small box, this last-mentioned article being the Eastern equivalent for the Western carpet bag. Dr Gordon's habit was to travel through his large constituency with small baggage and a big heart.

The chair-bearers did not seem to take any offence at the halt in the journey before it was begun, as caused by Pun Kwi's arrival. They were opium-smokers, and a respite, however short, was most welcome. The periods of rest and refreshment, which come as a boon and a blessing to Chinese chair-bearers, would, if studied, yield valuable object-lessons on the harmlessness of opium. Opium-smoking chair-bearers are always large-hearted in giving to the occupant of their chair good value for his money. Thanks to opium, Dr Gordon's journey westward was to be like a seat in a long Parliament; and Dr Gordon, foolish man, is an anti-opiumist!

Dr Gordon and Pun Kwi found their way to Ming Kuang's house. Still a young man, the doctor had already seen a good deal of cholera during his years of wide experience among the Chinese people. When he looked at the patient, he at once shook his head. He asked one or two questions, and shook his head again. 'Had you sent for me ten hours ago, this disease might have been checked,' he said; and with a few solemn and tender words, which included an earnest exhortation to the dying woman to put her trust in the God of Salvation, he left the sick-room.

Tek Chiu listened anxiously to Dr Gordon's words. During the night he had slept soundly; for sleep as one of the subtle forces of nature had exacted obedience from the son, while it failed to succeed with the husband and father, who tremblingly and assiduously nursed the dying wife and mother throughout the weary hours of night till dawn came. Then Tek Chiu awoke, only a few minutes before Pun Kwi with Dr Gordon had entered the house.

The boy heard his mother's moaning, the sound of which was much feebler than it had been when he lay down to sleep five hours before on his couch in the adjoining room. He looked at his father's anxious face. Hitherto the father had been a perfect pattern to the son, whose little world of everything gave greatest place to look and gesture. 'Mother is very ill,' thought Tek Chiu, 'and father is anxious about her. I ought to be anxious too.' The thought of his mother's death was not yet present to him in such a way as to make him realise it in his boyish mind. As to the very meaning of death, it was for Tek Chiu an open question. He was like a soldier at preliminary drill, not yet ushered into the real field of warfare and struggle. But when Dr Gordon, on leaving the house at the close of his brief visit, gently touched him on the shoulder and half-playfully exhorted him to be brave, Tek Chiu, for the first time, seemed to understand the deeper meaning of his position, and suddenly gave vent to involuntary sobs. The medical missionary's words broke the spell of Tek Chiu's peaceful world. Already he felt himself bereft of his mother. The actual bereavement, which took place a few hours afterwards, bringing with it the suddenness belonging to events that are even most expected—a suddenness that gives a shock to the old and to the young alike—awoke the lad from the dream of life's morning. The light through which he saw a sorrowful real world did not gradually dawn on him. It came to the motherless boy, as it comes to many other children, through a lightning flash. His childhood for him belonged now to the dead past—dead and buried out of sound and sight, but the living echoes and visions retained by memory, to grow vaguer and dimmer with advancing years.

Tek Chiu is the very image of his father. So far as physical qualities count for anything, the law of heredity has worked with wonderful exactness in reproducing the father in the son. As for moral qualities, Tek Chiu is not yet old enough to stand scrutiny by way of comparing or contrasting him with his father. If you were to critically examine through these thirteen years of babyhood and boyhood, you would doubtless find the usual components of reverence for superiors and generous impulses blended with self-will and selfishness. Candid specialists in the study of human character would find it difficult in surveying Tek Chiu thus far in his young life to see much standing out in distinct relief that would serve as an index to his future or his fate. Tek Chiu has not yet done anything extraordinary. The only child of his parents, he has grown up under their sedulous guardianship. Both his grandparents on his father's side had died before he was born, and in these special circumstances, as the child of their old age, his father and mother have been to him parents and grandparents combined.

The father and the son, now left alone, are more than ever in each other's company—the father to instruct, the son to learn. Already the boy is able to read a considerable number of the hieroglyphics of his native literature, and to repeat from memory large passages of Confucius and Mencius. His mind has for four years been steeping in the best of moral precepts as to the duties of individuals and the well-being of the State. A few doors from Ming Kuang's house is situated one of Black Rock schools, where Tek Chiu has been reading books with other boys. If the schoolmaster wearing the huge brass-ringed spectacles is to be believed, Tek Chiu has already shown himself to be 'ten parts clever.' But the old dominie has possibly overreached himself in giving this high testimonial to his pupil. Tek Chiu is the son of his father—a graduate who daily inspects his son's work, doing what every father has a right to do in the way of giving help and encouragement. Few if any of the other boys in the school have such advantages as Tek Chiu. Yet the schoolmaster does not make it his business to gauge circumstances, and his praise of the graduate's son is therefore unstinted and unreserved. In China, as elsewhere in this faulty world, everything depends on the work being actually done, and, apart from a few mechanical conditions and restrictions, subtle questions as to how the work is done or who does it are left out of account.

Tek Chiu cannot escape his environment. Nor is it desirable that he should. These elements in the boy's education being the materials out of which his personality is being formed—for the process of formation has but begun—are evidently of a valuable sort. Tek Chiu is the child of Chinese conservatism at its best.

Oftentimes—and now especially after the mother's death—the father has taken the son aside to exhort him and to warn him of future dangers.

'Be filial and love virtue, my son! So shalt thou prosper.' Ming Kuang's is a simple creed. It is the creed that must' be handed down unimpaired to the younger generation. It has stood the test of four thousand years. And what are the practical precepts for the observance of this creed? Surely it means a son's manifestation of a filial spirit to his parents during their life, assiduous and scrupulous attention to the ceremonies of burial as soon as they are dead, and ever after, while the son's life lasts, regular and constant offerings to their spirits! In this way, Tek Chiu and unborn posterity will be safeguarded from whatever is improper and transitory. But if, as Ming Kuang continually warns his son—if in an evil day Tek Chiu should be tempted to forget the faith that has been handed down to him from his parents and remote ancestry; if he should, either by indolence or indifference on the one hand, or by scepticism or positive disbelief on the other, turn his back on a father's counsels, the spirits of his ancestors will rebel against him and disown him.

The venerable Teacher Bruce had called the graduate's attention to the Chinese belief, held, if not by literary men, at all events by the common people—that the influence of ancestors over posterity is a dread rather than a love. What the evil consequences are for those neglecting the rites of ancestral worship is everything; in any other respect, ancestral worship is nothing. So said Teacher Bruce. But Ming Kuang has refused to entertain such a view. The very fact, indeed, that he once on a time, in the throes of an intellectual struggle, had doubted this truth of his native religion, has doubly armed Ming Kuang to combat by anticipation the difficulties of posterity. His words of warning to his son are therefore charged with that terrible moral earnestness of which a thinking mind is capable. Ming Kuang, it is true, admits the utility of fear and dread as a preventive against the non-observance of traditional rites. That the unthinking masses should fear their ancestors' revenge, and that they should be destitute not only of any other fear but even of anything else in the nature of religious feeling, is due simply to the raw condition of their own untutored and unthinking minds. Let China's sons but understand what these rites mean, and they will then recognise one of the great causes that have maintained the preservation of family life, and with it the preservation of family honour and purity. And as the family is the cradle of the nation, how is a nation to have a healthy life if it be weakened and crippled in its infancy?

. . . .

It was early in autumn — the hottest part of the year. Only a few months before, Tek Chiu's mother had been called away from earth by the visitation of cholera. At that time there were but few deaths in Black Rock from the disease, Tek Chiu's delicate mother being one of the few victims. The excessive heat brought about, for the second time in the same year, a fresh visitation of the fell disease—this time sadly more sweeping. In and around Black Rock the Angel of Death smote young and old, rich and poor alike. The people were dying in tens and hundreds.

But four months ago his father had taught Tek Chiu the rudiments of nursing a sick patient. It had been for Tek Chiu the beginning of many lessons, learnt within that brief period—lessons that he would never forget. All the son's education was now needed, for his father was smitten down by the plague. Ming Kuang lay sick and helpless. He was under the arrest of death.

The boy discerned a strange glare in his father's eye. Ming Kuang was sinking rapidly. He spoke with difficulty.

'Come near me, my son,' he said.

Tek Chiu bent over his father.

'Avoid vice, and cleave to virtue, my son. Never abandon the right path.'

Reverently Tek Chiu knelt at his father's bedside, as a proof that he would remember and cherish his father's words. Tek Chiu's father and his father's God were to him as one and the same person. Therefore he knelt. It was his duty.

The dying man seemed to get a new lease of energy. His voice suddenly grew stronger. But life's candle flickers brightly and suddenly before going out altogether, as if defying death.

'Tek Chiu!'

'Yes, my father!'

'Always study the sages' doctrine deeply—and— never forget your father!'

Tek Chiu, in tearful agony, promised obedience. Ming Kuang, who had raised himself up in his bed, looked satisfied with his son's promise, and lay back, to raise himself no more.

A heavy sigh, and all was over.

Tek Chiu was left alone.

CHAPTER V.

THE GRADUATE'S FUNERAL.

As with the ancient Greeks, so with the Chinese, the burial counts for a good deal.

Ming Kuang's death was notified to a sorrowing community.

Tender hands dressed the corpse, clothing it with the liberal supply of nine garments, made according to the pattern of the dressing customs of the earlier dynasty of the Mings. The abhorrence of change that had filled Ming Kuang's later life is a subject for contemplation here in face of this treatment of his own dead body. Ming Kuang loses his queue. This change in hairdressing means the restoration to him of his liberty—a progress backward to the good old times which Ming Kuang had habitually idealised, and for which he had sighed. His creed is honoured in his dead body.

A well-known Black Rock astrologer having fixed the dates of burial, the names of the chief mourners, and the respective dates of sacrificing to the spirit of the deceased and of burying the mortal remains, were with customary propriety announced. At the northwest end of Black Rock, on an oblong plateau of turf, astrologers of a bygone day had fixed Ming Kuang's last resting-place. Ming Kuang was to sleep with his fathers.

Two weeks of characteristically Chinese inactivity, a quiet season to Tek Chiu for grief, passed by; and then began the funeral preparations. These befitted the dignity of Ming Kuang's station as a graduate, honoured and revered. Friends came to the house bringing scrolls, extracts from the Classics commemorative of the graduate's virtues. Animal food in three forms— duck, chicken, and pork—emblems of three lives, and a pot of wine are presented as offerings to the spirit. With these votive gifts, the friends come in procession to the house of mourning. The uniform white dresses and official caps without tassels, as worn by each mourner, add to the imposing character of the ceremony. The friends inspect the coffin, walking in procession round it. The master of ceremonies with his two assistants, one on each side of him, presents three joss-sticks. This official bows low in reverential worship to the spirit of Ming Kuang. This done, one of the assistants fixes the burning joss-sticks at the foot of the coffin. A visiting mourner then falling on his knees sobs loudly, and his example is soon followed by others. Near relatives of the deceased graduate lift up the fallen ones, the grief is accepted as vicarious; and as a reward for sympathy thus shown, three cups of wine, one at a time, are put into each mourner's hand. Each invokes the spirit of his dead friend to partake of the wine offering. The Chinaman, in the hour of bereavement, if he be guilty at times of feigning grief, makes no effort to appropriate consolation, except it be that to be exported from the unseen world. At such a time wine is the drink of dead men. The offerer pours out the contents of the cup on the ground.

And now that the swellings of Jordan divide Ming

Kuang from the friends he has left behind, a letter of affectionate greeting goes after him. Standing by the coffin's side, Scholar Wu, on behalf of the friends, reads it aloud:—

'The eternal world has claimed thee, O wise and trusty friend, resplendent in virtues, honoured in years! These things can never be but as they are. We have lost thee, our scholar and our guide! As a token that our friendship disturbed by Death remains yet unbroken if Memory does not mock us, receive from us, O excellent teacher, these viands and these wines. All these we offer to thy Manes. Ours is a grief that baffles word and thought.'

The earth drinks the wine, and Ming Kuang's spirit soars in the air around his friends.

The ground in front of the altar is still wet with the poured-out wine when the viands are removed. But the letter has yet to be sent off. Two things—fire and money—are needed, and these are forthcoming. The letter with silver paper, the current coin of men's spirits (gold is the exclusive currency of the gods), passes through the purgatorial fire into the receptive hands of Ming Kuang's translated self. Imitation money satisfies the dead, who are not so fastidious as the living. The eternal efficacy of money, and even of its counterfeit, and the preserving and transmitting power of fire, give solace to the weeping friends.

Two days later Ming Kuang's body was committed to the sod. The procession started from the house at an early hour, in order that ample time might be at the disposal of the mourners to complete all the obsequies without undue haste. Banners, the insignia of the greatness of Ming Kuang's family, were carried in front. Bands of music, gongs, flutes, cymbals, drums, were played; and the scrolls presented by friends were borne with regularity in the procession.

The canopied chair containing the burning joss-sticks and the tablet still untenanted is carried in front of the coffin. On the return journey this chair will take the place of the bier. From the moment that Ming Kuang's breath went out of him joss-sticks have been kept burning. This fire prevents the spirit from wandering too far afield. Tek Chiu, as chief mourner and heir, walks slowly and mechanically on the left side of the bier, carrying the Buddhist banner consecrated by priests to frighten away the devils. To carry this banner is a son's sacred duty. With the other hand he holds a mourning stick, dressed at the top with a small flag of sackcloth. Tek Chiu himself is dressed in sackcloth. His queue loosened out, his head-dress—a curious contrivance made of straw-braid arranged in strips, making conspicuous his dishevelled hair—his straw shoes, his alternate kneeling and sobbing on the way from the house to the place of interment, his studious acts of obeisance when crossing Black Rock bridge or rounding one of the many corners, lest the spirit at such tempting places should go astray—in such garb and in such posture Tek Chiu is one of a countless procession, past, present, and future, of China's mourning children.

Other relatives, clansmen, and friends—a Chinaman has more relatives than anybody else—follow in the procession. Ming Kuang's only and younger brother is next of kin after Tek Chiu, and he walks on the right-hand side of the bier. At a short distance behind follow other mourning relatives, among whom are females covered with the usual extra supply of sackcloth.

The procession has now reached the open grave. By careful reckoning, the astrologers have already determined the exact time to lower the coffin. A last offering, the usual three kinds of flesh, is now made; and a careful observer will afterwards notice that the ultimate function of the offered food is to enrich the stomach of the sexton. The due burning of gold paper —a bribe given to the god of earth—precedes the lowering of the coffin. This done, dust returns to dust. While the remains of Ming Kuang are being covered with earth, a mourner throws into the closing grave a piece of broken sod, and his example is followed by others.

The grave is now closed, and the master of ceremonies gives a signal to throw up the blocks. Ming Kuang must tell those burying him whether or not he is comfortable by signifying to them if his grave-heap is tall enough. The fortune-telling blocks ere long come to terms with their experimenters, and the burial of Ming Kuang is at an end.

But the spirit—the spirit over which no grave can close—must find its resting-place. An old and honoured man of Black Rock, well stricken in years, and blessed with posterity even to the extent of great-grandsons, and thus superior on account of his good fortune to all malign spiritual influences, is cordially invited to perform the last act in the funeral ceremony. The old man's function is to dot the tablet.

The vacant ancestral tablet is placed in front of the grave. Joss-sticks are kept burning in a new censer specially procured for the ceremony. Into the hole prepared at the back of the tablet has been inserted a paper recording information as to the name and years of the deceased. As for Ming Kuang's age, three years are added to it,—one for heaven, one for earth, and one for Ming Kuang himself. These are years added to the sum of Ming Kuang's honour and fame. In this record also are stated the place of burial and the names of heirs, according to priority, and of mourners. It is a wise arrangement, for in the event of subsequent family disputes, this record may be resorted to. In such a contingency the record does the work of judges and lawyers, while it saves payment of lawyers' modest fees.

Reverentially carrying this tablet on his back, Tek Chiu kneels down, with his back towards the grave. The old man, then, dressing himself in official robes, takes the vermilion pencil, and with it points to the sun, to the heavens, and to the earth, summoning these as witnesses. He invokes the spirit of Ming Kuang to reside in its resting-place; and then with the pencil the old man adds to the Chinese character that has already been written in black the indispensable red dot.

The canopied chair now receives the tenanted tablet, which is placed there behind the burning censer of joss-sticks, and the procession returns homeward. The tablet then gets a prominent place on the sideboard in the chief room of the family abode—the old room of Ming Kuang's wine party—from which Ming Kuang is now and henceforth absent in body, but where he is still present in spirit.

At the funeral, where Pun Kwi, and still more his daughter, occupied an important position, Tek Chiu and Niang caught a glimpse of each other. During the months intervening between Min Niang's return with her parents from Canton, and the present mournful occasion, the betrothed husband and wife had never met. Min Niang knew her place and kept it; if not, her parents would have kept it for her. To her, as to Tek Chiu, the age of discretion had come early. They were both old-fashioned, having been born to parents in old age. Now, at the age of thirteen, the pair are strangers to each other, such mutual ignorance being the necessary condition for a lawful love. Although Min Niang had previously done her part at the funeral rites of Tek Chiu's mother, she did not see Tek Chiu on that occasion. It was now after a lapse of six years that the betrothed pair exchanged an unavoidable, furtive glance. They kept looking away from each other. These six years, the second and later period of their lives, had almost wholly obliterated the first and earlier period. Boys and girls alike seem to despise their own babyhood, and with it most of its associations. Reasons that do not baffle analysis disposed Tek Chiu and Min Niang to mutual repulsion, and not attraction. If Love be the great agency that constitutes and rules the universe, then it is quite possible to interpret this mutual antagonism as being Love itself, clothed in the garb of its contrary, and manifested here in its capricious infantile stage. Be it so. It is the Chinese history of a courtship.

Tek Chiu knew by implication that his marriage was a great and necessary institution, arranged for him wisely enough by hands other than his own. To question the wisdom of such an order of things was not in Tek Chiu's line. A wife was a pre-determined institution quite as much as was a father or a mother.

And, moreover, he was not quite old enough to be susceptible to the normal emotions of an infatuated lover. The loss of his father was what lay nearest his heart; nor was he disposed, lonely as he was at that juncture, to learn the expulsive power of a new affection. Accordingly, when in the midst of his sore bereavement and genuine grief, he met Min Niang, he naturally appeared careless. It was the proper thing to do.

Min Niang was accompanied at the funeral by a girl companion, shorter and stouter and slightly older than herself. Ah Ho was Pun Kwi's maid-servant, purchased at Canton during his second term of sojourn there, for a respectable sum out of his hard-earned savings. Ah Ho was no mere menial. She had been taken into the family as a suitable companion for Min Niang; and from the date of purchase till now the two girls had been companions indeed.

Ah Ho's antecedents, as well known to the members of the Pun family, can, like the history of most people, be put into brief space. She was one of a family of two children, the son and daughter of a widow. Village pirates had on a certain fatal day attacked the old homestead at Peaceful Shepherd, a place several miles north of Canton, and mercilessly levied on the hapless widow a heavy tax which she was compelled to pay. And to pay her debt to her exactors the widow had no alternative but to pledge her son, until such time as she might find a market for her daughter. Ere long Pun Kwi was the timely purchaser of Ah Ho, and the boy was restored to his mother.

With the usual diplomatic skill that distinguished

him, Pun Kwi was understood about the time of Ming Kuang's death to be receiving tenders for Ah Ho's hand and heart from aspiring fathers-in-law. Competitive negotiations, which were taxing Pun Kwi's genius, were at that juncture in process of being sifted. It was no small matter. Ah Ho, as she had come to Pun Kwi, was an investment to the extent of the round sum of sixty dollars. To give the girl away for less than a hundred per cent. on that amount would be an inexcusable financial blunder. Ah Ho's future was therefore being carefully weighed in the scales of Pun Kwi's judgment, and the girl herself, meek and patient, was waiting with a characteristic display of submissiveness and devotion. For five years she had enjoyed a comfortable home in the bosom of her guardian's household. She was not unhappy. As a dutiful inferior, she honoured and revered Pun Kwi and his invalid wife, while she loved Min Niang, whom she had unconsciously taught herself to regard more as a confidential friend than as a mistress.

The two girls had returned from Ming Kuang's funeral to their own house.

'You saw your betrothed husband to-day, Missie,' Ah Ho began.

'I could not avoid seeing him,' was the answer.

'Of course not! I had greater freedom to survey him carefully. He looked very sad, as he stood at the grave. And truly sad he must feel, now that he has lost both father and mother.'

'I overheard my father say that he must henceforth be under the guardianship of his uncle. He must spend the next three years in dutiful mourning for his dead father.'

'His uncle will not likely be so kind to him as his father has been.'

'Not likely! Scholar Ming Kuang had more kindness than most men. But the son is now better able to look after himself. He is no longer a child.'

'Yet he is still very young.'

Ah Ho ventured this remark, feeling as she did that the betrothed husband of her young mistress needed sympathy in the circumstances.

Min Niang's mind was no doubt quite responsive to Ah Ho's words of feeling. But she was verbally combative.

'Many people have lost both their parents at an earlier age than Tek Chiu.'

Ah Ho was importunate.

'I wonder if your wedding will take place as soon as the three years of mourning are over,' she said.

The remark was meant to be, if not quite a question, the beginning of a discussion.

'Neither father nor mother has said anything on the subject, and I dare not ask them.'

Min Niang here began to speak in more subdued tones. Ah Ho had pierced through Min Niang's veneering of girlish indifference. The two girls were now no longer playful. They spoke as only girls at the threshold of womanhood can speak. They were straitened as to their knowledge of the world and of human affairs in general. Yet both alike knew that in youth's fair morn, when life should be at its brightest, there was much to perplex and overawe Chinese girls such as they were.

Their exchange of confidence, intended for mutual consolation, seemed but to solemnise both girls by the admission to their minds of apprehensive probabilities concerning their future lives. They were not, of course, in a position to compare their own fortunes with the fortunes of girls in Western lands, where individual liberty belongs to woman almost as much as it belongs to man. But this much these girls knew—that theirs was a position of unqualified dependence on the varying fortunes and destinies of others—others who might or who might not be trustworthy.

It was a world of chance. Knowing this, they feared; their past and present happiness seemed to be slipping away from them.

It was Ah Ho's references to herself in particular that had coursed through, as a vein of melancholy, the words and thoughts of both girls. Ah Ho had taken for granted that the future of her young mistress was one to be envied. The graduate's son would be like his father—Min Niang would be happy. But she herself, happy in the present though only a maid-servant, her lines having fallen in pleasant places, with a still happier past, for she once was a daughter, and her young mistress well understood that Ah Ho's was no blameworthy regret—what of the future, regarding which even a girl could not avoid being curious? Even her master's kindness might not save her. The unknown world was not to be trusted.

Both girls understood each other perfectly. Their thoughts grew with their conversation. For them, the blade, the ear, and the stalk of corn were doubt, distrust, and alarm. If Ming Kuang, graduate, had had his gloomy moods, these unsophisticated maidens had theirs too.

CHAPTER VI.

THE COACHING DAYS.

THE kind Head-man of Black Rock, now in a grey old age, changed much by the hand of Father Time since the long-past Autumn Festival, had as a tribute to Ming Kuang's memory shown some solicitude for Tek Chiu's orphan condition. That public-spirited man, along with Pun Kwi and a few other friends, had made arrangements to train Tek Chiu with a view to following his father's profession. This generosity suited Tek Chiu's own ambition. Scholar Wu was made the lad's surety and tutor. He welcomed his new charge. As a pecuniary consideration, the tutoring of Tek Chiu did not mean much; but it was something. Scholar Wu had other five pupils, lads of literary ambition, who came daily to Wu's special class to be coached. These Tek Chiu joined in their studies. By arrangement with Tek Chiu's uncle, who was now in possession of his deceased brother's house and patrimony, Tek Chiu went to stay with his tutor. In this way he came to have an intimacy with the teacher that the other pupils had denied to them.

Wu's private income was no more a settled thing than that of the other members belonging to the rank and file of Chinese literati. China honours her scholars, but does not pay them. Giving their good offices in cases of litigation, and acting as coaches to younger men, who, if these succeed in the examinations, become as poor as their tutors, the Chinese literati have many a struggle to keep the wolf from the door; and although their minds are thoroughly conversant with the morality of the sages, the pinch of poverty gives a proneness to laxity in their observance, if not in their interpretation, of that moral code. Since the Chinese order of things makes the acknowledged moral law difficult to keep and easy to break, critics of China must considerately gauge her circumstances and deal gently with her people's weaknesses. The patriarchal system of Government has put a hard crust round China, conserving it, yet limiting it; and this limitation not only checks new possibilities of moral growth in the individual lives of the people, but it prevents these lives from being consistent with their own native national morality. It is the old difficulty felt in places other than China—the consideration that whereas the life ought to be determined by the doctrine, the doctrine is rather determined by the life.

Scholar Wu was a gambler. He was interested in the trade. Near to his own cottage was a gambling-house, from the profits of which a percentage was paid him, in lieu of his protection. As a graduate whose recognised duty it was to preserve the high tone of morality in his district, Scholar Wu's official status acted as a potent check upon the exactions of the magistrate's runners, the underlings of the Yamen. The gambling-house keeper well knew that Scholar Wu's influence was not to be despised. Therefore, in addition to the regular percentage premium, Wu was on festive occasions the recipient of handsome presents.

He gave protection to the establishment, and on occasional evenings gambled himself.

It was the card-playing and the four-sided teetotum species of gambling that commended themselves to a literary man of Wu's tastes. The mid-day lottery, with its thirty-seven constellation animals, had no doubt its charms for illiterate men and dreaming women. Drawing lots in the daytime was not for Wu; but ere the sun set each day, the nett drawings that swelled the coffers of the gambling-house treasury — the grand results of each day's constellation system—commanded the respectful patronage of the scholar. The sun set every day; and business, with its usual fluctuations, kept prospering.

Tek Chiu, gifted with an extraordinary memory, worked hard at his books. He had begun to question his tutor on the meaning of the Classics they read. The epigrammatic dicta of Confucius, and the multitudinous meanings taken out of them by the tutor, did not seem to arrest the pupil's mind so much as did the 'Way of Virtue Classic,' a work attributed to the metaphysician Lao-tse.

'What is meant by saying,' asked Tek Chiu, 'that the way that can be defined is not the eternal way? the name that can be named not the eternal name? If the eternal way cannot be defined, and the eternal name cannot be named, what have we to say or think about them at all?'

It was a very natural question.

'Lao-tse says many mysterious things that Confucius does not approve. Lao-tse is a dreamer,' was Wu's reply.

'Teacher, if Sage Lao-tse were in this room just now,

do you think he would be able to explain the commencement of his book?'

The equilibrium of Wu's mind was disturbed by the question. He admitted to his pupil that it was quite possible Sage Lao-tse would be able to answer for himself.

Tek Chiu was beginning to cultivate a love for the mysterious. He became fond of Lao-tse, not because he did, but because he did not, understand the interminable series of contradictions that constituted the warp and woof of the Chinese Hegel. Ming Kuang lived again in his son. The love for Lao-tse was the appetite of a mind as yet but dimly conscious of its own wants —a mind pre-determined, as it seemed, to break asunder the bands that fettered Confucian and Chinese thought.

The boy's wild passion for learning was astir. He greedily devoured everything that came in his way, and he was hungry still. It was no easy task for Scholar Wu to discipline his pupil. Tek Chiu was often rebuked for a want of clearness in his essays, written by the pupil as expository exercises on prescribed portions of the Classics. And Tek Chiu was a very bad writer of the characters. His hand was clumsy and careless—so much so that Wu constantly warned him that, unless he took more pains with the strokes, curves, and symmetry of his writing, he would be 'put down' when he presented himself in due time at the examinations. In this matter of handwriting Tek Chiu was constantly reminded how unfavourably he compared with his father.

But in spite of his faults—and what student is without faults?—Tek Chiu spent these days very happily with Wu. When times of recreation would come, Tek Chiu would manifest anxiety to follow his teacher's footsteps. Only on some occasions did Wu encourage Tek Chiu's companionship; for a gambling-house, thought Wu, was no place for a boy. The Chinese, while not considering occasional gambling to be wrong, have nevertheless a conscience with respect to it as a habitual practice.

During the first few months of Wu's guardianship Tek Chiu was excluded from the precincts of the gambling shrine. But after a time, whether it was that the influence of Lao-tse made Tek Chiu particularly curious and importunate, or that Scholar Wu felt the irksomeness and inconsistency of demanding from another a higher standard of morality than he demanded from himself, the teacher conceded to his pupil an occasional visit to the gambling-house.

This Black Rock gambling-house was in two senses 'out of the way.' Although close to Wu's house, it was situated in an obscure corner. The regular gambling saloon, as a practical result of the gaming system, was a foreign invention, the Portuguese having introduced it into Macao and made it fashionable. Black Rock was not to be behind the times — hence this dark, alluring corner established by private enterprise, the resort of young and old, rich and poor.

To the Chinese Government it might be said: 'So long as men are what they are, a channel must be opened up for vice. Then why not recognise and sanction it?' But the Chinese Government in general, and the Fokien Provincial Government in particular, are obstinate. The district Superintendent of Instruction, a subordinate of the Literary Chancellor, would forget his high office and bring the Education Department into disgrace, were he to give formal recognition to a gambling den. Such is the law, though not necessarily the realised ideal of the Chinese Government. That the Chinese have not a tender conscience does not warrant the assumption that they have no conscience at all.

For although, following up the establishment of gambling saloons by Portuguese in China, the Canton Provincial Government has now opened up for itself a source of revenue in the State-regulated gambling-farm —a system of betting, not on horses, but on men, and these no ordinary men, but literary graduates—the Provincial Government of Fokien gives no such direct sanction to regular gambling. In Fokien, the literary guess competitions, which receive honourable acknowledgment, inasmuch as their proceeds go to pay State officials, belong really to the chance art, although success in the competition necessitates the possession of thinking and literary capacity. There is issued at frequent intervals a verse of poetry, complete, excepting two characters, which those taking part in the game are meant to fill in. The two characters—'the missing links'—of the verse as it was when originally composed, are carefully noted down, locked up in a box, and taken out when all competitive answers have been received. The lucky guessers get valuable prizes, and the large profit percentage fills the pockets of the State officials.

But Chinese betting, whether it be Cantonese betting on scholars, or Fokien betting on scholars' mental diet —Chinese betting, less heinous and less silly than the betting of the Western turf, is the least disreputable spot within the area of Chinese gambling pursuits.

The ordinary copper box and card species of gambling has an almost irresistible fascination for the Chinese. Chance, like Prospero's wand, exercises a strange spell over this most materialistic of peoples, as though their materialism goaded them betimes to spiritual madness.

Scholar Wu, Confucianist though he was, became more and more intoxicated with the gambling drug. He lost oftener than he gained. He began to make heavy stakes and to lose them. It was several months after Tek Chiu became Wu's pupil that the teacher, in one dark disastrous night, lost a sum of money equivalent to forty Mexican dollars. It was a big loss for Wu, who fell into arrears. Till now he had kept his head above water. But now relatives and acquaintances began to be cynical both behind his back and in his presence. Till now, as a gambler, Wu had gone as far as he could with impunity, but on that single night, when heated and excited with wine, he grew desperate and risky, and crossed the threshold of respectability. Even a scholar may lose his good name, as Wu's case shows. Wu's prestige had now taken a leap downwards, like the silver dollar in times of commercial depression. The gambling-house keeper began to be less obsequious; the duns became more importunate. Wu was in difficulties.

At this point Wu was more than ordinarily disposed to be confidential with Tek Chiu. So sweet are the uses of adversity, that Wu seemed unconsciously to set aside his patronising attitude to his protégé. One afternoon, Tek Chiu, having found out the cause of his teacher's unusual dejection and apathy, repaired to his father's house to speak with his uncle.

The uncle was a quiet man, without literary qualifications, who cultivated a small patch of ground, tended pigs, sowed and reaped his crops, and fought his daily battles against want. He cordially welcomed his nephew, who on this occasion approached his father's representative in the most reverential of postures. Tek Chiu had come to ask a favour—money, if his uncle had any. Reluctantly Tek Chiu told the cause of his request—it was to help Teacher Wu out of his difficulties. The uncle remonstrated, pointing out to the lad that Wu's debts were beyond the compass of any possible help such as a son of Ming Kuang could offer. After payment of the funeral expenses, which was largely a matter of charity, Ming Kuang's property, in addition to his house and patch of land, was the humble sum of ten Mexican dollars and a few odd hundred cash. A son had doubtless the first claim on that money, but there were other relatives, each of whom would expect a share in the final distribution. That money was in the uncle's possession undisturbed, and laid up in a napkin—a reserve for some rainy day.

Tek Chiu listened patiently to Uncle Peng's expostulations; but his heart remained resolute to help Teacher Wu if he could. He was entitled to the lion's share of his father's money, house, and lands. At that time he needed money for a benevolent and desirable end.

'Venerable uncle, let my share of the remainder of my father's property be all the smaller, and help me in this matter by advancing to me my father's money.'

Had Tek Chiu been asking the money for his own use, he would doubtless have been less courageous with his uncle. But Teacher Wu's dejected look kept haunting his mental vision.

'You give that money to Teacher Wu, and you'll never see it again,' was the uncle's last word before the final surrender to Tek Chiu's wish—for Tek Chiu importuned successfully. The napkin with its contents was handed over to him, in exchange for a formidable receipt such as only a young scholar could compose. Tek Chiu's caligraphy was more leniently viewed by an indulgent uncle than by a critical teacher. The old man seemed satisfied with the stylish character of his nephew's production, and, accepting it in return for the money, he stowed it away carefully in a corner.

Scholar Wu stared with surprise at his pupil's beneficence. He shook his head, manifesting professed unwillingness to accept the offered help. To refuse what one is gasping to accept is an art known to people of all races in this world-loving world. For Wu, a Chinaman and a scholar, it was both an art and a science. Wu took the money, but he did not pay his debts with it. Before that night was over he had gambled, and Fortune frowning on him once again, he had lost all. Wu of course had meant to win. A few successful hits at dice would have put him completely on his feet again. But China has its Alnaschar's castles as well as its pagodas, and Wu became more demoralised than ever.

Uncle Peng's napkin remained. The fate of the contents Tek Chiu never knew. He had helped his teacher. Next to a father and mother, a teacher ought to be revered and loved. Teacher Wu's coaching in the high morality of the Classics had brought out into free activity the chivalrous emotions and generous sentiments of the pupil. Tek Chiu had done his duty by helping his teacher, and he had brought himself to believe that the teacher had a merrier face and a lighter heart for many days subsequent to the sweet surprise afforded him by the timely aid.

Tek Chiu had begun also to enjoy close companionship with his fellow-students. At a critical moment, one of the scholars, Leng Kee by name, introduced Tek Chiu to the mysteries of the animal constellation lottery. Tek Chiu had no money, but Leng Kee removed this obstacle by lending him the necessary amount to try his luck. Tek Chiu staked on the tortoise, and to Tek Chiu's bewilderment and delight the official distribution in the afternoon announced that the tortoise had topped the pole. Leng Kee got back his loan with phenomenal interest. Tek Chiu staked again—this time on the rat. The rat was Tek Chiu's chance guess of the morning; and in the afternoon, to his increasing bewilderment, the rat led the way. Tek Chiu had by this second hit established his reputation among a number of people as a successful lottery gambler. He tried again and again, but his choosing hand seemed to have lost her cunning. He was dissatisfied, and found a channel for his dissatisfaction in card-playing, Leng Kee and other boys encouraging him. Card-playing had more dignity about it, and Tek Chiu's gambling habits became more openly known.

On the afternoon of a certain day, when Teacher Wu was laid up in bed with fever, the six pupils were reading aloud in the front room. Tek Chiu had already become *facile princeps* in the coaching class. His wonderful memory and his ready wit commanded the reverential awe of his fellows, although gambling had begun to divide his interests. Tek Chiu had in mind and knowledge grown apace. He had already mastered the 'Four Books' and the 'Five Classics.'

He could faithfully evolve, according to Teacher Wu's models, long essays out of each passage. His eagerness to recite and discourse on Lao-tse had not diminished. The morality of Lao-tse, less rigid and more elastic than that of the other Classics, seemed to have given the lad too tolerant a view of life and practice. His mind, occupied with the mysteries of existence and non-existence, had become cast in a philosophic mould. It had become therefore easy for him to be generous, while difficult for him to be stern either with others or with himself.

The task of reading books on a hot summer afternoon found a sudden respite in the interruption of gongs and cymbals playing in the street. Such interruptions during hours of study have a stimulating and soothing influence on boys. The gongs were no sooner sounded than the six students rushed to the door. In a vacant space of ground, about twenty or thirty yards from Wu's house, a theatrical performance had just been begun. The sight was a surprise to the boys. An elaborate scaffolding had been erected as noiselessly as though it had been erected in close proximity to a condemned cell.

Boy actors, dressed as women, with painted faces, were performing on the platform. A motley gathering of waifs and strays, including abandoned-looking loafers and hungry-looking beggars, immediately surrounded the scaffolding. It was a series of performances given in honour of a wealthy shopkeeper's grandmother. The more respectable people were surveying the play from a distance. The dialogue between the two actors was inaudible to everybody and to themselves owing to the clanging of musical instruments. Loud sound and intricate gesture count for much at Chinese play-acting.

These meaningless plays and deafening sounds of the itinerant theatrical arrangement do not seem to act as a stimulating agency to thought in one direction or another. To the pure all things are pure. But knowledge of the world as it is discloses in all their base vulgarity of conception the associations of these theatres as outrages on even the least human of human instincts—so inhuman and unnatural are their associated vices, which it were degrading human language to describe.

Tek Chiu at Wu's doorstep suggested to his companions that they should take a closer look at the play. These laughingly responded, and they all went in a body to join the crowd. Tek Chiu, more learned in books and more powerful in intellect than his schoolmates, was behind all of them in his knowledge of the dark ways of these theatre actors, and the still darker ways of those animals in human form whose practice it is to follow the pageant from place to place. The jesting innuendoes of the other boys were at first more mystifying to Tek Chiu than even the most incomprehensible of Lao-tse's sentences; but Tek Chiu was no exception to the bulk of mankind, in whose minds is a latent curiosity to learn the definition of a particular evil, although there may be utter abhorrence of the evil itself.

It was a black chapter in the book of human life that had been opened up to an inquiring mind; and to the honour of Chinese prescribed morality be it said, Tek Chiu had come to look at this chapter with the amount of intelligence with which a schoolboy, ignorant of the Greek alphabet, looks at a page of Homer for the first time. Nevertheless it was now given to Tek Chiu to ponder on the hitherto unthought-of depths of human degradation. Tek Chiu was at that time certainly no evolutionist. He thought neither of progress nor degeneration. He did not reflect that these theatrical myrmidons had once been little children with possibilities like himself for better things, and that they were and had been the instruments rather than the members of society. He therefore abhorred with indiscriminate abhorrence the sin and the sinner. Yet the effects of this attitude of the lad's mind was not the healthiest possible one. His conscience became more deadened in the contemplation of those evils that belong to the more natural order. Had a faithful instructor pointed out to him at this time that the more properly natural and ordinary forms of vice may ultimately lead men towards those that belong to a still lower level, Tek Chiu might have become here less compromising than he was in his attitude towards some evils that were militating against the precepts of the morality he had been taught.

Leaving the sights and sounds of the theatre show, Tek Chiu and his companions were walking back to their books, when they were about to pass by a small group of people, rapidly becoming larger. In the middle of this group was a European missionary, accompanied by a young Chinese preacher, whom Tek Chiu could recognise as a young fellow who once sold nuts and cakes, but who was now in the pay of the foreigners. The foreigner, a round stout man, was standing in silence while the Chinaman was preaching. "Repentance of sins" was the theme. Smoking opium, playing cards, attending theatre shows, were all denounced in the strongest terms. Men doing these kinds of wickedness and refusing to repent would be sent into hell. "And what is hell?" asked the preacher. "An eternally consuming fire," he added, answering his own question.

During the latter part of the young Chinese preacher's discourse, embodying denunciations of those overt acts and practices of sinning men, the European kept his eye fixed steadfastly on Tek Chiu. Tek Chiu, though disposed to laugh aloud with his companions at the definition given of hell, could not do so, feeling himself under the foreigner's scrutiny. Tek Chiu, a young gambler, had heard that the reward of gambling was the tortures of hell, yet he was unmoved. Not the preacher's words, but the foreigner's look, disconcerted him. He was much relieved when the preacher coming to a sudden stop, the foreigner began to turn his eye in another direction, and to hand out tracts.

Tek Chiu gathered himself together and spoke in a clear voice to the preacher who had just concluded his exhortation. 'May I ask a little about the doctrine you have been preaching? Where is the hell of which you speak? Is it in the clouds, or under the earth, or on some island, or where is it?'

'I cannot say where, but I know that it is somewhere, and a place of torments for lost spirits.'

'Torments of fire,' asked Tek Chiu.

'Yes,' replied the preacher.

'Then if the torments are of fire, that fire must have a particular place; and you cannot tell where it is, whether north, south, east, or west.'

Tek Chiu was really serious and argumentative. But the young Christian preacher thought his questioner simply jesting, and he got angry. No doubt the behaviour of Tek Chiu's companions gave him some ground for thinking Tek Chiu insincere.

'The natural man cannot know the things of the Spirit of God,' said the preacher.

Tek Chiu turned to his laughing companions and they left the crowd.

The foreigner's name was the Reverend Joseph Richmond, and the Chinese catechist was named Yew Lay. Teacher Richmond, who had been engaged in a copious distribution of tracts, observing that Tek Chiu had turned his back on the crowd, asked his companion if he knew who the questioner was. Had he ever come to the chapel to hear the doctrine?

Yew Lay replied that he was a deceased graduate's son, who, while still in mourning for his father, had given himself up to all sorts of bad practices; he was a constant visitor to one of the worst gambling-houses in the town. He had asked questions simply because he wished to controvert. He was a bad boy—not a sincere seeker after the true doctrine.

CHAPTER VII.

EVEN WAY.

THE Missionary Hospital in the city of Even Way is a place where many a good day's work has been done. The worker's name is Angus Gordon, M.B., C.M. In the city itself, and for many miles in the region round, the Chinese people know long ere now that if urgent medical aid is needed, at sunrise or at noon, at sunset or at midnight, Dr Gordon would rather die than refuse to give it. For the last twenty years the great adamantine wall of anti-foreign feeling has been crumbling down in and around Even Way. No other region within the eighteen provinces of the Middle Kingdom can present a more conspicuous example of the power of one strong man. Angus Gordon, a Scotchman, has an iron will, a deft hand, a clear head, and a generous heart.

It was a Tuesday forenoon. In the stream of patients with ulcers, abscesses, eye-cataracts, and other nameless ailments, who were passing through the operating-room when Dr Gordon and his Chinese students were hard at work, was Pun Kwi. Pun Kwi, accompanied by two helping friends, one of whom was Tek Chiu, had travelled from Black Rock to get cured by the foreign doctor of his ailment—a tumour in the neck. The operation was painful but speedy; and with directions to keep the wound clean and well dressed, Pun Kwi with his companions was on the point of leaving the Hospital, when the doctor, successively eyeing Pun Kwi and Tek Chiu, remarked—

'Where do you stay? I must have seen you before.'

'Yes,' said Pun Kwi; 'one morning, many months ago, in Black Rock.'

'Surely,' said the doctor, 'you asked me to see this boy's dying mother.'

'That is so,' said Pun Kwi.

But other patients were awaiting operations; and the doctor had simply time to say—

'Remember, brother, that there is a much more important thing than the need to get your body healed, great as that need is. See that you give heed to the doctrine that we are sent here to preach. That is by far the most important matter.'

The doctor proceeded with his next case—the dressing of a hideous-looking ulcer. He had begun to toil with some mysterious medical fluid when all of a sudden he stopped and shouted out in English from the railed window of the dispensary into the porch—

'That old fellow whose case I have just treated is rather an interesting person. He has travelled in his day.'

The person whom Gordon here addressed was Henry Bell, a young missionary who had just come to the place to sojourn for a time with Dr Gordon.

Bell saluted Pun Kwi and his two friends. Asked if he had obtained benefit at the Hospital, Pun Kwi replied in the affirmative with emphasis. No doubt, he said, the pain of the operation had been considerable; but the tumour had been removed. He was grateful beyond measure, and even surprised. An old Chinese proverb said that a man would have to take a tumour in the neck to his grave with him. Dr Gordon had cheated the proverb and the grave.

'Have you heard of the gospel of salvation?' Henry Bell went on to ask.

'O yes, often,' replied Pun Kwi.

'It is very mysterious; I cannot understand it,' volunteered Tek Chiu.

The young missionary was gratified to hear the lad speak out, even although it was to express a difficulty. The remark revealed an ingenuous youth.

Bell explained to these three pilgrims that God was the Father of men, and that Jesus Christ His Son was their Saviour and Brother, and that those who trusted in Him and served Him would gain an undying reward. In a few sentences Henry Bell preached the gospel of forgiveness of sins and eternal life, Pun Kwi and his companions nodding approval at intervals. These three Black Rock travellers then left the Hospital.

It was evening, and Dr Gordon sat in his usual evening seat within Even Way Mission-house. It was a seat which he vacated only when he went to bed, or not unfrequently when he was summoned away by a midnight call for medical aid.

'Draw in yer chair, lad, and gie us yer crack,' said the doctor, addressing Henry Bell, who was leisurely entering the room.

Bell claimed Celtic descent by his mother's side. He therefore rightly interpreted Gordon's Scotch Highland dialect as the very effusion of homeliness and hospitality.

'And how are you going to like China?' asked the doctor, who had lit his pipe, and who, in the midst of vigorous puffs producing thick volumes of smoke, readily awaited his guest's answer.

The homeliness of the man and the smoke saved Bell from being formal. In usual circumstances he would have said, 'Very well, I think.' But Gordon seemed to have the power of drawing men as well as pipes.

'Well,' said the other, 'I have been now over a year in China, and I have tried to keep my eyes open, and, except in the way of learning the language, I have tried to keep my mouth shut. In some respects I am gratified; while in other respects I am disappointed with the prospects of a missionary's life.'

'That's what I should have thought, lad,' said Gordon. 'And what are your disappointments?' Gordon's face suddenly beamed with merriment. He felt he was putting a poser to the young missionary.

Bell responded to his friend's humour. 'In the first place,' he said, in a low sepulchral tone, mimicking the Scotch country parson, 'no European missionary has yet succeeded in speaking the Chinese language very well. If any one has succeeded, he died long ago. It is rather discouraging to an ambitious fellow like me to think that if I would be an exemplary speaker of Chinese I must die first.'

'You see,' continued Bell, not allowing his friend to interrupt, 'I speak from the ripe experience of European missionaries themselves. Missionary A speaks of the linguistic attainments of missionaries B, C, and D

Each of these three has his conspicuous faults, varying in their degree of heinousness. A similar criticism is passed by missionary B on the linguistic attainments of missionaries A, C, and D; missionary C deals similarly with A, B, and D; and lastly, missionary D with equal warmth points out the relative imperfections of the tones, or the idiom, or the extent of knowledge, of missionaries A, B, and C. The criticisms, while partially appreciative, are all quite in accord with one another. Harmony among missionaries is a consummation devoutly to be wished—but that is a digression. I have already come to my conclusion: Wherefore no missionary can in the actual become quite proficient in Chinese. Q.E.D.'

'Ha'e a cigar, lad,' said the doctor.

Before he sailed from England, Bell had thrown away a formidable pipe and a beautiful tobacco pouch; but time works wonders. He had met missionaries who were intemperate in their condemnation of the weed; and their apostolic counterblast to tobacco had converted him into a moderate smoker, as was evident from his acceptance of the cigar offered him by Gordon.

'Did you speak to that boy at the Hospital this morning?' Gordon asked of his friend.

'The boy who accompanied the old man?'

'Yes.'

'I spoke to him as well as I could. It is a hard business to discourse on the serious questions of life in a language that one knows so imperfectly. And even, given a perfect utterance, there are those whose minds are hard to influence.'

'Yes! I am glad you spoke to the boy. The old man's mind belongs, I fear, to the beaten way-side track order; but that boy has a wonderfully sharp and attractive look about him. I remember having met him two years ago and more. When passing through Black Rock, I was called in to see his dying mother. The old man whom he accompanied to-day is some relative of his. He is not his father, for his father is a graduate —a Siew Tsai.'

'Indeed!' said Bell. 'Is that boy's father a graduate?'

'Yes—a heathen, of course,' replied Gordon.

'Is he a heathen because he is a graduate?' asked Bell.

'These literary men are hard to reach.'

Gordon had got back once more to his deliberate style of moral earnestness. Both friends voluntarily allowed the subject to drop. They talked far into the night on many topics successively suggested through that strange association of ideas which regulates a mind playing freely round its object, and that cannot be quite reduced to a system. China and missions in time had passed out of sight, and 'Caledonia, stern and wild,' had come into view. Old college days came back again. The august professor, with his ballad quotations and his solemn but all too gentle rebukes to exuberant youth, had, as through a phonograph, been made to speak once more. Abortive experiments of the Natural Philosophy class-room were painted in their realistic and tragic colours. Even Way Mission House had transcended the limits of time and space; and youth and hope had been made to live again.

Next morning another missionary, travelling and hungry, entered the sacred precincts of Dr Gordon's sitting-room—the room hallowed by the talk and smoke of the preceding night. The Reverend Joseph Richmond was a married man, and therefore hated tobacco both in itself and in its effects. He had often denounced smoking to Gordon as idolatrous burning of incense, while Gordon would reply that it was praiseworthy burning of the idol.

'Gordon should ventilate this room,' was his remark to Bell, while his nose kept vigorously inhaling the poisonous atmosphere. But the new-comer was neither a cynic nor a scold. He was in the best of humour, a hungry yet not an angry man.

Breakfast was already over, and Gordon had gone to his Hospital. Bell welcomed his friend, and in the absence of his host himself gave command to the boys to hasten and feed the traveller.

Mr Richmond had passed the previous night at a place halfway between Black Rock and the city to which he had just come. Heaven's Tavern, a place famous for bed-bugs, enjoyed no sinecure fame: to the eager appetite of these creatures, the stout and jovial missionary had been an easy and welcome prey. But cruel as these creatures had been—may not the struggle for existence be justified?—they had not deprived the reverend gentleman of his own appetite or his good humour. Indeed, there seems to have been good humour all round, for if the bugs of Heaven's Tavern had not, in so many words, said, 'Come again soon,' they had meant to say it.

The preliminary salutations over, and the allusion to the bugs duly and decorously made, Richmond began to unfold more important news.

'I must tell Gordon that one of his patients died yesterday at Heaven's Tavern village.'

It was a transition from the gay to the grave—a transition which Bell evidently felt was too sudden.

'I am sure Gordon has not killed him,' said Bell. 'Gordon is not the man to do any such thing.'

'No. Eating an overdose of oysters can hardly be said to have been part of Gordon's prescription,' said Richmond, giving information while suitably indorsing Bell's protest. He added, 'It's very unfortunate in more ways than one. The relatives of the dead man and many others will attribute the cause of death to us. There will be more superstitions than ever about foreign medicines and medical treatment.'

'They'll lose sight of the oysters,' said Bell. 'Who is the man that has died? Perhaps I know him.'

'His name is Pun Kwi, an elderly man. He belongs to Black Rock, and he was on his way back to his place.'

'Dear me! I think I do know him. Did a middle-aged man and a young lad accompany him?'

'It is quite so,' said Richmond, answering in idiomatic Chinese.

'And it's the old man that's dead, is it?'

'Yes. Gordon had removed a small tumour from his neck. The poor old fellow had severe pains after eating what proved to be poisonous oysters, and he died in three hours' time. When I arrived at the village last evening, I found the village people much excited about the matter. Naturally enough, the two companions of the dead man were in a sore state. They conveyed the corpse to Black Rock this morning, leaving before daybreak.'

'I spoke,' said Bell, 'to these men when they were about to leave the Hospital yesterday. Gordon was remarking last night how bright and promising the young lad seems to be. When Gordon takes a fancy to any one he is not half-hearted about it. The lad is a graduate's son.'

'Yes,' said Richmond. 'But his father is long since dead. The old man that died yesterday is the boy's father-in-law. But Gordon has been looking merely on the lad's outward appearance. He is a bad boy.'

Bell heard this last remark with disappointment. Richmond, a senior missionary, familiar with almost everybody and everything in Black Rock, and indeed in the whole surrounding region, was in a position to know the truth, if going often to Black Rock counted for anything.

'The boy is a gambler, and keeps the most disreputable company,' continued Richmond. 'Although still so young, he is a positively hardened heathen Chinaman.'

But ere Tek Chiu's character began to pass under review Richmond had already finished his morning meal. Richmond's terse sentences exhausted the topic. He rose to go to the Hospital. He was a man of action. Bell was deeply interested in Richmond's remarks, but it was no time for further questioning, much less was it an occasion for moralising.

Bell prepared to accompany his senior colleague. While tying his shoe—a suitable time for a brown study—he was picturing in his mind Pun Kwi's face, and recalling the conversation of the previous day with the old man now dead, and also the ingenuous, questioning words of Tek Chiu. That young lad was almost, if not quite a hopeless case in Richmond's eyes. Gambling and bad company had made the lad a hardened sinner. It was heathen hardness.

CHAPTER VIII.

SALISBURY.

GOLDEN DOOR, sixty miles south-west of Black Rock, with its three hundred thousand inhabitants, has barely escaped being a sea-port city. A river—Mud River is its name—narrow at Golden Door, widens itself as it travels seaward. Junks and sampans float upon its waters, while its banks for many miles are fields of rice and sugar-cane, dotted here and there with a house or a pagoda. Mud River is the diameter of a wide, circular plain, the circumference of which is a range of high hills. These heights frown on the level land below. At frequent stages of its course Mud River receives tributaries flowing down from different points of the surrounding hills, and irrigating the whole plain. These tributaries, as their crooked windings attest, grudge their respective contributions of water to Mud River, which, however, in spite of such stinginess, is at last the proud absorber of them all.

Near to Golden Door, as if anxious to keep it from having a view of the distant ocean, the hills, suddenly approaching Mud River, fall precipitately into it. At some distance up the slope of the most presumptuous hill are two European houses of so large a size that when first built they bewildered the Chinese, who have now, however, through lapse of time, become insensible to their strangeness and their glory. These two buildings, the one a house and the other a school, stand out in distinct relief from one another, and still more from the fantastically-topped Chinese houses.

The dwelling-house has been named by its builders 'Salisbury Villa,' known simply as 'Salisbury,' and called after the distinguished statesman, whom it thus honours on account of his spirited foreign policy. 'Salisbury's' position is precarious. It threatens to slide into Mud River. But this is not all. An enormous round boulder, claiming to be a part of the hill, but having a dangerously top-heavy appearance, that seems to belie such a claim, projects over the villa. European visitors to this place have passed many cruel jokes about this boulder. A gifted blue-stocking lady is reported to have referred in this connection to the doctrine of Linnæus, that 'fossils are the parents, not the children of rocks.' This lady had inconsiderately compared 'Salisbury' to a fossil, and by careful deductive reasoning spoke of the impending disaster threatening 'Salisbury' as the case of a parent being destroyed by its own offspring. But 'Salisbury' is much too modern to be a fossil.

Two missionary ladies occupy 'Salisbury.' They do not concern themselves about the boulder, or what the boulder may do, for their minds are absorbed by more ethereal pursuits.

In one of the two front rooms on the first floor sits Miss Minnie Sand, plying her needle and thread. The letter-carrier has just left Golden Door on his way down the river, and Miss Sand has had a busy morning of it writing off her letters to catch the European mail.

Her friend and colleague, Miss Stonebridge, who is just expected back from the school where she is teaching, defies the European mail. She is an American.

Miss Sand, as she sews leisurely, the bustle of writing and despatching letters being over, has her eyes wide open, so imperious is the demand of the seam that requires small stitches. Now and then she holds the seam up almost to a level with her chin, her shoulders being bent downwards by way of adaptation to her special task. A faithful camera at the present moment would picture Miss Sand free altogether from that objectionable self-consciousness which makes every ordinary photograph more or less unreal.

Miss Sand is a little over being quite a young lady, for her age is about thirty, while she is considerably under the average height. A glance at her reveals a plump face, with the large eyes that need the assistance of eye-glasses to look at distant objects; a cheek bone pronouncedly jutting out from beneath the outer corner of the eye, a blue circular vein, like the small arc of a large circle, specially visible on the upper surface of one cheek, a beautiful chin, altogether elastic but for compressed lips, a mouth over the average size, yet in neat symmetry with the large, majestic, massive head that sits comfortably on powerful shoulders. Some years' residence in China have been prejudicial to Miss Sand's teeth, but like the women of China, among whom this devoted little lady's lot is cast, the grinders are kept well indoors. Only when Miss Sand's sense of humour becomes too strong for her do her front teeth insist on being seen; then the lips that are usually so forbidding relax to a degree that quite compensates for their habitual staidness.

Miss Sand's temperament belongs to the nervous type. Therefore it is that a close friendship, deepened and ripened by years, exists between Miss Stonebridge and herself; for Miss Stonebridge, who is ten years her friend's senior, is in general outline a vastly different type of individuality, being quite as lymphatic as Miss Sand is nervous.

As Miss Eva Stonebridge enters 'Salisbury' by the front door, her friend's voice accosts her—

'Is that you, Eva, dear?'

'Have you got all your letters off?' is the answer which is yet a question, a proof that Americans—one at least—may be schooled in Scotch civilisation.

A thin lady enters the room, to sit on a chair opposite her friend. Miss Stonebridge is not much taller than her junior colleague, but being of slim physique, the difference between the two young ladies in respect of stature is conspicuous.

'O Eva,' said the younger lady in high and excited tones, to indicate an important announcement, 'I have sent in my letter to *The London Missionary Astonisher*, and I have given a description of Min Niang's case. But it is so difficult to get home people to understand the outs and ins of these matters. I really begin, now that the letter is off, to think that I have been trying to describe the indescribable.'

'Have you made a copy of the letter? I should so much like to see it.'

'O Eva! I have had pity on your literary taste, and have torn up the rough draft I had previously sketched out, and that was the only copy I had. You will see it soon enough—too soon, indeed—when *The Astonisher* arrives from home. The decent editor would do me a

F

kindness if he would consign my letter to the waste-basket.'

'Minnie, you do talk nonsense.'

'I'm afraid I have written nonsense.'

'Do you really expect,' asked Miss Stonebridge, 'that I am going to shower compliments on you for your charming style, and in Chinese fashion humour your latest whims? I am angry with you, Minnie, for not allowing me to see the letter. But now tell me what you have said about this affair of Min Niang.'

Miss Sand made an effort to draw from the storehouse of her memory to satisfy her friend.

'Well, I began,' she said, 'by saying that on the death of the girl's father, Pun Kwi, some months ago, a lady missionary, Miss Stonebridge by name, had been visiting Black Rock, and had made the acquaintance of Min Niang's mother. Through the instrumentality of the amiable and charming qualities of Miss Stonebridge——'

'O Minnie, be serious, and tell your story as you wrote it,' said the listener, suppressing with difficulty Miss Sand's laugh, of which she herself had caught the infection.

'Well, then, I said that you visited Pun Kwi's widow, and that the poor woman, whose sanity of mind seemed to be slightly affected by her bereavement, had come to like you very much.'

'Oh, I see now,' interjected Miss Stonebridge, with wicked sarcasm; 'I see now why you think you have written nonsense.'

'Eva! you are a horrid thing,' said Miss Sand, as though she would proceed no further. Up went the industrious stitch to its former position, this time like the signal of a ship in distress.

'Well, then,' said her companion soothingly, 'I won't again interrupt, although I wish you had left me out of the story altogether.'

'I said,' continued Miss Sand, not seeming to notice the concession, 'that you had recited Gospel stories to the woman, and taught her about the Saviour, and that she gradually became interested. I recounted her observation on the Loaves and Fishes incident. It looks like mixing up the sublime with the ridiculous, but I could not resist the temptation. Then, again, you had persuaded the mother to send her daughter to our school. As well as I could, I described the story of the slave-girl bought at Canton by Min Niang's father, and brought to Black Rock. As pathetically as I could also I related how this poor slave-girl suddenly disappeared, carried off, as it is most likely, by some Cantonese boatmen, and that she has never been heard of since. There, now, haven't I satisfied your thirst for knowledge?'

'Did you not say anything about the unfortunate marriage engagement?'

'Yes, of course, I had to refer to this matter in particular, since it gave point to my story. But it was here I felt how difficult it is to write a missionary letter. I glided over painful details, simply summarising the matter by saying that the girl, who, as we hope, has become a sincere Christian, is in misery on account of her betrothal to a heathen boy. The betrothal having taken place at her birth, the poor girl seems to have no control over her future. I closed the letter by saying that Min Niang's case gives striking proof of the sadly rigorous character of the Chinese marriage customs, and the great hindrances that these customs present to the progress of the Gospel.'

The missionary letter was allowed to go on its undisturbed way to England to add to the columns of the *Astonisher*. Miss Sand's review of Min Niang's case set her friend a-thinking. Miss Stonebridge was accustomed to think, and that too with ingenuity and determination.

'I say, Minnie, we must do our best to save the poor girl.'

'Surely,' said the other. 'What is your opinion of the matter?'

By a subtle process of association, Miss Stonebridge's opinion, even to minute details, had become necessary to Miss Sand's life. Personality that is said to eternally resist obliteration is yet, it seems, capable of being so leavened by the influence of others as to come dangerously near self-extinction. It is a danger to which strong as well as weak minds are liable. To identify another actual personality with one's own ideal is an easy thing for men to do; and it is a task equally tempting for people of vastly different calibre.

'What really can be done, Eva?' said Miss Sand, repeating her question in a slightly different way.

'The boy's uncle must be approached with as much discretion as possible. If he, as the boy's guardian, yields to reason, we need have no difficulty with the girl's mother, and the matter is thereby brought to a satisfactory settlement.'

'Eva, you ought to have been made a statesman or some great diplomatist.'

. . . .

Min Niang's six months' residence at the Mission-school had greatly widened the expanse of her hitherto narrowed life. She had already become passionately attached to the two ladies who had been daily teaching her of Heaven and happiness, and who had shown her all the kindness that a girl of sixteen could wish. The girls' school was no dull nunnery. The two lady missionaries, who combined cheerfulness with purity and goodness, had made the school and its pupils a tolerably successful reproduction of themselves. Of course there were differences of character and temperament, varying degrees of mental and moral excellence, amongst these twenty-three school-girls, whose ages ranged from ten to fifteen. Old Adam at times was not without his place even there. Girls are usually girls, quite as much as boys are boys; and full well Miss Stonebridge and Miss Sand knew that the training of these girls was a struggle upwards, a struggle alike for teachers and taught, and not simply a negative process of studied exclusion from the positive and palpable evils of an outside world.

Min Niang's beauty of person, sweetness of temper, and frankness of manner had from the first day of her entrance into school commanded a wide and widening space in the hearts of her two teachers. They constantly prayed for her and with her. Min Niang was already half conscious that six months of the school, having lifted her as from a valley to a mountain-top, had widened the expanse of her vision. She had begun to think of life's meaning and purpose. Of course, even now she knew only a little. But the little that she knew and the much that she felt were quite enough to wean her from the tastes of her earlier uneventful years. With a few exceptions, and these confined to the children of great and wealthy people, Chinese girls are precluded from learning to read books. But these ladies—mandarins' daughters they were—who had come from places very far across the sea, were teaching the people that every girl ought to know how to read and write. Pity it was, thought Min Niang, that so few parents in Black Rock and elsewhere would allow their girls to be put under the care of such good people. Of course, if many girls did come to school, there would not be sufficient accommodation for them. But new and bigger schools could then be built. And other mandarins in the far-off country might send their daughters too.

Min Niang's mother willingly paid a sum of money for her daughter's boarding expenses while she remained at school. It was quite a modest allowance, and the money was well spent. When Min Niang, after four months' residence at the foreign ladies' school, had come back to her home in Black Rock for a fortnight's holiday, she was able to tell her mother many wonderful things that she had learnt. By that time she had come to know a good many of the Chinese characters and she could also read Chinese "white" words printed in foreigners' letters, and very cleverly too. Therefore the mother was well pleased that her daughter was under such good guardianship. It was hard for mother and daughter to be separate; but the time would soon come when in due course of things her daughter would be still much more beyond her mother's control. Many a mother in these circumstances would have kept her daughter all to herself as long as possible. Not so with this mother, who thought of her daughter's good rather than of her own immediate happiness. As for herself, she was a helpless and lonely widow now, in subjection to her crafty brother-in-law and his family. These relatives, and this brother-in-law in particular, had already succeeded in frittering away a considerable proportion of Min Niang's patrimony. An opium-smoker, who, in obedience to the relation between cause and effect, manipulated money rightly or wrongly when he could get it, the brother-in-law found out of course that beyond a certain point he could not with impunity satisfy his selfishness and greed. Thus it was that the widow of Pun Kwi, becoming more miserable from day to day, like a ship finding a peaceful harbour from the storm, welcomed the many kindnesses shown her by Miss Stonebridge. This lady had been to the woman as an angel of peace in the times of her bereavement and perplexity.

In these circumstances, both mother and daughter have been led into close friendship with the two ladies whose abode is 'Salisbury.' The most powerful of Christian instruments, the magnet of human sympathy and consolation, has done its great work of attracting a Chinese mother and her daughter. Perplexity in matters that men are wont to despise as worldly and ephemeral had produced in the mother a motive—an unworthy motive, it may have been—but still a motive, leading her out of the beaten tracks of her past surroundings. And the new path is to have its briars and thorns, if not for herself, at all events for her daughter, whose future, as well as her own, this Chinese mother has been unconsciously shaping. Men are makers of one another's destiny.

Miss Stonebridge and Miss Sand are in 'Salisbury,' sitting at evening tea, when the bell rings. The boy announces one of the school disciples, who has been ushered into the sitting-room. It is Min Niang, not the bright happy girl whom Miss Stonebridge left at school but a few hours ago, but a girl suppressing violent sobs.

'It's Min Niang, Eva,' cries Miss Sand, as she enters the sitting-room where Min Niang is waiting. Miss Sand is about to salute her pupil in the language of gutturals and nasals that so badly befit the little lady's powers of utterance, so admirably and peculiarly adapted to her own English mother tongue. She is about to ask, 'What's the matter?' but Min Niang anticipates her.

'Mother is dead. She died two nights ago.' The orphan girl has suppressed much of her emotion and her grief till now, but when conscious that the sad event of her bereavement has come to her teacher's knowledge and inevitable sympathy, she instantaneously loses control of herself and cries bitterly.

'Who told her?' asks Miss Stonebridge, who has just entered the room. Min Niang's bitter weeping makes both the ladies speak of her in the third person.

'Here is the letter,' said Miss Sand. 'It is written by that wretched brother-in-law. There is nothing said about the cause of her death. No one here knew she was ill.'

'Who gave you the letter, Min Niang, dear?' asked Miss Stonebridge coaxingly.

'The keeper of the Chapel got it from the letter-carrier,' said Min Niang, expressing herself through her grief with difficulty.

Miss Stonebridge looked sternly at her colleague, the deep sympathy leaving her face, and giving way to what looked like indignation.

'This won't do, Minnie. The letter should have

come here first. The keeper of the Chapel has no right to receive letters for our girls in any circumstances. We must keep up the dignity and good name of the school.'

Miss Sand warmly corroborated.

But the way in which Min Niang had received her letter could not have changed the news. Min Niang was now an orphan. She was now to cling to these kind ladies more than ever.

CHAPTER IX.

ARRESTED DEVELOPMENT.

THE uncle has always been a prominent figure in history. He may have his virtues, but he is the indispensable agent in tales of cold-blooded cruelty. Richard the Third was an uncle. Macbeth should have been one. The Babes in the Wood had an uncle. A brother's or a sister's children are a nuisance—for this cause the uncles of history are famous. There are Chinese uncles, and Min Niang's was one. Pun Lun was his name. Of course, some uncles, like the uncle of Helen's Babies, have real grievances. But these are exceptional cases, most uncles being wicked. Pun Lun was wicked; but only some people knew of it.

Pun Kwi's hard and patient toil, if made commensurate with the dollars, which, through oyster-eating, he had been compelled to relinquish, had been as love's labour lost; Pun Kwi's property had for a long time been riddling through a bag with holes in it—holes sufficiently large to make the contents of the bag become gradually smaller. But all was not lost. Pun Lun combined miserliness with self-indulgence. His habits of indolence and selfish passion imperatively demanded the appropriation of his brother's money.

Yet his was not the unscrupulous generosity of the spendthrift. He looked before him and schemed.

Unlike the drunkard, the opium-smoker has a method in his madness. Drunkenness, being a more social, is a more contagious disease, the drunkard feeling most at home in the company of others like himself. Within such surroundings the property of friends is common. Opium-smoking, on the other hand, treats society more as a combination of independent, separate beings. The confirmed opium-smoker loves the corner where he may be left to darkness, and to himself. He is not so much a social animal as a lover of self and pelf. Hence it is that, given each of these two men, the drunkard and the opium-smoker, a money fortune which they may spend, and on which they may spend themselves, although whisky is cheap and opium dear, the whisky-drinker is a shorter-lived being than the opium-smoker.

And again, drunkenness is often the shadowy means towards the darker ends of sins against social purity, since drink goads men to sensuality. Similar to that general effect is the effect of opium-smoking, which however, beyond a definitely prescribed point, has quite the opposite effect. Being conformed to the image of the opium-smoker, a man soon loses in relation to social purity the power to be either morally good or morally bad. That universal animal impulse, the gift of a wise Creator to ensure the preservation of the race, the opium-smoker ere long gets rid of; and the opium-devil, as a sort of disembodied spirit, is free to consecrate himself to his own special ministry.

Chinese domestic economy made Pun Kwi's brother's

residence the house contiguous to his own. The patrimony of the family to which the brothers Kwi and Lun belonged had many years before been divided, and Lun had therefore no legal claim on his deceased brother's property. But the sudden and untimely end of Pun Kwi gave Pun Lun special moral powers over the property, powers which, had Pun Kwi died gradually, he would not have possessed. Yet a Chinese widow has rights, and Pun Lun was not inhuman. The widow, from the time of her husband's decease till her own, had access to her husband's money, and in matters of food and dress lived comfortably. But the social restrictions of Chinese family life put the widow without sons largely under the nominal and real control of her deceased husband's relatives; and the helpless widow, in the performance of her own duties, virtually lost those rights that were hers, and that she, being no Amazon, was too weak and passive to persistently claim. Ere long, however, such war with her husband's relatives as she was strong enough to wage soon ceased; she did not long survive her husband. And when she died much that concerned the orphan girl was vested in the hands of this indispensable uncle, who, although he lived for self-indulgence, could speak agreeable and smooth words.

From Golden Door Mission-school, Min Niang had come to Black Rock soon after receiving the news of her mother's death, and immediately after the funeral (a Christian burial, conducted with a simplicity and a facility that forcibly contrasted with ordinary Chinese funerals) to Golden Door Mission-school Min Niang went back again. Uncle Lun himself was no Christian, yet, amid the vacant stares of many, and the indignation of some, he had allowed Mr Richmond and the Black Rock Christians to bury Min Niang's mother in accordance with the simple creed of the Resurrection Hope. It was rumoured among heathen neighbours that Pun Lun was about to become a Christian too; but the members forming the small body of Black Rock Christian Church knew and thought otherwise. Pun Lun would unequivocally cheat such sanguine expectations as others might hold about him. Pun Lun clung more than ever to his heathenism, his opium, and his brother's money. Special devotion to this last-mentioned idol was the central article of his creed.

Other relatives, more anxious on the question than Min Niang herself, began to enquire about Pun Kwi's property. Min Niang had hurriedly left Black Rock, not without her uncle's sanction. He had given his niece a sum of twenty dollars, he had spoken kindly to her, he had volunteered the promise that he should soon let her know what amount of her parents' property it would be competent for her to receive. Min Niang, not quite insensible to her uncle's weaknesses, nevertheless trusted him, and went back to her guardians at Salisbury. She instinctively felt that her teachers would guide and advise her how to obtain what she, as the only child of her parents, had a right to get.

A jealous and keen critic of all these events was Scholar Wu. A guest at the wine party seventeen years before, a witness to the solemn betrothal agreement, a guardian and tutor of Ming Kuang's son, a consistent and bitter opponent of everything connected with Christianity and foreigners, an insolvent debtor, and an unlucky gambler, not ungrateful to Tek Chiu for a conspicuous act of past kindness, Wu read, or thought he read, between the lines. As soon as he learned that Min Niang had once again left Black Rock for the foreigners' school at Golden Door city, he urged Tek Chiu to enter into speedy negotiations with the uncle of his betrothed. Wu well knew Pun Lun's character. He was peculiarly competent to judge the man and his movements.

Wu's strong recommendation to Tek Chiu was that he should consummate his marriage without delay. Had the wedding taken place before the death of Min Niang's mother, Tek Chiu's betrothed would have less of a legal claim than she now had on her parents' property. Undue haste having thus been avoided on the one hand, it remained for Tek Chiu, on the other hand, if he was to be true to those interests that so closely affected his own, to avoid needless and dangerous delay.

Wu was urgent in his counsel. As for Tek Chiu, he was rather platonic when the question was first raised by his teacher. He was much more bent on literary honours and fame than on matrimony. Yet Wu's painstaking efforts to show to his disciple that plotters were taking undue advantage of him were not to be without practical result.

'Your betrothed has gone back to the foreigners' school,' said Wu, 'and her uncle is left to hold undisputed sway over what belongs to her and to you. These mischief-making foreigners are at their tricks again.'

'They have taught Min Niang to read and write,' said Tek Chiu. 'Many people have told me, teacher, that the foreigners are doing works not of mischief but of great benevolence.'

'No scholar has ever told you that, I am sure.' Scholar Wu could be fierce, and he was in his fiercest mood.

'My father often praised the foreigner,' said Tek Chiu.

'Your venerable father's generous nature made him gentle even with blackguards,' answered Wu. 'For that reason your father died a poor man.'

Scholar Wu's was a clever retort. Tek Chiu's own generosity—the contents of the napkin affair—was not at that moment before Wu's mind.

Tek Chiu made a deeper plunge.

'At Even Way Hospital a friend of that foreign doctor, who visited my mother when she was dying, explained to me that all men are brothers, and that the Supreme Being is the Father of us all.'

'Will you too become an attendant of the foreigners'?' asked Wu. 'Just think for a moment. At the funeral of your bride's mother these foreigners conducted the proceedings with shamefaced impiety. No Taoist or Buddhist priest was present; no paper money was used; no crackers set off. Yet these irregularities are as nothing, compared with others about which you know full well. Those relatives, who in the circumstances were not self-respectful enough to absent themselves, were prohibited from kneeling at the grave. In addition to this, the tablet was kept out of the way —tablet there was none. What words can be found strong enough to denounce these people? They are not people at all, but foreign devils. And now your bride is in their complete possession. To remain at her parents' house seemed misery to her. Her very home she now despises: and all this the work of these foreigners. But your father-in-law's brother, Pun Lun, no doubt feels grateful that these foreigners are in this region. "It's an ill wind that blows nobody good."'

'Well, teacher, you know it is very improper for me to do anything in this matter. Had you not better advise my Uncle Peng?'

There was no delay with Wu. He went to Peng, who cordially welcomed the graduate's visit. Peng had, at that very time, been thinking in his own mind that he owed to Tek Chiu a duty in the direction suggested by Wu. Wu's energy resulted in an immediate conference between the two uncles, guardians respectively of the interests of two families.

Peng took the initiative. He went to Pun Lun's house, and made application for Min Niang as his nephew's betrothed bride. Peng spontaneously acknowledged that the death of Min Niang's mother, not yet cold in her grave, made the proposal for a speedy consummation of the marriage appear in many respects untimely: but the orphan condition of Tek Chiu and his affianced lady might reasonably claim respectful consideration as being a case of exceptional merit. A period of—say at most—three months' delay for Min Niang to mourn her mother's death would satisfy relatives and friends, who, having respect to the circumstances, would not be too exacting in their demands. It was well known to Min Niang's guardian, as well as to Peng himself, said the diplomatist, that Pun Kwi had during the later years of his life repeatedly refused to entertain the suggestion to adopt a son who might bear his family name—so great was hiss olicitude for his intended son-in-law. Therefore, Peng suggested, an early marriage was what Pun Kwi and his newly deceased widow would have desired.

Uncle Peng was no doubt correct in his reading of the lamented Pun Kwi's thoughts towards Tek Chiu; but he had not the same just reasons for assuming that Pun Kwi's widow had, after her husband's death, cherished the usual hopes of a Chinese mother. If the truth must be told, that woman's contact with Christianity had changed for her the entire face of things. The new faith had made her 'unearthly.' Specious whisperings in her ear about a degenerating youth, who, if not already enveloped in prodigality, was at any rate falling rapidly into it, had disposed her to await events rather than to shape or hasten them. But Uncle Peng, honest man, spoke only as he thought. And even although he had an adequate grasp of the situation, skill in diplomacy was awanting to him.

Pun Lun courteously listened to his visitor's words, and effusively expressed readiness to make negotiations for the marriage. He declared to Peng that the happiness of the young couple had been his constant thought. Next morning he would start for Golden Door city, and make his niece aware of the arrangement to which Peng and himself so cordially agreed.

Teacher Wu, who was in literary pursuits so excellent a coach, had not explicitly tutored Peng on the question of the bride's dowry; and Peng, in view especially of such a cordial reception, was not the man to raise the question at that stage. It appeared to him at that time that everything would be done according to propriety. Quite satisfied with his visit, he left Pun Lun to start on his promised journey to Golden Door.

G

Miss Stonebridge received Pun Lun at Salisbury. Her mind became disquieted by the announcement that Min Niang's marriage had been fixed for so early a date. Nor did she conceal from this uncle the cause of her alarm.

'I have thought long and anxiously,' she said, addressing Pun Lun, 'on this matter of the marriage of your niece to a lad who is living a bad life. Do you not think, sir, that it is your interest, as the helpless girl's guardian, that her future happiness be made tolerably secure before you consent to surrender her?'

Miss Stonebridge fastened her large eyes on Pun Lun, who could not well return the gaze. He held down his head. Pun Lun was not accustomed to the remonstrances of a woman. Like Satan confronting Gabriel he seemed to feel at that moment how awful goodness was. Miss Stonebridge seemed to be charged with supernatural power—she held her captive spell-bound. Pun Lun felt uncomfortable, while Miss Stonebridge discoursed in strongest and most earnest tones of the necessity for all men of a new life. Miss Stonebridge never minced matters when speaking to anyone on the central theme of her mission; and her love for Min Niang fanned the flame of her zeal in this interview with Pun Lun. But practical difficulties in this matter there certainly were; and Miss Stonebridge at last in more measured terms suggested that three months for Min Niang to mourn for her mother was quite an inadequate time. It was not, she maintained, in conformity with Chinese custom to take a step which would certainly not commend itself to the public mind as either reasonable or proper.

Pun Lun felt relieved when Miss Stonebridge,

avowedly washing her hands clean of the matter, concluded by saying that she supposed he must now talk with his niece. He sent the servant to call Min Niang from school. Miss Stonebridge anticipated with accuracy what Min Niang would have to say in the matter. As for Pun Lun himself, he would not in ordinary circumstances, as a Chinese guardian, have taken into account the individual willingness or unwillingness of a betrothed girl to fall in with a marriage arrangement. To approve or disapprove is not in the line of Chinese womankind. But Miss Stonebridge, as a Christian, was a champion of individualism and of her own sex, and she indoctrinated Pun Lun with this article of her creed, not by open controversy, but by tacit implication. Pun Lun was glad on any condition whatever to let the issue of his errand to 'Salisbury' be decided between his niece and himself.

Min Niang decorously saluted her uncle. He, with almost no preliminary ceremony — a most unusual thing for Pun Lun to do—plunged *in medias res.* Addressing Min Niang, he declared it to be the will of her betrothed husband's guardians that she should within three months' time enter into the bonds of wedlock.

The words were scarcely uttered when Min Niang burst into loud and bitter weeping. Marriage and misery were as one and the same thing for poor Min Niang. The first outburst of grief over, she begged her uncle for a respite of at least three months more. Min Niang named this further lapse of time, not as a coy damsel whose prerogative it is to name the day and be happy in doing so, but as one simply anxious to keep at a distance from the day of doom that, like a dark cloud, overarched the horizon in front.

The tears of his niece seemed to soften Pun Lun, whose words of gentleness were, in the estimation of Miss Stonebridge, a redeeming feature of his otherwise worthless character. He left 'Salisbury,' having given the promise to Min Niang that he would not consent to the marriage taking place earlier than six months from that date.

Pun Lun was as good as his word. He got back to Black Rock, and without delay informed Uncle Peng that the girl, still in great grief for her mother, was urgent in requesting that six months should elapse before the marriage. Pun Lun added that, reluctant as he himself was, considering the terms of Peng's request, to accede to the wishes of the importunate girl, he felt that, in view of the mother's recent death, it were better to allow it to be as Min Niang desired. Pun Lun told his tale with the utmost politeness and frankness, and Peng did his best to rival him in courtesy by the patient way in which he listened and submitted to Pun Lun's verdict.

A delay of three months' time might to many people seem trifling. But it was too much for Scholar Wu, who heard with indignation Peng's faithful recital of Pun Lun's story. In Tek Chiu's presence, he discussed the whole matter with Uncle Peng.

'These foreigners must know full well that every week's delay in your nephew's marriage means to his wife so much loss of her father's property.' Then Wu became sarcastic. 'Six months' mourning for her mother! How careful are these foreigners not to offend against this one custom and practice! In more important matters they are absolutely indifferent.'

Teacher Wu then launched out into a sea of invective,

He attributed all sorts of sinister motives to the foreigners. He would not be astonished to learn that they also, as well as Pun Lun, were covetous of the deceased Pun Kwi's money. 'Did not the foreigners receive a monthly allowance for Min Niang's boarding expenses?'

Tek Chiu had preserved a thoughtful silence throughout the storm of his teacher's denunciations. But when it was suggested that the foreigners were bent on worldly gain, he took speech in hand. He did not think that these foreign teachers had the motives Teacher Wu attributed to them. Their great desire, he believed, was for Min Niang's highest good. If an allowance of money was made to them on Min Niang's account, it was only a trifling amount. All the foreign teachers that he had yet met had a benevolent purpose in their minds. A great many things that they taught the people Tek Chiu himself did not believe, but he was quite sure that the purpose of all their work was good. He humbly ventured therefore to suggest to his uncle and to Teacher Wu that his betrothed wife's wishes should in all respects be complied with. Six months would pass full quickly.

Wu and his pupil agreed to differ. But a short time before, and Tek Chiu would have trembled to dissent from anything his teacher would say. Now it was otherwise. They were still as close friends as ever—closer, if that were possible—although Tek Chiu's independence of manhood seemed to have grown up in a single day. Such sudden growth, however, seemed but to intensify the mutual confidences of teacher and scholar. Wu needed now more than ever a friend.

Despite frequent dissipations, Scholar Wu had worked

hard to train his pupils. But already, ere Tek Chiu's marriage negotiations had come to occupy such a large place in Wu's thoughts, the other pupils had left off receiving Wu's tuition. Wu felt keenly the withdrawal of these five pupils in whose prospects he had come, in the painstaking toils of coaching them, to be deeply interested. Whether it was that the parents and guardians of these lads had lost confidence in Wu's social influence and good name, or that the lads themselves had become possessed of that love of change which makes ninety per cent. of the world's young men restless, it is not easy to determine. Wu was left alone with Tek Chiu. And although Wu did not conceal from others his own sincere belief that his only surviving pupil was the ablest and best of all the students that had come to him for coaching, there were those among Wu's enemies and friends who interpreted the breaking up of Wu's class as an unlucky omen. Not otherwise than as when the rats leave a ship that the fire is destined to destroy, did men think and speak of Wu and his falling reputation. But Wu and Tek Chiu plodded on.

In the dark ways of the corner house Tek Chiu with Wu became more deeply versed than ever. It was a moonless night, about eleven o'clock, when Wu, accompanied by Tek Chiu, sat in the gambling-house busy at cards. A middle-aged man, about Wu's own age, who had already won his spurs as a player, challenged Wu for a heavy sum of money. The two men had already played together with varying fortunes; although at the moment the heavy challenge was made Wu's star was in lucky ascendancy. The heavy stakes were made—twenty dollars a side. After quivering excitement Wu won. It was a lucky night for Wu, if wins count for anything. But the losing man, chagrined at his own bad luck, threw out an unhappy suggestion that reflected on Scholar Wu's honour. The beaten player insinuated that Wu had won by trickery.

Straightway a dispute arose. The underlings of the gambling-house were divided amongst themselves. Some favoured Wu, others Wu's opponent. A free fight ensued. Wu demanded that the imputation should be withdrawn, but without success. Blows supplanted words. The Wu-ites were bent on upholding the honour of their scholar and superior. Seizing as weapons a number of thick bamboos that had been resting peacefully in a dark corner of the room, Wu's myrmidons, much the stronger of the two factions, fell mercilessly on the insulter. Before the fury of the avengers had spent itself, the victim lay motionless on the ground.

Tek Chiu, in the utmost perplexity, was helpless in the fray. In vain he pled with the ruffians to desist, and lay down their weapons. But his efforts were really vain; for although he seemed to prevail at last with the mob, the beaten man was prostrate on the floor, having the appearance of a corpse. Tek Chiu, wringing his hands in despair, applied restoratives and changed the public sentiment. The man, now at death's door, ceased to be the foe of anybody, and became the friend of everybody. He still breathed—but heavily. Tek Chiu succeeded in getting him to swallow some spirits, which seemed to call back life. But the pain of the sufferer was terrible. He could only utter plaintive moans. Men carried him stretched on a plank to his own house, where he spent a night of agony, and where next morning at daybreak he died.

Wu's wins of that night were now turned into losses. When he heard of the man's death, he devoutly wished he had never gambled at all. 'Gambling is always a losing game,' thought Wu to himself, when the probable consequences of the previous night's brawl began to be uncomfortably present to his mind.

The relatives of the murdered man were soon astir. They petitioned the district mandarin for satisfaction. As to those implicated in the charge, these relatives cast the net as wide as possible. To accuse merely the actual murderers, the wielders of the death-inflicting bamboos, would be perversity and folly. These were mere underlings, with neither money nor influence. It was alleged that the chief party in the crime was Scholar Wu. All others within the gambling-house during the time of the murder were implicated as responsible parties. The 'Coroner's inquest' sustained the allegation.

Wu lost, not his head, but his diploma. No skull, encased in a wayside cage as a terror to evil-doers, marked the expiation of the Black Rock gambling-house tragedy. Money—an enormous sum, that Wu could guarantee but never pay—took the place of a life that Chinese law nominally demands in return for a life. Wu's loss of his professional badge, and still more his guarantee of money, met and stopped the claims of avengers, and Justice still sat enthroned.

And what had become of Tek Chiu? With the events of one short morning endeth the first lesson.

On the night of the tragedy Tek Chiu had not gambled at all. But he had sat with gamblers.

On the morning, when the dire consequences of the brawl came to light, Tek Chiu's heart bled for Wu.

He went to his Uncle Peng to tell all, but ere he got there the old man had already heard of the calamity. His own nephew and Teacher Wu—so ran the dread rumour—belonged to a gang of gambling-house murderers. The old man's heart was sinking.

What was Tek Chiu to do? He had not yet been cast into prison; but he knew not when the runners of the Yamen would come to seize him. Escape for Wu there was none—he was too well watched. But Tek Chiu might fly somewhere for a time, at least—in this way the grief-stricken Peng advised his nephew. Tek Chiu in Black Rock, whether in prison or out of it, might give a world of trouble to the few relatives that he had. The friends of the murdered man would squeeze everybody.

There was no time even so much as to deliberate. Uncle Peng managed to scrape together seven Mexican dollars. Handing it to his nephew with his benediction, he bade him an urgent and painful farewell. Tek Chiu was to leave his old homestead, his father's friends, his father's grave, his father's tablet, where restfully reposed the spirit to whom Tek Chiu owed everything valuable in life—leaving these behind, he was to explore unknown lands beyond Black Rock and China.

Tek Chiu obeyed his uncle's urgency. Towards Golden Door city he would set his face. He left Black Rock, casting not one longing, lingering look behind him. He feared the Yamen and its intricate machinery.

CHAPTER X.

TURNABOUT.

ON the rocky mainland coast, some thirty miles distant from Golden Door city, yet closely linked to that city through the kindly aid of Mud River and the sea into which Mud River flows, is the town of Turnabout. Turnabout is a seaport place, regularly Chinese but for a few warehouses—hongs as they are called—built in European style, and occupying the most advantageous part of a spacious harbour. The European population of Turnabout is small. Three mercantile firms, managed by active partners and their assistants—as for sleeping partners, they have gone home; the British Consul, worthy representative of Her Majesty, whose flag waves proudly aloft above the Consulate house; the Collector of Customs, who, along with three or four assistants, reminds Chinese traders of 'duty' to the advantage of the Chinese Government, that has lost faith in the integrity and collective powers of its own publicans—these are the heads as well as the rank and file of Turnabout European 'society.' Three or four European houses, the largest of which is a 'mess,' are situated on the sea-shore at the entrance to the harbour—a level plain that has some length without much breadth, small in itself, yet comparatively large considering the rocky coast of that region. On that plain also, but nearer to the compact masses of Chinese, is the Missionary Compound. The Compound is a group of houses, chapel, and schools. The houses are tenanted by missionaries and their families. Although some of the missionaries are constantly occupied in journeying through the region, building and confirming the churches, they have their fixed place of abode in Turnabout.

The Chinese summer having already set in, these houses of the Compound are now well occupied by regular tenants, and also by visitors who stay all the year round in inland cities and towns, and repair for a week or two to Turnabout to enjoy a well-earned and much-needed holiday.

One of the houses, a plain square edifice, is the home of Mr Richmond with his family. This house belongs to a tennis lawn; for the lawn which faces the sea is large, while the house that sits inside of it is relatively small. The house must have been a kind of afterthought, a building reared out of the few remaining bricks that had escaped a place in the large capacious chapel standing off from the sea, out at the distance of a stone's throw from the nearest point of the lawn.

It was a Tuesday afternoon. The sun was sinking, while the mercurial thermometer was stubbornly remaining high at 86° in the shade. A setting sun means little or no respite from the heat of a Chinese summer.

'Thirty off,' said Richmond, in the fever heat of tennis. He was playing on his lawn. Ground, net, and balls were all his own—hence his fearless speaking.

'We are forty and you are thirty,' said Bell, one of Richmond's two opponents. 'But,' he added soothingly, 'I may have counted wrong. We'll say thirty off. Fire away—it's your serve.'

'Honour bright,' shouted a voice from the spectators' gallery. The gallery was a modest wooden seat, with a back that almost leaned against a grass embankment. The good-natured spectator was a burly man, small of stature and ruddy of face, with hair half black, half white, that told of life's winter coming on. But the heart of the old man as he eagerly watched the play was as boyish as the heart of the youngest of those on the lawn. He rose and walked leisurely down the lawn to be an impartial umpire, leaving the seat still tenanted by two young ladies, who were thus handed over to the charming pleasantries of mutual greetings and confidences. They were old friends—Miss Sand and Miss Oldham—who had now met each other for the first time after a lapse of two months.

'I cannot tell you, Bessie, how lonely I feel since Eva left for Japan.' Miss Sand began the remark simultaneously with a sudden dropping of her eye-glasses. She had been witnessing the players and their movements, chuckling at the blunders of the play, blunders which only missionaries could make.

'How long is it since she left?' asked Miss Oldham.

'Why, it's exactly eight weeks since we all met on this lawn, and that was the day before the cruel ship left the port. And to think that other four or five months will yet pass ere Eva returns—it is simply distressing. My father used to condemn unsparingly the question "Is life worth living?" as a silly question. But he might have qualified his condemnation had he considered the case of Eva Stonebridge in Japan and me here.'

The 'set' by-and-by came to an end. Richmond's side was victorious, Bell's vanquished.

'There is still time for another set,' said Richmond, who was master of ceremonies. 'Miss Sand and Miss Oldham might play.'

Miss Sand asked to be excused.

'I wish to speak to you, Mr Richmond, on a matter of business,' she said, after four players had taken up positions at their respective posts, Miss Oldham and Bell being among them.

Mr Richmond was all attention, and Miss Sand assumed her most business-like attitude.

'I wish very much to know, Mr Richmond, if this Black Rock affair can now be satisfactorily settled?'

'Yes, I certainly think,' responded Richmond, 'that it can be settled, and very satisfactorily too. That heathen boy has decamped to explore foreign regions. He is now in the position of an outlaw. Your young *protégée* has gained her freedom at last.'

'What a relief to Eva's mind when she comes to know of this!' exclaimed Miss Sand. 'I would like to give the girl to Yew Lay. Mrs Gilmore is of the same mind too.'

Richmond meditated. 'Yew Lay is at present a Black Rock man—that's a drawback,' he said. 'But, of course,' he added, more reassuringly, 'there are talks among us of transferring him to be both preacher and teacher at "Three Tree Well." In that case there would be no difficulty in giving effect to your proposal. My only difficulty in the matter is that if Yew Lay were to remain preacher at Black Rock and marry that girl, an unpopular prejudice might be excited against the Mission, and we cannot afford at the present stage to give needless offence to the heathen community.'

'Of course not,' said Miss Sand; 'that would not be desirable. You will do your best in the matter, Mr Richmond, won't you? Yew Lay does not belong to Black Rock, and if you transfer him to Three Tree Well, as you propose, any difficulty on that score is thus removed.'

'Yew Lay's mother has eighty dollars, Mrs Richmond tells me,' said Richmond.

'Yes,' said Miss Sand. 'I should think that even an avaricious man like Min Niang's uncle might be persuaded to bargain for that amount, although of course a heathen family would willingly give more for Min Niang.'

'That uncle will make as much as possible out of the transaction, you may be sure,' said Richmond. 'But,' he added, 'the scoundrel has got fat already by property not his own by right at all. The property belonged to that girl's father, and should now be hers.'

'Yes,' said Miss Sand; 'it is a complicated case. But Min Niang, noble creature that she is, has declared that she will sacrifice all possible chances of ever getting any of the money in order to escape a heathen family. Poor girl, she has put her hand to the plough, and she refuses to look back.'

The conversation was interrupted by a stoppage of the tennis-play, sudden darkness having arrested the game. The players, in groups of twos and threes standing at the head of the lawn, began to talk 'shop.'

'You go off again to Golden Door on Friday, I suppose, Minnie,' said the tall, stately Miss Oldham, who had been doing wonders with the tennis-racket.

'O yes, Bessie; the cares of the school sit heavily upon me. When will you come up to see me at Salisbury?'

Miss Oldham was answering the question to her friend's satisfaction when Mr and Mrs Richmond broke in upon their confidences.

'Now, Mr Richmond,' said Miss Sand, 'as I understand you are going south to-morrow, and as I leave here on Friday, I shall not see you again for some time. Will you promise me to do your best for my girl, Min Niang? You have a good head to manage these matters, Mr Richmond. Hasn't he, Mrs Richmond?' Mrs Richmond, a quiet lady, blandly smiled, and Mr Richmond himself gave an assuring answer to Miss Sand's petitions.

Mr Richmond was a man on whom lay the care of all the churches. Everybody confided in him. He was held by all his colleagues to be an authority in matters of church discipline. And the matter of Min Niang's future happiness was one of these things about which, as Miss Sand felt, he could give ready and judicious counsel and help.

The absence of Miss Stonebridge in Japan, an absence necessitated by an indifferent state of health, imposed many extra duties on her junior colleague. Miss Sand's capabilities were now, through the straining force of her situation, being tested and indisputably proved. To rightly train the girls under her care was a matter of time, while to rightly marry them was one of seasonable opportunity.

Henry Bell, a junior missionary and a stranger to the subtle problems of marrying and giving in marriage, was labouring to satisfy the more rudimentary requirements of his calling—to use his limited knowledge of the language, and to increase it as speedily as possible. He selected Black Rock as a suitable spot. His purpose was to reside where there would be no European beside himself. The choice of Black Rock had practically been determined for him by the Mission Council at Turnabout. Yew Lay, the Black Rock preacher, was to be transferred to Three Tree Well; and for a few weeks to come Black Rock would have no native evangelist. It was accordingly with the cordial approval of his senior colleagues that Bell left Turnabout to sojourn a few months in Tek Chiu's native town. Armed with a good stock of books and provender, and solemnly enjoined by his friends in Turnabout to be mindful of his health, Bell took up his bed and walked northward. He arrived at Black Rock to find Yew Lay, the preacher, making preparations to flit.

Yew Lay, still a young man, had for three years consistently preached Hell Fire to the people of Black Rock; and his preaching had done good. Not that he had kept back from his hearers occasional glimpses of Heaven: his was simply the case of a man whose mind was most at home in the doctrine of Divine judgment as taught in its more concrete aspects. He had been trained along with other preachers in a Mission college that insisted on students having a competent knowledge of the Bible from Genesis to Revelation. Of Hebrew and Greek he knew nothing; and being quite a stranger to the English language, he was, as he himself acknowledged to Bell, shut out from access to good Bible commentaries that so often serve as effective substitutes for a knowledge of the original languages of the Sacred Book. But Yew Lay had made good use of such means as he could call his own. His College training had made him a dogmatist and a puritan in theology. He had a wonderful memory for Bible texts, all of which he could neatly make to fit in to a system of doctrine that had been instilled into him by his foreign teachers. Indeed, Yew Lay was a greater architect of dogma than any one of his teachers. For, although even the most dogmatic of these teachers had left him some latitude on certain questions of Christian doctrine, Yew Lay had a strong bias towards the definite and the severe.

Henry Bell spent his first two hours at Black Rock in uninterrupted conversation with this young Chinese preacher. In answer to Bell's question, Yew Lay stated that his two themes of the previous Sabbath had been—

Morning—" Elisha, the Mocking Children, and the Two She-Bears."

Evening—" The Rich Man and Lazarus."

On the first of these two subjects Bell was silent. But as to "The Rich Man and Lazarus" he ventured the remark that he had never felt himself sufficiently able to deal with such a subject.

'It is a subject that requires great delicacy from the preacher who would deal with it,' said Bell, in the best Chinese phraseology he could command. 'I have always found it much easier to discourse on such subjects as " The Great Supper," " The Prodigal Son," or " The Syro-Phœnician Woman."

'Why are you leaving Black Rock?' asked Bell, after the two hours' talk.

'Teacher Gilmore and Teacher Richmond think it better that I should go to the south region. I have been three years here already, and it is more suitable that I should go somewhere else to make way for another preacher of greater gifts than myself.'

'I pray that you may have much success in your new sphere. Mr Richmond told me that you are to get married at an early date.'

Yew Lay blushed. Matrimony is a subject about which a Chinaman speaks to others as little as possible. Yew Lay therefore handled this subject as anyone would handle a hot potato.

Bell, already accustomed to Chinese modesty, understood Yew Lay. He could understand the Chinaman whether as to his depreciation of his own preaching powers or as to his discomfiture on the marriage question.

'I wish you every happiness in your marriage.'

Yew Lay profusely thanked the young foreigner.

CHAPTER XI.

TRANSITION.

By an arrangement in which Uncle Peng passively, and Uncle Pun Lun actively acquiesced, Yew Lay and Min Niang were formally betrothed. Three months later would be the wedding. All that the Rev. Joseph Richmond, carrying out the wishes of Miss Sand and her absent colleague, had to do, was to come to terms with the two uncles; and with tolerably good grace he succeeded.

'Well, teacher, you are preparing your heart to preach the doctrine,' said Richmond in Chinese to Bell, as he suddenly invaded the young missionary's sanctum at Black Rock. Richmond, who could say serious things in Chinese to Chinamen, was accustomed to use that language as a vehicle for a playful attitude of mind when he met an intimate European friend.

'It is an unexpected pleasure to see you here,' said Bell, who had been steeped in sermon-making, and who was thankful for this respite.

'I am up to look after a wife for the young preacher that has been working here.'

'A benevolent mission,' responded Bell, as yet unfamiliar with the facts of Min Niang's history.

'Gordon has given me strict charge to get you to go up his way,' said Richmond, changing the subject.

'I have a mind to obey the summons. You are on your way back to Turnabout, I suppose?'

'Yes!' said Richmond. 'I have had a very encouraging time of it. The work at Even Way is going forward by leaps and bounds. I baptized a graduate on his death-bed. We had much difficulty in persuading the relatives, especially the women-folks, to surrender to us the ancestral tablets. But in the end we prevailed. We have every reason to thank God and take courage.'

'Talking of graduates,' said Bell; 'I had often intended—but it has always escaped my mind—to ask about a graduate's son whom I met some time ago at Even Way Hospital. He belonged to Black Rock, if I remember rightly. He accompanied an old man, who died at Heaven's Tavern Village on his way back from the Hospital. Do you know what has become of that lad? I liked his look.'

'I suppose he is in Singapore long ere now,' said Richmond.

'In Singapore!' exclaimed Bell. 'What has sent him away there?'

'It is strange,' said Richmond, 'that you have been these weeks here, and have not heard of the gambling-house tragedy. But, of course, it took place some months ago. The lad took a short cut out of his difficulties by emigrating. I suppose it was the best thing he could have done. His departure has brought relief to us, I assure you, and to Miss Stonebridge and Miss Sand in particular.'

Without wasting words, Richmond told Bell the

main facts of Min Niang's early betrothal, and how she had become an object of solicitude to the lady missionaries.

'It's rather a pathetic story,' said Bell. 'And so the graduate's son loses his bride!'

'Rightly too,' said Richmond. 'The way of transgressors is hard.'

'And Yew Lay is the gainer,' said Bell, as if speaking to himself. Yew Lay, along with brother Christians, was having some refreshment downstairs in the cook's quarters at the time of the missionaries' dialogue.

'I confess,' said Bell deliberately to his friend, 'that if I were a Chinaman, and had my choice of marrying that girl, even although she were a veritable angel, I should prefer to do without her.'

Richmond silently smiled at his young colleague's harmless notions.

'There is a strange romance about the whole affair,' continued Bell, speaking now in more subdued tones. 'A betrothal before birth—a change in the girl, converted to Christianity—an exiled bridegroom—a revolution in the Chinese social sentiment. Positively, Yew Lay, the interloper, is not to be envied. But of course Yew Lay, poor chap, is not to blame. An individual in China has nothing to do with his own marriage.'

After Richmond had resumed his journey towards Turnabout, Bell's curiosity led him to search for the young exile's relatives. An old Christian brother, whom Bell regularly accompanied on out-door preaching expeditions, and who constantly painted, to Bell's delight, old scenes in Dr Bruce's heroic life among the Chinese of Black Rock, agreed to escort him to the house of Tek Chiu's uncle. This old man seemed to know everything and everybody in Black Rock. He was one of the earliest Christians of that region, and had adorned the doctrine through good and ill report.

Old Uncle Peng wore a dejected look. Min Kuang's charge, the care of an only son, lay heavily upon him. That the lad had been compelled to leave the country to escape evil consequences was but the beginning of sorrows. Probably he had gone to Singapore. Would he ever return?

Although scolding was not quite an easy matter for Peng, he was tolerably successful in his efforts to scold Henry Bell. Ah Long, the old Christian brother, shielded the foreigner as well as he could by scolding Peng in return. Ah Long was older than Peng, and Peng could not well retort. But the simple facts that Bell was very young, and that he was comparatively a stranger to China, saved him from the vengeance that Peng would otherwise have contrived to wreak upon him. The foreigners had lent a helping hand to deprive his nephew of his bride, Peng had begun to say. Tek Chiu was absent, and could not defend his own rights; and Peng himself was helpless to vindicate his nephew's claim on the bride. Tek Chiu had gone abroad, and could not well return for years to come. Perhaps he would never return at all. The fevers of a hot country might have already killed him. Some evil beast might have devoured him.

'Only yesterday,' said Peng, 'a man who lived in Singapore for five years, and who is now back again here, told me that for every three men that go to Singapore only one comes back alive. That man's house is only two stones' throws from here. His friends will tell you that when he left here to go to Singapore he was stout and strong of limb; now he is a skeleton and a weakling. A breath of wind would blow him down. The only employment he could get all the time he was in that place was to run all day pulling the "son of a carriage."'

Peng's idiomatic Chinese for a jinrikisha was intelligible to Bell only after considerable mental effort. The phrase was a fresh addition to his vocabulary.

'But your nephew has ability for higher things than pulling a rikisha,' suggested Bell to old Uncle Peng, whose dull sense of hearing required the young missionary to repeat the statement by 'putting out' a louder voice.

While Bell was making himself audible, a middle-aged man in long robes entered the room. It was Scholar Wu.

Whatever Wu thought or said about foreigners, he was a Chinaman. He was not openly impolite. As he entered Peng's house, his ear caught the foreigner's reference to his pupil, and the minimum of ceremony over, he asked anxiously if there was any news of the lad.

'No,' said Bell; 'I should much like to know where he is and how he fares.'

Scholar Wu's anxiety to obtain knowledge of Tek Chiu was at that time considerable; and this sentiment expressed by Bell formed a bond of sympathy between the foreigner and himself. To turn an enemy into a friend is usually a perplexing task; to accomplish such a task belongs less to dynamics than to art. This slight pressure of a finger on the right chord and at the right time wrought here for Bell a triumph the extent of which he himself never knew. For the first time in his life Wu felt kindly towards a foreigner. At intervals in a conversation that traversed as subject-matter the regions known to the Chinaman abroad, Wu lauded the ingenuity and goodness of foreigners.

In his inmost soul Wu had for months been nursing a longing to follow his pupil. It seemed to Wu that life abroad must indeed be a hard thing were it no better than his life at Black Rock, as recently embittered by adverse fortunes. The loss of his diploma was an indignity that was bringing to him, to an extent greater than he had at first thought, the reproach of men. Some laughed at him, while others mocked him in his misery. And his debts, which he had now ceased to calculate, were hanging like millstones round his neck. What wonder, then, that Wu should be anxious to know all about his pupil? And what wonder that he should extend to Bell unusual consideration; since the time had come for Wu to learn as much as possible about foreign parts? He too would emigrate.

Scholar Wu's previous notions of foreign regions were crude. At different periods of the Ming dynasty the Emperor of China had sent embassies, which exacted large tribute from the native chiefs in various regions of Malaysia. This chapter in history was well known to Scholar Wu. But the details of modern Chinese emigration Wu had still to learn. He had already had many opportunities of knowing; but his anti-foreign feeling had led him to assume that it was beneath the dignity of a scholar to exercise his mind about such a subject. Now the much intensified struggle for life was making Wu an ordinary being.

From emigration and foreigners, the talk of Bell and

Scholar Wu soon launched into the still wider and profounder topics of religion. Wu propounded questions to which Bell gave answers, while asking questions in return.

The personality of a Heavenly Father, the Incarnation of a Saviour Christ, the Christian doctrine of immortality were, as Wu kept stoutly maintaining, mysteries which could not be realised in thought, and which could not reasonably be maintained. Over against Wu's contentions, Bell declared with emphasis that only by means of such great truths could the mysteries of man, the world, and God be made intelligible. Without these as fundamental truths, all else would necessarily be chaotic elements in a mystery of darkness. The mystery of light, indeed, was the system into which fitted the eternal immutable truths of all real religion. Wu's hatred of Christianity, almost born and assuredly fostered in him, had endowed him with a kind of spiritual preparedness of a special kind. Having proved himself capable of hating the Christian faith, his mind was much nearer a love for it than the minds of most Chinamen, whose spiritualistic susceptibilities are not simply non-Christian but almost non-existent.

Thus it was that in a few weeks' time a miracle was wrought in Black Rock. Wu enjoyed the friendship of Bell for several weeks after meeting him at the house of Uncle Peng, and then suddenly became a changed man.

The suddenness of Wu's change was real, if sudden change of life there ever has been among men. But the student of this phenomenon is not true to the whole facts of the case who does not take into account the entire range of Wu's past life, character, and circumstances, as the great vantage-ground from which God may be witnessed as communicating to this anti-foreign Chinese graduate the purposes of His love. Past and present are as one to him who thinks the thought of God. Wu's great sin that needed great forgiveness; his poverty and desperation that set him adrift from the ease and luxury that militate against spirituality; his loss of that official dignity which he, as a typical Chinaman, would almost sooner die than lose; his decision, now matured, to leave his home and emigrate, and his consequent openness of mind to foreign testimony; his tender happy memories of Ming Kuang, who, notwithstanding that he had died ere crossing that Jordan which separates the religions of China from the promised land of Christianity, had often remonstrated with others, Wu among them, for their want of open-mindedness; his knowledge of old Dr Bruce, as that knowledge lingered in his memory, testifying to the power, fragrance, and beauty of that teacher's life; and lastly, his friendship with Henry Bell, who, discoursing with him for some weeks past as one enquirer after truth talks with another, had put forth the sickle and reaped the harvest of Wu's moral earnestness and final conviction as to the worth of Christianity and Christ,—such were the missionary forces that at last had passed into their resultant. It is a mere question of words, that has hitherto been the bone of contention among different schools of Christian theology, whether these circumstances be termed causative forces or channels. In the light of highest, widest truth, that deals with the subtle question of the relations between the Divine and the human, all human forces are also channels, the stream and its confines being one and the same thing. Missionary facts, like Kant's Practical Reason, are corrective things which do not surrender all to vagueness and verbiage, but which, on the contrary, assign to these their proper posts and put labels on them.

Other forces, of course, had been pulling Wu in the opposite direction. The natural, resisting deadness of man's heart to spiritual life; the abhorrence of change, that makes the Chinese mind what it is; deep-seated Chinese prejudice against the foreigner, a prejudice at its very strongest in Wu; the wound still open and sore caused by missionary high-handedness in the matter of Tek Chiu's bride—such were some of the obstacles that, like a wall of sand before the incoming tide, had loosened and disappeared.

Wu's public profession of allegiance to the Christian faith would have been much delayed—it might indeed have never been made at all—but for another change that now took place.

Henry Bell was seized with sudden illness one night; and when the grey light of next morning dawned, he was very weak—so weak that he could with difficulty call for Beng Guan, the chapel-keeper below. Great was the distress of the attendant when he found the young foreigner so ill, whose comforts Richmond by word of mouth, and Gordon by letter, had enjoined him to promote. The young Chinaman had been doing his work right faithfully; but his sedulous care did not ward off that sickness which in some form or other comes sooner or later to all.

When Beng Guan ascended to the little room tenanted by Bell on this morning of sickness, he found his charge prostrate on the floor. He had fallen out of his bed, and evidently was too weak to find unaided his way up to it again. A brother from below came up to the chapel-keeper's aid; and, with gentle hands, both of these friends in need stretched the young missionary on his bed. A little Chinese wine caused him to revive somewhat, and gave him strength to speak; for it had seemed to the attendant when he entered the room that Bell's speech had gone.

'Send for Gordon,' said Bell, speaking in English. The two Chinamen looked at each other.

'I should much like to see Gordon, but I am afraid the way is too long,' continued the sufferer in his own mother-tongue.

Beng Guan, leaning down and speaking into the patient's ear, desired to know his wish. Bell recovered himself somewhat; and, smiling at his mistake, spoke Chinese. Within a few minutes' time, one brother had left for Even Way, and Scholar Wu was at the bedside.

'Teacher,' said Bell, 'I must leave you. I cannot tell you what is wrong with me. Perhaps it is cholera; but I'm not sure. But I well know that in a few hours hence I shall be no longer with you. I am therefore anxious to speak with you.'

With much difficulty Wu came to see that the missionary was dying. Gazing straight into the sufferer's eyes, Wu asked if his heart had peace. The Chinaman asked this question as though he himself were under the spell of some enchantment, so solemnly curious was he to know how his own new faith could confront death.

'For me there is perfect, unfathomable peace,' said Henry Bell, returning Wu's gaze with an intensity that made the Chinaman, matured in years as he was, feel overwhelmed with a sense of the young foreigner's seniority. For one Chinaman, at least, Bell was now no longer the foreigner.

The invalid was very weak. He could not tell his own ailment. During the night-time he thought it was dysentery, and he was now in a burning fever. He could not make a diagnosis of himself after a technical, scientific fashion. But he knew, as he repeated to Wu, that his summons had come. Of his imminent death Bell spoke with unfeigned certainty. Nor did he speak of the matter with surprise or alarm. One would have imagined that the date of Bell's death had been known to himself for years past; and Wu was not quite kept in bewilderment on the subject, for Bell himself gave him the explanation.

'Like Joseph, whom you may have read of in the Book of Genesis, I have been through my life given to dreams. This power, given me, was the answer to a prayer I made when I was yet a child. I used to pray over a large solid block of coal in my father's coal-cellar—do you know what a coal-cellar is, Wu?—and, with this large block of coal as my altar, my special prayer was that I should be as a man like unto the prophet Elijah. My prayer has somehow been answered. Certain important events that have taken place in my life I had already dreamed of and seen beforehand. And when I awoke last night and found myself in pain, I remembered a dream which I had some years ago. I saw myself then as I now lie here. I saw you, too, Teacher Wu. I shall die at noon to-day. Show me my watch, Wu! It hangs on a nail behind this bed. It is now almost ten o'clock, I should say.'

Wu showed Bell his watch. It was ten minutes before ten o'clock.

'We have still two hours, Wu. Let me speak with you as our Father may give me strength. Through no merit of mine, Wu, I have been privileged to get occasional glimpses of the spiritual world, that is,—so far as I am able to explain it—the spiritual world has occasionally become materialised in dreams to me as simply temporary accommodations to the limitations of human vision. But, remember, the spiritual is not the same thing as the material.

'But oh! Wu, the inadequacy of my powers to speak in your language troubles me much. And even did I know all your words well, I suspect that there are many glories that even then would fail of expression. Would that you knew English, Wu; I could then explain to you more clearly what I know of the Person and work of Christ.'

The young missionary was all the while speaking Chinese with amazing aptness. Yet he seemed much perplexed about the weakness of expression.

It was now half-past eleven o'clock. Bell was consciously much weaker; but his speech and powers of mind had not yet failed him.

'I now speak through you, Wu, to my loved ones at home, and also to all my friends here in this region of China, and to the Chinese people of the Christian future. Charge them to magnify the Saviour Jesus Christ, and to rejoice in Him always. And you, Wu, turn your back on all your past life! The great Sin-bearer will relieve you of all your burdensome weights. Forget the things that are behind! Turn your face towards the future! And may the Grace of Almighty God be with you, through Jesus Christ our Lord!'

Henry Bell ceased to speak. Wu spoke to him, but

got no answer. Five Chinese brethren stood round the front of the missionary's bed. Three were in tears, Wu being one of them.

The sallow, clearly-cut face of the youthful missionary (his age was twenty-seven, but he looked even younger than his years), the quivering lips, his head, which he playfully tossed as a boy does who nestles on his mother's lap, the occasional looks of boyish delight which he kept distributing between Teacher Wu, Beng Guan, and the others—such is the chronicle of Henry Bell's last half-hour on earth. He spoke no more to those around him. But to Wu, who kept scanning him with earnest, loving gaze, the young missionary, now Wu's greatest earthly creditor, whose presence he sorely grudged to lose, seemed with quivering lips to be speaking and conversing to some one, not in Chinese tones, not even in earthly sounds, but yet in a language that the Person whom he had served and adored could surely understand.

Then the lips and eyelids ere long protested in their weakness against their being the media of such unaccustomed sounds and sights. Their work was finished. And as the hour closed, there closed with it Henry Bell's earthly toil, the whole workshop of the body and its busy members; the weapons, too, of thought and emotion, changed all at once from work to rest. The heart that lived to know, because it had lived to feel, ceased now to beat. And while the Black Rock prophet's chamber was being irradiated by the sun, that passed through the topmost seams of the window shutter and the door, and when that sun reached its greatest altitude in the heavens, then rose aloft the spirit of Henry Bell, attracted to the glories of a triumphant immortality by the Light that is above the brightness of all created suns.

The flush of life lingered on the missionary's brow as Wu, with one heavy sigh and a big irrepressible sob, laid his hand tenderly and reverently upon it. So deals a mother with her first-born babe as he sleeps in his cradle. 'Had he really gone as he had said?' asked Wu of himself, gently arranging the bed-covering and the pillow of him that slept. And the perfect stillness answered 'Yes.'

'I have never till now seen man die thus,' said Wu to the Christians beside him. 'Our mournful burial customs would badly fit in to such a death as this. He has died, not as dust going back to dust, but as a bridegroom preparing for his wedding.'

CHAPTER XII.

THE COOLY.

WHEN Tek Chiu reached Golden Door city in his flight from calamity, he had six dollars in his possession. It was, he thought, a small sum with which to begin life. Hoping therefore to add to his income, he soon staked in gambling all he had; and lost it. And when abject poverty came to stare him in the face, he met a friend.

The friend was a crimper, a recruiting agent for the supply of emigrating Chinamen as labourers for the Malay Archipelago. The meeting was timely. Tek Chiu at Golden Door was lying by the wayside, bruised and bleeding in heart with the sorrow of leaving Black Rock behind him; and the crimping agent, Samaritan-like, ministered unto him. This functionary offered to advance as a loan enough money to pay a passage in the ship *Sai Phung*, notified to leave the port of Turnabout in little over twenty-four hours' time. The recruiter comforted Tek Chiu by calling upon him to dismiss needless anxiety. He would get abundant opportunities for making money in the Straits. That land was a land of Goschen.

'I am a student,' said Tek Chiu, 'and I wish to continue to read books.'

'You can get good employment, then, as teacher; and you will have splendid opportunities also to learn foreign languages.'

To learn foreign languages was indeed a new idea to Tek Chiu, and he liked it.

'In what way shall I pay back my passage-money?' asked the aspiring emigrant.

'When you get to Singapore, your destination, a very skilful and well-disposed man who manages matters there will receive from you a regular sum of money each month until you pay off all your debt. And it is only just and fair, of course, that you should pay him a little extra, as interest for the loan.'

'But suppose I do not speedily get employment, what then?'

'The managing man will do all he can for you in that case. But since there are others in this city who are anxious to go abroad, I must leave you meanwhile. In three hours' time the tide will be favourable for us to sail to Turnabout. If you choose, you might meet me at the jetty at that time.'

The speaker pointed to a place at the side of Mud River where were a number of junks that had the appearance of being impatient to start. The bustle of the boatmen showed that preparations on a large scale were going on.

'Or, if you like,' continued the recruiter, surveying Tek Chiu in a business-like fashion, and speaking as one who feels himself to be making a generous concession, 'you may come with me and I'll give you a few dollars to buy your bedding and clothes. But remember,' he added solemnly—so speaks a man when he appeals to the conscience of another—'you must pay me back this money with a little interest within a reasonable time after you get to your destination.'

'That I shall do, you may be sure,' said Tek Chiu, as

tears of joy gathered in his eyes. He followed his instructor, and procured a piece of matting, a red blanket, a varnished bamboo pillow, and some smaller pieces of raiment. These articles cost seventeen hundred cash. They were purchased at specially low prices, the recruiter being a friend of the shop-keeper. The four hundred cash that made up the balance of two Mexican dollars were handed over to Tek Chiu by the recruiter, who thus became Tek Chiu's creditor.

In less than another hour's time, Tek Chiu found himself housed in a junk that swarmed with intending emigrants and their friends. The buzz of conversation, which comprised discussions on various matters public and private, was made harmonious by praises of Singapore. Singapore at the Equator, a shining buckle on the belt of the earth, is the golden hope of many a Celestial. In that free and friendly port thousands of Chinamen, discontented with their lot, and oppressed by poverty or by fear of the mandarins, seek shelter and fortune, leaving their native land in almost daily shiploads. And many an impecunious Chinaman, still confined in the discontent of China, as he meditates on the good luck of emigrants who have preceded him and reached Singapore, puzzles himself with the problem, how those fortunate ones (like Pope's flies in amber) ever got there at all. But this puzzle is confined to inland villages and towns. In the larger inland cities and in the treaty ports, no Chinaman who keeps his eyes and ears open need be ignorant of a way of access to sunny Singapore. The recruiter is on the spot to guarantee a passage and also prosperity at the end of it.

The recruiter's timely aid gave Tek Chiu a new start in life. Landing at Turnabout late in the evening, after seven hours' sail, he spent the night in a depôt, a place crowded with others who, like himself, were eager to leave China. Tek Chiu, along with the newly found shipmates of his voyage, was now committed by the Samaritan recruiter to the charge of the depôt-keeper. As only one night remained to be spent in China, the recruiter's acts of benevolence soon came to an end. Next morning Tek Chiu was in most polite fashion introduced to the K'eh T'ow who, so the recruiter told the lad, would be as a father to him on the voyage.

Tek Chiu did not like the appearance of his new father. During the previous night while in the depôt, he had already met this person, a red-faced sensualist; and from the attentions paid him by the inmates of the depôt, Tek Chiu had inferred that he was some one in authority. This K'eh T'ow had treated Tek Chiu very blandly, even to the extent of offering him a share of his opium. Tek Chiu's answer—'I have never yet smoked opium, and I don't intend to do so,' made the tempter smile mischievously, and Tek Chiu from that moment avoided him as he would avoid small-pox.

When, therefore, next morning the recruiter, taking leave of Tek Chiu, introduced him formally to the K'eh T'ow, it was with disappointment that the lad recognised him as the opium-smoker of the previous night. 'I shall put no dependence on *him*,' said Tek Chiu to himself. 'His business must be to deceive men; his habits are neither proper nor right.' Self-reliant and circumspect, the lad inwardly resolved that, so far as that would be possible, he would be faithful to his father's last commission. The morality of the old graduate had, like an oak, taken deep and firm root in the soil of his son's life. It was Chinese morality at its best—a morality which Ming Kuang in his conservation had thought was morality unalloyed. But this morality Teacher Bruce, in days gone by, had helped the graduate to formulate and value. Maintaining a nominal resistance to Christianity, Ming Kuang had unconsciously taught himself to use its Light as the medium through which he viewed his own native morality. That Light, Ming Kuang, being no soientist, had no thought of analysing.

At such critical junctures, therefore, came the precepts of the father to the aid of the son. Tek Chiu's cultivated taste for gambling showed clearly enough, forsooth, that he had hitherto failed to keep all his father's precepts. But have not Christians, too, as well as 'heathen' Chinamen, their faults?

But it is time to go on board. The K'eh T'ow, with over forty men, led the way to the jetty: ere long the great steamer, with its mystery of size and power, received a new instalment of passengers, like the Trojan horse receiving into its belly the host of brass-clad Greeks.

Thus it was that Tek Chiu, a young man of eighteen according to Chinese chronology, constituted one of the 876 parts of the cooly cargo. The Chinese cooly ship is a miniature Chinese city or town. The coolies are huddled together. Crowding is Chinese orthodoxy; and the good ship *Sai Phung* could not during that voyage be convicted of heresy.

The darker doings of Spanish barracoons and Portuguese desperadoes have been succeeded in these latter days by the more humane treatment of the emigrating cooly. Steam has shortened the time of transit. Coolies are not now battened down under hatches in ill-ventilated, poisonous holds, or left there to sickness or death. To make an attempt to reach the deck does not now mean being shot. The peculiar horrors of the historical 'middle passage' have been swept away—horrors that were wont to beget mutiny and self-immolation among exasperated passengers. The modern cooly ship is more a creature of civilisation.

The modern shipowner is, nevertheless, a shipowner first and a humanitarian afterwards; and the boarding officer is still far from being immaculate. The millennium has not yet come. Of food there seemed, so far as Tek Chiu's modest opinion was concerned, to be a fairly liberal supply—rice being, of course, the staple article. But people ought to know that the arrangements as to food supplies on board these ships are conducted with an ingenuity that deprives the cooly of the most valuable and nutritious portions of the victuals professedly bought for him. The estate of these Celestial coolies is almost as bad as that of the Skye crofters.

The cooly's loss is the purveyor's gain. At the port of destination a good market is usually found for what might have been consumed on the voyage. The amount of salvage stock is seldom small. Such are the cooly ships that plough the China Sea. These bearing aloft the British flag, the emblem of almost world-wide Empire, appropriate to themselves the sacred name of Liberty by way of compensation for the Slavery that this sacred name so oftentimes even now, in contact with China and the Chinese, effectively creates and conceals.

During the earlier and larger half of the voyage Tek Chiu, when not sea-sick, had felt the loneliness of a crowd. An aspiring graduate, he had begun to feel now the incongruity of his surroundings with his past career as a reader of books. Disgrace at being a cooly was not of course quite obvious to the young adventurer. Conspicuously high, indeed, is the place given in China to the scholar. Yet the line of division as drawn between trades and professions is drawn in China in such a way as to vindicate the dignity of manual labour. The great middle classes, the merchants and shopkeepers of China, are the possessors, in theory at any rate, of a dignity which is inferior to that of the agricultural labourer. A cooly may be a movable piece of merchandise; but the creed of China demands that the 'article' that is in this way bought and sold should be considered of greater value and dignity than the money-making trader through whose hands the 'article' passes.

Tek Chiu's constitution, temperament, and past training had evidently destined him for mental more than for physical labour. The lad had consulted his own predilections when he came to verbal terms with the Golden Door crimper. His ambition was to obtain work in the Straits as teacher, and still more as learner. But in this ship no one excepting the K'eh T'ow and himself seemed to be able to read. He had, therefore, no friend on board with whom he could satisfactorily exchange views on the subject of his prospects in Singapore. Tek Chiu's mind was thus left to answer its own puzzles, most of which therefore till the end of the voyage had to remain unanswered.

When still a day's sail from Singapore, as Fortune would have it, Tek Chiu had a talk with a man who was travelling to the Straits for a third time. His name was Song, and he was old. This wanderer could not, it seemed, endure the monotonous life of his native Fokien village. He gladdened Tek Chiu by telling him what Tek Chiu already knew from others—that Singapore was a better place than any part of China; but in almost the same breath Old Song warned Tek Chiu against being deceived by greedy and worthless men.

'You will be compelled to work among jungle in tobacco plantations,' said Old Song, knowing that Tek Chiu was a sold cooly. 'You will get no chance to read books at all.' (The lad had uttered his expectation in the hearing of the old man.) 'The recruiter has deceived you to make his own profit.'

Long before Old Song—once a bought and sold cooly himself—concluded his testimony, Tek Chiu's heart had already failed him. Since the hour when he agreed to accept the recruiter's terms he had been in a fool's paradise.

Old Song had come from the other side of the ship—the starboard side near the engine—and at the port side near the forecastle head had met Tek Chiu. To accommodate himself to the restrictions imposed on Tek Chiu as an unpaid cooly, this old man had removed his camp. He had brought forward his piece of matting, and made it run into the piece possessed by Tek Chiu. There, at intervals between his opium-smoking doses, he imparted minute information to the young and raw recruit, who, notwithstanding the opium fumes, kept close to the old man and learned the sad truth.

Old Song, perceiving the effect of his words on his youthful companion, asked him: 'Do you feel disappointed at what I have told you?'

For the first time since his father's death, Tek Chiu burst into tears, which he struggled hard to repress. He was the saddest of the 876 passengers. Unlike a sheep going to the slaughter, he was aware that he was going there. His knowledge was his sorrow; and his thought, the product of his mind's training, was the sting. As for the other unpaid coolies, these had been better fitted for hardship. Their ignorance was their fitness and their bliss. Coolies, like poets, are born, not made.

Old Song had paid his own passage. He knew better than attach himself to the unpaid class. His past experience had given him quite enough of the hardships of an indigent sold cooly. His story, as he told it to Tek Chiu, was one the first half of which stretched back to a time prior to the efforts of the British Government to regulate the cooly traffic. These were dark days, days when the darkness of the cooly trade was visible. And the second half of the old man's story—the modern version—like the second half of the Jewish decalogue, was like unto the first— with the important qualification, that now, with foreign officials greatly multiplied, the raw cooly had more abundance of opportunity to be bamboozled by the complexities and subtleties of Western law. Old Song had no ill-will towards foreign barbarians. On the contrary, he commended them. For although in knowing men's hearts, their ability was not so great as that of his own countrymen, still they were wonderful people on account of their many cunning contrivances, of which the telegraph-wire and steam-engine were samples. Old Song was a debtor to the foreigners: he had received much benefit from their hospitals, and several times he had been rescued from death by the happiness and splendour of their jail.

'Their jail!' exclaimed Tek Chiu.

'Yes,' said Song, not appreciating Tek Chiu's bewilderment. 'A man who works in Singapore for any length of time feels in need of a few holidays. Wealthy merchants in Singapore have their great houses out in the country, and poor men have the foreigners' jail. In red-haired foreigners' territory, poor men, too, can be happy. The foreigners doubtless had this in their mind when they built the prison. It is a wise arrangement. In the jail opium is prohibited.'

Song made this last remark while he was laboriously preparing to smoke a fresh dose of that drug. How Old Song spent his holidays in Singapore was a matter that surprised and amused Tek Chiu. He questioned his old friend a little further.

'How do you gain admission to that institution?'

'For me it is not now so easy as it used to be,' said Song. 'But as yet I have never had much difficulty. During the time when I worked in Singapore on my own account as a rikisha-puller, my plan was to forget lighting up the rikisha lamps when darkness set in. Sometimes, however, such a course was not necessary. Malay policemen are very skilful in arresting men without cause. The best plan is to cheat the policeman by going with him to the prison-office. He expects you to "tip" him and save him all this trouble of escorting you. It was by a mere accident once that I was compelled to go to jail. Till that time I had always been afraid of the jail, but since that lucky arrest I have despised the policeman, except at such times as when I have felt in need of a holiday for my health's sake.'

Old Song's implication that he had frequently courted policemen to get 'run in' slightly brightened Tek Chiu. From that point Old Song proceeded to speak about his life as an agricultural cooly, and in that connection he gave his notions about the well-meaning foreigners. After his second voyage to the Straits, he was for a time employed as a garden cooly at a short distance from Singapore city. Dissatisfied with small pay and poor prospects there, he left that vocation; and one day when in Singapore city, whither he had come in hopes of bettering himself, he met a man who promised him high wages and light work. Grasping at the proffered help, Old Song followed the man to confer with the new employer. But ere he knew it Old Song had fallen into a bad hole. Entering a house, which proved to be a depôt, Old Song was made a prisoner, the depôt-keeper claiming him quite avowedly as part of a quantity of special preserves which it was his intention to forward with due decorum to Siak, for cooly labour in sago plantations there. Thus kidnapped, Old Song was with due ceremony brought to the foreigner's place, called the 'Chinese Protectorate,' where he stoutly denied the charge of being a cooly who was under obligations to the depôt-keeper. The depôt-keeper, knowing well his business, in words of surprise and indignation produced by Song's remonstrances, claimed his man; and the black-faced official at the Protectorate told Old Song that he must settle his account with the depôt-keeper as best he could, while he charged the depôt-keeper that, as his cooly was not willing to go out of Singapore, the proposed transfer to Siak could not be allowed. 'I was conveyed back to the depôt,' said Song, 'and I was closeted in a cellar upstairs. A fire made of coarse rice-husks was kindled in the place immediately below me. The smoke, coming up from a hole in the ground where I was standing, filled the cellar in a few minutes.'

'And what did you do then?' asked Tek Chiu, thrilled with the story, while gasping and trembling for an answer to his question.

'I growled like a tiger,' said Song; 'and the depôt-keeper declared that so long as I refused to sign the foreigner's document the fire would be kept going. Paddy-husk, he told me, was cheap; nevertheless, I did not burn to death.'

Old Song was pulling breath from his opium pipe as he discoursed on his purgatorial experience, and made his last statement in a reassuring manner.

'After a time,' continued Old Song, 'the depôt-keeper came and asked me if I would sign. He promised me freedom from the cellar, five dollars in money, and other inducements, which I shall not enumerate in the hearing of a lad such as you. To be suffocated with paddy smoke is bad; but to be allured into such places as those into which that depôt-keeper allured me for the sake of my signature is worse than paddy burning. At last I consented to become friends with the depôt-keeper. I agreed to accept all his bribes and to sign his contract, and he opened the cellar door.

'I went to Siak; and in four months' time, when I was very ill and about to die with jungle fever, my younger brother, having found out where I was, secured the influence of a big man in Singapore, and got me away from Siak. It was there I learned to smoke opium. I was told that opium was a good medicine for fever, and so I was persuaded to smoke it.'

On the subject of opium-smoking Old Song had a conscience. He spoke of his first schooling in the smoking habit as the most thrilling of his jungle experiences. And Tek Chiu, like a sensible Chinaman, appreciated the emphasis which his old companion gave to the matter.

With melancholy interest, Tek Chiu, as he listened to the old man's experiences, had the cruel conviction that he was listening to the history of his own immediate future. Discerning the lad's state of mind, and looking on him with some feeling of tenderness, the old man, in face of his own paddy-husk story, gave Tek Chiu the wrinkle that he should appeal from the black-faced Protector to the red-haired foreigner, whom Old Song differentiated as the 'great dog.' The black-faced man at the Protectorate was a mere underling. But the man with the power would surely listen to the story of anyone who stated his case clearly. Tek Chiu was then instructed to make it his business to refuse to go to a malarial district such as a plantation or a mine. Any one going to such a place would likely die very soon. A lad so young and so able to read books, as Old Song pointed out, would do well to take every possible precaution on reaching Singapore that he should be sent to a healthy spot. Tek Chiu gave heed to this advice. He did not wish to die.

'The foreign mandarin will extend protection to you,' said Old Song. 'But you must take great care to claim that protection. Men who newly arrive from China know nothing about the foreigner's generosity; and the foreigner's protection is therefore simply a "show." In nine cases out of ten, protection is of little or no use whatever. Most unpaid coolies are eaten alive by four sets of people: first, the recruiter and his agents in China, including the K'eh T'ow, who travels with the coolies; next, the depôt-keeper in Singapore; next, the planter's agents—sometimes a foreign merchant's firm; and lastly, the planter himself. Now, young friend, be bold. Take my advice, and use your great ability to assert your rights.'

The old man smoked himself to sleep. But Tek Chiu kept awake, not because of his being an abstainer from opium, but because, seeing the future more clearly than he had seen it before, his mind persisted in thinking about it. Old Song's panorama had saddened and forewarned him.

CHAPTER XIII.

PROTECTION.

THE mysteries of the ship's engine had overawed Tek Chiu on the day when he embarked at Turnabout; but since he had throughout the voyage become familiar with other terrors, the engine had by the morning of arrival at Singapore tamed considerably. The sun had not yet risen on that morning, when he was roused from sleep by the violent shuddering of the ship caused by the discharge of waste steam. The old *Sai Phung* was casting anchor in the bay opposite to a place called Johnston's Pier; and as Tek Chiu rubbed his eyes and looked, it was to become bewildered and charmed by the beauty of the city that stood before him. But his wonderment was short-lived; for his thoughts soon became absorbed in the work of leaving the ship. Some there were who, ere the anchor was yet cast and the boarding officer arrived, jumped into sampans, baggage and all. But Tek Chiu was under guard. *He was to be* taken *ashore.*

The thoughts and feelings of the young immigrant as he set foot on the landing-place were those of a stranger and an exile. The peremptory and gruff ejaculations of the tall Sikhs, who spoke in a language that Tek Chiu did not understand, signified that he with the rest of the herd was to follow. Through large and beautiful openings the pageant passed. The European buildings, familiar in a small way to Tek Chiu in China, were specially imposing here on account of their number and variety. Beautiful carriages drawn by stately horses, rattling gharries with their wicked ponies, flying rikishas pulled by running, reckless Chinamen—it was a pleasing, overpowering spectacle. In addition to the crowds of Celestials, men of the queue, were large numbers of Malays and Klings, varying in their degrees of blackness and nakedness, and an occasional European.

Singapore, a free port, had its custom-house for Tek Chiu. That house was the cooly depôt, the hotel where for a time he was to lodge, where Tek Chiu was to pay as duty his own person.

Seven days in a cooly depôt certified to accommodate 80 men passed slowly and in dull monotony. Tek Chiu, although not disposed to be petulant, complained of a bad smell in the house, but as neither the depôt-keeper nor the other coolies felt it, he was watched with some suspicion. Pity it was that the lad was not informed and set at rest on the matter, for the cause of his uneasiness had its correct explanation in the fact that within fifty yards of the back room where he had his sleeping space a durien-eating family resided. This young cooly, albeit a Chinaman, reared amid the least modern of sanitary surroundings, had found here a new misfortune in the durien-fruit smell, a misfortune from which neither distance from the duriens nor the iron bars of the depôt could aught avail to protect him.

Two Europeans visited the depôt during Tek Chiu's sojourn in it. They could not speak Chinese—at any rate, if they could, they were not disposed to do so. Tek Chiu in vain taxed his ingenuity to get a chance to speak to both of these men, who came at different times and on separate business. One was a doctor—a young, dark-haired foreigner, who did not commend himself to Tek Chiu as Dr Gordon in bygone days had done. The other was a man with a camera, who scanned Tek Chiu carefully, charging him by means of signs to look at the bull's eye. Tek Chiu, remembering Old Song's hints, was glad to be a subject of the foreigner's treatment. He stood the ordeal like a man.

During Tek Chiu's seven days' sojourn at the depôt the keeper's conduct was tolerably courteous and considerate. On the eighth day that functionary made the announcement to Tek Chiu that it was now time for him to go to the Protectorate and sign the foreigner's document. Tek Chiu, having revolved in his mind Old Song's information, had already presaged something of this sort, and asked his father superior for particulars as to the contract he was expected to sign. Without compunction, the keeper informed him that it was arranged he should work out his passage-money in Deli. Deli, in the island of Sumatra, was a place which, as Tek Chiu well knew, killed men and grew tobacco. In silence he obeyed the summons, and, under escort, was conducted to the Protectorate.

A hubbub of men, chiefly Chinamen, stormed the entrance to the building. European and Malay police constables, exhibiting by their bearing higher and lower degrees of official authority, kept exercising that authority, and a little more, over the several groups. Tek Chiu was one of a special batch of coolies. Those around him were utterly indifferent as to whether the 'water and soil'—the idiomatic Chinese for climate—of the place for which the depôt-keeper had booked them favoured longevity or not. No man can be more indifferent to hygiene or life than the average Chinaman. This apathy of his companions much perplexed Tek Chiu. He had his own thoughts, and these he could only keep to himself.

He determined to avoid Old Song's misfortunes if possible. Yet he was between the horns of a dilemma. What was he to do? If he protested against going to Deli, he would be carried back to the depôt and badly treated; unless, as he hoped, he might make his case plain to the foreign officials. But he could scarcely avoid thinking of paddy-husk fire and smoke, and shuddering as befitted the thought. Again, if he submitted to sign the document, his prospects were undone. Willing as he was to endure hardship for a time, and work off a debt which he assuredly ought to pay, Tek Chiu—such was his education—had still higher notions of his life and prospects than to think that a steamboat passage from China was an adequate equivalent. After a final process of reasoning, Tek Chiu made up his mind to run the risks of subsequent cruelty from his creditor, the depôt-keeper, and try to explain the merits of his position to the foreigner at the Protectorate. He determined to put the worth of Old Song's counsels to the test.

A good-natured Scotch policeman was standing at the fringe of the crowd of expectant Celestials outside the door of the Protectorate. Seeing him, Tek Chiu, in his mother tongue—he had no other—took courage and spoke. 'Here is a European and a ruler,' thought the lad to himself; 'he is my court of appeal.' Disregarding the cooly-house myrmidon, he accosted the foreigner. 'I shall not go to Deli. I shall not sign the agreement,' he said resolutely.

'Apa?' said Donald, speaking in Malay, using a word the Scotch equivalent of which is ' *Wha-at?*'

'That man is not the big dog,' said a brother in bondage. 'You can state your refusal when you get inside the building. The man with power will ask you to sign the paper after your name is called.'

Tek Chiu was compelled to be satisfied with this brother cooly's explanation. The myrmidon, a Fokien Chinaman, who of course had overheard Tek Chiu's premature protest, which had been completely wasted on Donald, looked cynically at the young rebel. This myrmidon did not take the trouble to be fierce.

The batch of coolies to which Tek Chiu belonged was, after a patient period of waiting, brought together in a slump before the acting Protector, whose deportment and behaviour could not readily dispose Tek Chiu or anybody else in a cooly's position to be argumentative. My Lord Protector had little time to spend with those at his tribunal. Cromwell was not a European, but a Tamil, who spoke the Fokien dialect of Chinese with fluency.

Those preceding Tek Chiu in the batch passed Cromwell's scrutiny in single file, and freely signed themselves away to Deli. That those who preceded Tek Chiu were illiterate and could not write their names nor read their agreement redounded all the more to their credit as qualified coolies; and the business of Cromwell was thereby facilitated. To expedite matters still more, the depôt-keeper himself had appeared upon the scene, and had been handing to each cooly, as he passed in front of Cromwell, a sum of money as so much advance for the cooly's outfit and private use. Those receiving the money looked as though their lines had fallen in pleasant places. Then the name of Liu Tek Chiu was called, and Cromwell spoke.

'You are willing to go to Deli and work according to contract, are you not?'

'No; I agreed to work in Singapore. I shall not go to Deli, as the climate there is bad.' Tek Chiu spoke with firmness.

'He must not go then,' said Cromwell, addressing the depôt-keeper, who was waiting with a sum of money in his hand. Tek Chiu looked solemnly and beseechingly at the two men alternately, and took no notice of the money. He then asked to see the Great English official, emphasising the middle word. It was a slight to Cromwell, and Cromwell did not like it. Tek Chiu was about to speak further when the depôt-keeper and his myrmidons, unhindered, hurried him out of the Protectorate, and Cromwell proceeded to deal with the next cooly.

Back went the pageant to the depôt, the keeper, at the Protectorate House door, delegating power to his servants, while he himself returned to Cromwell's tribunal to defend his interests there.

Although not lodged in a cellar, as he had feared, Tek Chiu found Old Song's history repeated, inasmuch as the previous seven days of this young cooly's hotel experience were now to him as the joys of a Paradise Lost. The absence of fire and smoke notwithstanding, he spent the next two days in hell. He got the barest scraps of food, and these were given him with growling and grudging. He was the pity and the laughing-stock of probationers, new arrivals from China, who were awaiting their turn to go to the Protectorate and sign their agreement, that prerogative being the gift of freedom-giving England.

Tek Chiu was indeed within the firm grasp of cooly-depôt law; and the treatment to which he was now being subjected was meant to be a warning and a terror to such new-comers as might be designing rebellion against cooly dealers by following the example of Tek Chiu's protest.

The British law provided that no cooly should be kept in the depôt longer than ten days; and Tek Chiu had now reached his ninth day of sojourn there. He had no option but to suffer indignities and await the turn of events. He had heard of the glories of British law, and he had some hope in the midst of his desperate fortunes that the law would protect him even now. While he was thus moping, he did not know that on the morning of that ninth day his name was signed for him in the books of the Protectorate. In Singapore, Chinamen are very like each other, and for such special purposes as those of signing an agreement one Chinaman is as good as another. Thus it was that while one man, a personator, wrote the name, another man, Tek Chiu, was to labour thenceforth with the sweat of his brow to fulfil the conditions.

He was told on the afternoon of this ninth day at the depôt that he must leave that place for another. He was in debt to those who had paid his passage; and this consideration compelled him, a stranger in a strange land, to be more than ordinarily passive. He felt that to assert such rights as he might have from British law was to go quite contrary to the ordinary arrangements of the cooly-trader. With fear and trembling, therefore, he had assumed the attitude of a pervert. Such fear and trembling were mainly due to the fact that he was decidedly a debtor to those who had, by advancing to him a passage, befriended him in China.

Tek Chiu was no loafer. He reasoned with himself. 'I shall gladly work hard here in Singapore in terms of my agreement which I made with the man whom I first met in China. But it is no part of my agreement to go to Deli, where the climate is likely to kill me as it has killed so many others.'

Guarded by an unusually large staff of depôt officials, he was conducted he knew not whither. On leaving the depôt he had asked the keeper as to his destination, and got the short answer that to eat and drink in a hotel was a poor return for passage-money. 'You will likely be taken to another depôt,' suggested an old man, as Tek Chiu passed out under guard into the open street.

The procession came in sight of the sea. Then Tek Chiu began to suspect foul play. From the movements of those escorting him, he inferred that they were to board a ship. He was right. His suspicions became convictions when they reached the sampan jetty.

The horrors of tigers and crocodiles, of jungle malaria and death, vividly and with terrible realism mirrored themselves in the mind of this young cooly. Around him were strong escorts and guardians, the efficient weapons of the cooly trade, while he, poor youth, was all unarmed and all alone. No such picture as this had filled his mind while as yet he was in China. The most depressing of the tales told by Old Song seemed to be light compared with this present, actual hardship. For a moment the boy stood still; but his hesitancy was the signal for his guardians to be all the more urgent with him. He was to enter a sampan. He refused.

'Your sending me on board ship is not according to law. I refuse to go. I claim that I am in the territory of the Great English Kingdom. The black-faced Protector declared that since I was unwilling to go to Deli, I must not be sent there.'

'Who told you that you were to be sent to Deli?' asked one of his gaolers.

'Here is the sampan and there is the ship,' said Tek Chiu, pointing successively from the sampan to a yellow-funnelled steamer at anchor out 'in the roads.' He had made an accurate guess, which astonished those around him.

Two Sikhs, Goliaths of Gath, came on the scene. The language common to all in Singapore — the resource of a polyglot population — is gesticulation. These Sikhs gesticulated; but they did not quite overawe Tek Chiu who, like a cornered rat, met officialism with defiance. But resistance was vain. For at the last, and the last soon came, the young cooly's body, but not his will, consented. Such consent was amply sufficient to satisfy the demands of surroundings in which body is everything and soul nothing.

Tek Chiu wrestled and struggled against an enormous preponderance of brute force. Nor did he take time to return blows, even if he could. His aim was to escape the sampan. He grew careless in his desperation, and then might inevitably triumphed against right. Lack of solid and regular food during the previous two days had weakened the youth, and he was lifted like a toy into the sampan and rowed to the ship.

The romance of cooly-life among Chinese immigrants to the Straits Settlements contains countless chapters; and the fortunes of Lin Tek Chiu, migrating cooly, make up one of these. By his obstinacy at the Protectorate, and afterwards at the wharf, this young man had wrecked his reputation. But the loss was inconsiderable and temporary, for he speedily passed into other hands; and the coasting steamer having ere long weighed anchor and sailed, all motive for offering resistance to keepers disappeared. While in Singapore, he fondly thought that his departure for Deli was an open question; and he therefore felt the glow of idle hopes. But he now inferred that while the English foreigners spoke a great deal of freedom, they cared little for coolies. He had desired liberty to do his duty, and it had been kept back from him. Every beat of that ship's engine took him further away from his rights and nearer his dark future. So mused Tek Chiu. He knew, or thought he knew, enough of Europeans to make him expect just treatment from them; he did not know that the planting business had to be protected. Had he known this, he might have felt less keenly the hardness of his lot.

How to supply cheap labour for the Strait Settlements and Malaysia was an urgent demand, the supply for which was to be met by the immigrant Chinaman. Whatever any Government could do for the protection and comfort of a cooly, in these qualifying circumstances, the British Government was doing. It had established a Chinese Protectorate in Singapore, and would it not, in course of time, appoint a commission to enquire into

—*the state of labour?* The treatment of the labourer would be a matter of investigation, provided always such a matter should be made subordinate to the more important question as to the number of labourers obtainable. Malaysia had been opened up in days gone by, as the outcome of a European demand for spice, and it must seem fitting for Governments to be consistent with the past, by placing spice before men's eyes as the primary and supreme object of contemplation, however well-intentioned they might feel towards the immigrant cooly.

The planter's cry of 'More coolies' as a call to arms has, since the days of Tek Chiu's cooly life, set the Government into action to protect the citadel of the depôt-keeper. Enemies from different sides, displaying different tactics, have made successive assaults, but with little avail. A Chinese Governor-General, presumably the mouthpiece of the Chinese Government, has condemned to extinction the unpaid cooly, and with him the depôt-keeper's trade.

'Now,' says this Governor-General—a Chinaman, 'no matter howsoever the regulation prepared [for the professed protection of the cooly] might be, when the contract was once entered into the emigrant's movements could no longer be free, and from this fact a thick crop of opportunities for evil would arise. Would it not then be better to allow each emigrant to provide his own passage-money, and so leave his movements unfettered? The request [by the Straits Government] that in future the credit-system should not be interdicted, it is impossible to comply with.'

Learned judges, too, in Her Britannic Majesty's Courts of the Strait Settlements lately decreed that the depôt-keeper had no power to forcibly detain emigrants, even although these were debtors. The depôt-keeper by this decree was discomfited, but only for a time, for he has obtained revenge by the Government coming to his rescue and pounding the judges with the heavy club of special legislation. And all this to protect the depôt-keeper, and through him the planter, and the planting interest. And the Chinese Protectorate, in a broad spirit, has included the depôt-keeper among those deserving protection.

Thus the planter, with his cry of 'More coolies,' has moved legislators, crushed opponents, and silenced everybody. The planter has no affection for the depôt-keeper. He never had.

But a system in which the depôt-keeper reigns supreme humiliates planters, and makes doughty champions of depôt-keepers out of them. The depôt-keeper vitiates remedial legislation, and gives a certain status to the Chinese Protectorate by making the work of that institution easy. And the depôt-keeper's atoning merit is that he makes cooly-labour forthcoming. The depôt-keeper will continue to be the colonial governor until the planter, learning a more excellent way, and prepared to suffer a temporary loss, will cease to play the rôle of Passion by turning himself into Patience. As the old order changes and gives place to new, some people must suffer loss. The extinction of the unpaid labourer and of the depôt-keeper would doubtless produce, as an immediate result, scarcity of labour; but such obstruction to the flow of the stream of Celestial labour would prove, by the test of time, to be but an unstable wall of sand over which a stream of greater volume, constancy, and purity would ere long flow. But time is short; and the planter prefers an abortive and premature harvest to 'the hundred-fold' even of this world's prosperity. 'Life everlasting in the world to come' is not supposed to influence the planting interest.

Travelling Missionary Evangelists, too, have hit against this trade in human beings. As good marksmen, they have sometimes hit the target; yet again, like some excited, clever 'shots,' they have quite as often as otherwise hit the wrong target altogether. Their zeal, not always well directed, has given cause for the enemy of Evangelical Christianity to blaspheme. Among European communities in the East, and in small Asiatic circles whose views and convictions are supplied ready-made by Europeans, 'faddists and Exeter Hall' are treated with the tenderness and consideration that sane men owe to—those unlike themselves.

CHAPTER XIV.

HOME RULE.

AFTER two days' sail from Singapore the little coasting steamer cast anchor in the harbour of Penang. Penang was a place that to Tek Chiu looked much more like his own home-land than Singapore. The high and rocky hills were there, but these seemed only to mock him. Such suggestions of China made him all the more conscious of his condition as a prisoner. He had spoken to nobody on his voyage from Singapore. But now a new detachment of his countrymen came on board as additional supplies for Deli tobacco-labour; and the crowding of the little ship gave Tek Chiu less room for silence.

On board, hailing from Penang, was a young man, who, hearing Tek Chiu's story, accurately solved for him the riddle of his forced severance from Singapore. A forgery must have taken place. The British Government, had they known of the matter—but of course it was not a public question of Imperial or Colonial policy—would have severely punished the depôt-keeper. But why, asked the new-comer of Tek Chiu, was he in distress about going to Deli?

Ere he arrived at Sumatra Tek Chiu found in this young Penang Chinaman the Hopeful of his wanderings.

Hopeful was a Straits-born Chinaman, not literally a cooly, but a cooly's companion. He was proceeding to Deli to be a clerk in a tobacco-plantation at a place which, as afterwards transpired, was within measurable distance of Tek Chiu's field of labour. Hopeful's grandfather had, half a century earlier than his grandson's recital of the story, left the city of Even Way in Fokien, China, and found a home in Penang, the island of the betel-nut. Hopeful's grandfather, by his plodding industry, had thrived, and married a wife, by whom he had had a large family. All of these, Hopeful's father among them, had succeeded tolerably well in life. Hopeful, determined to sustain the reputation of the family, was making for himself a start. In addition to his having been taught Chinese, which was still the language of his home (for the Chinese of Penang, unlike those of Singapore, despise the Malay jargon), Hopeful had been taught to speak English at an English Government-aided school. In virtue of this education the youth had now succeeded in obtaining employment from the agent of a planting firm. He astonished Tek Chiu by telling him that his salary was to be the sum of twenty-five dollars monthly. It seemed a large wage.

Tek Chiu's intimate knowledge of the leading Chinese Classics commanded Hopeful's admiration; for, in this branch of his education, Tek Chiu, unpaid cooly, was superior to him.

'If you are diligent,' said Hopeful, 'and if you avoid gambling, opium, and other evils, you will very soon be independent. I have not yet been to Deli; but I know from the testimony of friends that there are many good chances of success for a man who can take care of himself.'

Hopeful, like others among the world's bright souls, didn't know that the words that cost him so little had for the young cooly's wounds the healing power of balm.

Tek Chiu, Chinaman though he was, found it difficult to avoid being rapturous.

'The climate of Deli,' continued Hopeful, 'is more trying than that of Penang or Singapore—a fact due, of course, to malaria, the germs of which rise out of newly cultivated soil. But if you are careful to avoid sleeping outside, and boil the water of the place before drinking it, there is not so very much danger of your losing your health after all. The climate in China has its own special dangers, too, has it not?'

Tek Chiu, having lost both his parents from cholera, could give a ready reply.

Hopeful was evidently of a practical turn of mind.

'If you are to travel by rail after you get on shore, be careful of yourself when leaving the train. It is better to wait till the train stops altogether. But if you must step out while the train is in motion, don't turn your back to the front of the train. Don't jump straight out from the door-step of the carriage to the platform. Run along with the train. Many Chinese, direct from China, through want of getting a hint, and not taking proper precautions, have broken their necks at that work.'

Tek Chiu vowed he would be careful. Yet he secretly wished that trains had never been. He had been cheered by Hopeful's words, albeit the train in motion was a fly in the ointment.

'I should advise you,' said Hopeful, assuming that Tek Chiu would escape a railway accident, 'to study English as soon as you can. After freeing yourself from debt, you would then be able, knowing English, to get a fairly good wage. And you might, with a knowledge of Chinese characters that we Straits-born fellows have not got, teach in a school, or get lucrative employment in some other way.'

'I am afraid I shall have no opportunities to learn English in a tobacco-plantation,' said Tek Chiu. 'The field work will use up all my time and strength, and besides the foreigners there are not English but Dutch people.'

But Hopeful, according to his manner, built a beautiful castle for his friend. And the steamer reached the Sumatra coast.

The poisonous effects of Holland's selfish policy towards the Eastern Archipelago—a policy that has consistently sought a monopoly of trade, to the exclusion of other European nations and the detriment of the Eastern races—are now palpable. The Eastern peoples of Netherlands India, whether native or Chinese, have no access to Western education, so far as the Dutch Government have aught to do with the matter. Social distinctions, too, have all the rigidity and degradation of caste about them. Orientals, with a very few exceptions, are prohibited from asserting the dignity of manhood in presence of their European superiors. Neither Chinaman nor native dare drive his carriage in front of a European. It is with a grudge that the Oriental is permitted to have a carriage at all. The Dutchman, as a being of superior creation, grudges social status to those over whom he exercises lordship. The Dutchman has the power; and like a small boy with his Christmas presents, he glories in showing, and telling, too, that he has it.

Holland holds sway over almost the whole of Sumatra. Deli, in the northern part of the island, north-west of Singapore and south-west of Penang, is only in a mediate sense under Dutch rule, since the Eastern races in theory enjoy self-government there. This order of things serves as a grand compensation for Dutch haughtiness. In this way government is rendered possible and existence tolerable for the Eastern races. A passport system that demands toll from every Chinaman entering Dutch dominions in the form of the payment of a poll-tax, redounds to the benefit of the entrant, whose chances of making money are perhaps greater than those of the emigrant to free ports under British rule. The poll-tax is supposed to keep disreputable characters out of Netherlands India. But Dutch narrowness does not stop there. It comes dangerously near to that of America and Australia. If a Chinaman does not, within three months after paying his poll-tax, find regular employment, he must leave Dutch India. Holland has no Chinese poorhouses. She hands over all possible inmates to England.

The Chinese in Dutch territory, unless they are mine or plantation coolies, act as middle-men in business transactions between the natives and the Dutch. Among themselves these Chinese are allowed to have a district head-man—the Captain China—and he with his lieutenants regulates affairs exclusively Chinese. Grave criminal matters are ultimately referred to the Dutch; but in ordinary matters affecting social life and conduct, the Dutch delegate their governmental powers to the Captain China, who in turn reaches the whole Chinese community of his district through delegated agents. In North Borneo, and in the British-protected

States of the Malay Peninsula also, there is the district Captain China, but no mediation between this dignitary and the masses of the community is recognised. In Malaysia, British rule is the Agnosticism, while Dutch rule is the Positivism of politics. For the joint action of this passport system, and Dutch toleration of Chinese governing bodies appointed from the members of the Chinese community themselves, has gained for the Dutch Government success against Chinese secret and dangerous societies in Malaysia—a success which the British Government has, till recently at any rate, failed to obtain.

But when European Governments are weighed and compared, Lin Tek Chiu, transferred cooly, will neither gain nor lose much advantage from the transfer. He is planter's property. The same protection that has not hitherto been denied to him will be extended to him still.

The port of call was Belawan, where, after little delay, Tek Chiu and his party entered a modest railway train. An hour's drive took them to Medan, where with due safety and ceremony they alighted, to proceed on foot —a distance of eight miles—to the Bindjie district, the designed field of Tek Chiu's labour. Though parted from his friend Hopeful, Tek Chiu determined that he would thenceforth give heed to his conduct, and 'breast the blows of circumstance.'

Till now Old Song's description had tolerably well survived the test of verification. But the best and not the worst was yet to be.. Fortunately, the old cooly's prognostications about the jungle did not prove to be so authentic as those which he made about the cooly-depôt. Tek Chiu, too, proved to be a first-rate gardener. As a lineal descendant of Adam, possessed of strong hereditary gardening qualifications, he succeeded well in his work. He reared his plants and pleased both his tindal and his European manager.

Tek Chiu used well his spare hours. The second Straits-born Chinaman of his acquaintance, a young man who acted as clerk to the manager of the estate, gave Tek Chiu an A B C book. Ere long, by the help of this Baba, Tek Chiu mastered the alphabet. And not the alphabet alone, but elementary combinations of letters by means of helping pictures Tek Chiu came to know. 'Dog,' 'hen,' and 'cat' soon fell before the attacks of the young cooly. But Tek Chiu, who had no difficulty with 'cat,' did not find matters equally easy with 'dog.' His Chinese tongue oscillated between 'dock' and 'doggie.' But in due time even that difficulty was overcome, and in the natural growth of Tek Chiu's powers of pronouncing, 'doggie' at last became 'dog.'

Thus by dint of perseverance Tek Chiu's tobacco and his knowledge of English grew apace. By the time that the drying season set in, he had a noble record. In his allotted patch of ground where, subject to reasonable interference from the Chinese tindal and Mr Van Dyke, the European manager, he enjoyed the blessings of self-government, Tek Chiu had avoided the blackguardism of his fellow coolies. He had stolen no hatchets, although two of these implements had been stolen from him. In accordance with his manager's instructions, he had set his tobacco plants at the prescribed distances from one another; nor had he taken advantage of tree stumps to thickly stud his plants around such interdicted spots. The cooly who worked the spot next to Tek Chiu had hoodwinked both manager and tindal with impunity, Tek Chiu in vain appealing to the man's conscience. A small stump had been excommunicated according to instructions; but that business-like cooly had not only taken out the stump according to orders, but had also in a quiet unobserved moment placed the stump back again to the old spot whence it had been wrenched. Such a wilful love of obstruction lent excuse for multiplying plants around the conservative stump. The strategic act meant an addition of two or three plants to the cooly's credit on the day of reckoning. Chinamen are born arithmeticians.

But Tek Chiu cared not for the day of reckoning. The simpleton did everything as he was told to do it by those in authority. He had many opportunities for falling in with the ways of the place. But such opportunities were completely lost on Tek Chiu, who throughout the whole planting and reaping season did not obtain a single flogging. He was bent on study; and while others gambled when they had money—a desperate love of learning armed Tek Chiu against this enemy—or did any other evil when there was opportunity, Tek Chiu husbanded his time, worked his plot, and burned the midnight oil in spelling, pronouncing, and understanding English.

A message from Cheng Ann, the Baba clerk, asked Tek Chiu on a certain night to come along for a short time to the bungalow, a small attap hut situated behind the house of the European manager. To Tek Chiu's glad surprise, Hopeful was there. During all these months Hopeful had been within three miles' distance from Tek Chiu; but whether it was that he was ignorant of Tek Chiu's location, or, knowing it, like

Pharaoh's butler, he had not taken the trouble to think with solicitude about the interesting prisoner of his short voyage between Penang and Belawan, he and Tek Chiu had been lost to each other. He welcomed Tek Chiu with enthusiasm, and Cheng Ann for the first time became friends with the latter. True, the clerk had lent the cooly one or two small books, and had taken pains to help him, but this evening of meeting was a time of making special friendship.

The Siew Tsai degree was discussed over Cheng Ann's tea and Hopeful's Siamese cigarettes. Tek Chiu, indigent cooly, was wafted back on these fumes to Black Rock and home. The cooly's broken sentences in English took the two Babas by surprise. Hopeful felt of a truth that the castle he had built for Tek Chiu on the coasting steamer had been built on the solid foundations of the young cooly's good calibre and conduct. Hopeful was not slow to acknowledge in extravagant terms Tek Chiu's achievements. And if such exaggerated praise did not gauge Tek Chiu's English education as it was, it was a suitable description of what it would be. Tek Chiu's passion for learning was now at work in this new channel.

Having settled the question of language, these three friends, Fokien Chinamen by descent all of them, betook themselves to discourse on thought and reality. People in Malaysia seldom get beyond language. Both Hopeful and Cheng Ann were brothers, as members of the Ho Seng branch of the Triad Society. Both of these Babas were anxious to form a contingent of their Society in Deli, and their imperfect knowledge of Chinese written character gave an opening for the assistance and sympathy of Tek Chiu.

'We wish you to help us in this important matter,' said Hopeful.

'I shall gladly help you to the extent of my limited powers,' said Tek Chiu. 'But you are aware, I suppose, that members of the Triad Society are beheaded in China.'

The two Babas laughed.

'In the British colony of the Straits Settlements, including Singapore, Penang, Malacca, Province Wellesley, and smaller places, there are nearly two hundred thousand members of Societies. Fancy two hundred thousand people losing their heads,' said Cheng Ann.

'My friend Cheng Ann and I,' said Hopeful, 'who are Straits-born Chinamen of Penang, are among those who desire to help their fellow-countrymen to enjoy their rights of citizenship. When Chinese like yourself come abroad, you are unskilled in the intricacies of foreigners' law, and your connection with our Society would protect you against insult and injury.'

'I heartily commend your view of the matter,' said Tek Chiu. 'The foreigners don't understand us; and, so far as my small knowledge serves, they don't seem anxious to do so. The foreigners are very much like us. They think too much of themselves.'

The two Babas simultaneously nodded approval of the sentiment.

'The English people treat us Chinese much better in their territory than the Dutch people treat us here,' suggested Cheng Ann.

'That is so,' said Hopeful, sipping tea. 'But the English Government is more like the Government of China. The English people are suspicious of our Societies. And again, they supply us with social conditions of their own making, and these badly fit us. The Dutch, on the other hand, are more liberal, being less grandfatherly. They allow us to do pretty much as we choose. Dutch liberalism is laziness. As soon as our social customs prejudicially affect their interests in the least possible way, the Dutch treat the Chinese much more shamefully than the English would ever have it in their nature to do.'

'The aims of the Triad Society in this part of the world, as I understand you,' said Tek Chiu, 'are not the same as the aims of that Society in China.'

'Your surmise is right,' said Hopeful. 'We have no Ming dynasty to restore here.'

'We don't care a straw for either of the two dynasties,' said Cheng Ann; 'although, of course, for the sake of form, our members pass through the usual ceremonies. We simply join these Societies to protect one another and ourselves, and to conserve our Chinese customs.'

'These aims are ten parts praiseworthy,' said Tek Chiu. 'But the Chinese who are born in this part of the world have lost, as it seems to me, a good deal of their patriotism. I hope I am not offending you.'

'By no means,' responded the two Babas with one voice. 'We are very glad to have your opinions.'

'Well, you know, of course, that the present Manchu dynasty is a dynasty of foreigners.'

'Yes, yes,' said Cheng Ann. Hopeful did not answer.

'The Societies here seem, therefore, to me to be essentially the same as those in China, with this difference, that under Chinese rule members lose their heads, while here members keep them on.'

'That is an important difference, to be sure,' said

Hopeful. 'But there are other differences. The Manchu dynasty is much less foreign to the Chinese people in China than the British or Dutch government is to the Chinese people here. On the other hand, Chinese government being what it is, members of the Triad Society in China are compelled to have revolutionary aims both in profession and in fact. Chinese administration of justice, for instance, is very eccentric and oppressive. A man who commits murder may, if money is forthcoming, go free; while a man may be beheaded for smuggling salt. Members of the Triad Society believe in the British administration of justice. But as our customs and social habits are so vastly different from those of Europeans, we seek in the Triad Society to protect these customs and habits from being unduly interfered with, while we seek also to give to our wandering fellow-countrymen the friendly aid and sympathy that they need.'

Hopeful's analysis of the facts satisfied Tek Chiu's patriotism, and the young immigrant was not slow to acknowledge this. It was clear that Hopeful, and not Cheng Ann, had studied the politics of China. Hopeful, in turn, listened with intelligence and appreciation to Tek Chiu's analysis of Chinese history and politics. The conversation stretched far into the night, and Tek Chiu's knowledge as communicated on that occasion established to the satisfaction of the members of the small evening party the claims of Chinese Home Rule.

To ascertain how and why Secret Societies existed and are prevalent in China, in spite of the heaviest penalties, it is necessary to study not only the political and social organisations of that country, but also the underlying elements and forces at work in producing and shaping them. The origin and development of Secret Societies will thus be found to be conterminous with the evolutionary progress of the national life. To the latter of these two problems the former is the corollary.

When the 'hundred families' of China first emerged from the patriarchal to a more complex system of government, the elective principle was enforced in the election of rulers such as Yao, Shun, and Yu. This was in recognition of the national demand that government should be vested in the hands of the real aristocracy—men raised by merit to that good eminence. With the introduction however of the hereditary principle in the appointment of successors to Yu, the Feudal system began to take root, and thenceforth dynastic superseded national interests. The vassal chieftains of the several States, procuring and holding their authority from the sovereign, usurped the popular rights and neglected the democratic interests.

The populace, however, retained in their hands one terrible remedial privilege—the right of rebellion. This inalienable right they constantly exercised for the overthrow of their oppressors, and in the defence of their own interests. It had been justified and upheld by the teachings of their own Classics, and to this right Secret Societies in China appeal for existence. In a country where popular rights are not specially defined and adequately safeguarded, the possession of retaliatory powers in the hands of the people, and the knowledge that such powers would be promptly adopted by them, act as wholesome restraints to arbitrary and capricious authority. And where the democracy has no controlling voice in the appointment or removal of a ruler, their compliance with the ruler's authority could only be exacted either from their fear of its irresistibility or from their tacit acquiescence in the good it produces. As champions of popular and local rights, and as exponents of the democratic element in their national life, Secret Societies claim to work for the benefit of the people and for ensuring the exercise of good or tolerable government.

A survey of the political history of China serves to show that the subsequent careers and influences of these Societies must be associated with those interests which they have all along professed to promote.

The feudal system continued throughout the long period of

the Chow dynasty, until its suppression was demanded in the interests of the nation. It had existed long enough as a denationalising process. Its internecine strifes and encroachments on suzerain as well as democratic rights led to inevitable collisions and struggles for supremacy. The subsequent Tsin conquest therefore resulted in a reconstruction wholly in accord with the national aspirations of the race. But the reaction was not thorough. Tsin-Shi-Hwang-ti, though sufficiently powerful to overcome all opposition and to inaugurate a new Imperial ideal in government, did not fulfil the national expectations in other respects. His government was too oppressive. And though consolidation under one ruler was a political necessity of the times, the democratic elements insisted on its combination with good government. The old strife for mastery therefore took a new form. Henceforth it became a popular, not a political movement, there being uprisings against oppression, not a mere war of States. And Tsin fell. The revolution introduced by Shi-Hwang-ti suggested the idea of national life, not its fulfilment; and in the accompanying struggle the democratic elements in the national system first asserted their place in the body politic and claimed a right to be recognised.

Though the Hans rose to power upon the downfall of the Tsins, they also were unable to meet in full the demands of national life. Owing to the frequency of Tartar raids from without, and of faction fights from within, the unity of the Empire was posterior; for the first demands of national life were not complied with till many years after these demands were formally made. A great nucleus for national unity was then formed; but local autonomy representing the democratic elements was also a national requirement, and until the former should have been assured, it would be dangerous to satisfy the latter. Conversely, however, so long as these democratic elements remained disregarded and unreconciled, they would achieve progress by retarding or even by contributing to destroy the consolidation of national unity. Hence, not the virtues of Han Wen-ti, nor the patronage of letters and the revival of learning, nor the military genius of Wu-ti and his long struggle with the Tartars; nor all the glories of the Hans—such as the invention of paper and ink and the emancipation of slaves—could prevent the division of the Empire into three kingdoms that warred with each other for a century.

But four centuries after the downfall of the Hans, the earlier monarchs of the T'angs realised for a time the Unity of the Empire, which had been slowly evolving for nearly a thousand years from its inception as an idea in the mind of Tsin-Shi-Hwang-ti. The Tartars excluded, T'ai-tsung, the second Emperor of this dynasty, established the educational system that now rules the Empire, and holds it fast together. This was also a concession, the most important concession to democratic demands ever made. It re-established, though on a modified and practical basis, the national ideals of government by the best and most meritorious. The degeneration of the later T'angs could not continue the glorious work thus begun. On the contrary, it led to another break-up of the Empire, this time into North and South. The instruments of this dismemberment were the Tartars.

To Southern China belonged the Augustan age of the Sungs, the great era of printing, speculative philosophy, and the later histories. But with the incorporation of the Empire under the Mogul dynasty, the instincts of national unity began at last to be realised. From that time forward there has been in every sense, except in the recognition of the democratic interests, a Chinese nation. The cry of the nomad hordes was 'One world,' 'One king;' and under their military ascendancy, dismemberment by foreign invasion as the one standing menace to the unity of the Empire was checkmated and staved off. True, the country has during subsequent times been subjected to foreign domination, but sufficient time having already been given to weld together into a unity the separate parts of the nation, such foreign domination, when it has prevailed at all, has prevailed over China as a whole. But notwithstanding the unity of the race, the Moguls also failed to satisfy the demands of the democracy. They thereby afforded grounds for the workings of Secret Societies, and ultimately were compelled, through the strain of the revolt of native patriotism, to give place to the Mings.

The Mings, by the codification of the national laws, the formation of libraries, and the compilation of huge cyclopædias and dictionaries, continued the consolidation of the Empire. But this dynasty also neglected to legislate for the representation of democratic interests; and through disunion and internal rebellions it was at length overturned to enable the Manchus to test their constructive faculties.

The earlier monarchs of the Manchu dynasty were highly endowed with governmental capacity, largeness of plan, and organising powers. But they were compelled to minister to their own needs first; and their assimilative faculties enabled them to absorb literature, social organisation, education, and religion from China. During the two centuries their descendants have been on the Throne, they have been unable to supply the great needs of the democracy; but they have greatly extended the borders of the Empire, and have given to China the greatest national organisation it has ever possessed.

The barriers of national prejudices and patriotic instincts separate the Chinese people from their Manchu rulers, who have only partially assimilated themselves to the people they rule. Hence the many and great opportunities for Secret Societies. In their first efforts to consolidate their own authority, the Manchus had not sufficient opportunity to attend to the workings of these Societies. Thus, ere the Manchu dynasty had been firmly established, the nation's contact with Western powers revealed to the democracy the uncertainty of their position. From this revelation arose in time the Tai Ping rebellion with its terrible results. The Manchus, having overcome that rebellion, have been devoting their energies to re-establish their authority. The watchword with their statesmen is still 'Imperial,' not 'National' interests. The machinery of Imperial centralisation is most complete, ranging from the Emperor downward to the District Magistrate. The organisation of the Democracy, on the other hand, centres in the village or community elders; but the status of these elders is not officially recognised in the body politic. They and their people are still regarded by the officials as little children, to be ruled, petted, or punished without the right of remonstrance. They have no recognised channel by which they may communicate their wants to their parents and guardians. Their position is therefore intolerable and inadequate, considering the age of the nation. Thus, though the national unity of China has been accomplished, the demands of a quickened and healthy national life remain unsatisfied. Rebel Societies, when first formed, invariably emphasise the urgency of these democratic demands. But in their sure expectation of success these Societies proceed subsequently to consolidate such authority as they have been able by democratic assistance to assume. Afterwards, these Societies, losing their first love, neglecting the end by their absorption in the means, remain a palpable danger to all governmental authority. So long, however, as the democratic demands remain ignored, so long will authority be susceptible to violent attack and over-throw. This dualism in Chinese politics can never be ignored, whatever the government itself may be nominally. This dualism accounts for the venality of the Executive Government on the one hand, and for the existence and strifes of Secret Societies on the other. Two forces of Government—the Imperial, working downwards, and the Democratic, working upwards—are indispens-able elements in Chinese politics.

With the admission of foreigners, *e.g.*, those from Western nations, into the interior of the Empire under treaty provisions, another ground of opposition is formed between the Imperial and democratic interests. These foreigners form another party in the triangular contest going on in China at present. But whether or not this third element may ultimately prove an effective cure, as the coercive force needed to reconcile the Imperial with the democratic interests, time alone will reveal. Foreigners are admitted under treaties made between the foreigners themselves and the Imperial authorities. In this way the democracy is ignored. So long as the democracy keeps in submission to Imperial arrangements, all three parties in this triangular contest exist through mutual antagonism. But as soon as foreigners prejudicially affect the democracy, the national aspiration of race will compel the Imperial authorities to alter or modify their policy. National patriotism will perhaps then provide the necessary means for a reconciliation between them; and the underlying unity between opposing interests will thereby be consummated.

CHAPTER XV.

THE SOCIETY MAN.

THE young Dutchman who managed the estate on which Tek Chiu worked had for a considerable time been observing Tek Chiu's abilities and habits of industry. Four hundred coolies are a large crowd; but Mr Van Dyke's keen eye had already, unaided by the Baba clerk, singled out the young cooly.

Soon after the evening on which the discussion on Chinese history and politics took place, Cheng Ann took occasion, in conversation with Mr Van Dyke, to recount the salient points in Tek Chiu's history and circumstances. The young Dutchman was much interested in the story.

'I have for a considerable time thought that there was something exceptional about that lad,' said Mr Van Dyke. Pleased with Tek Chiu's history as Cheng Ann had just recounted it to him, and still more pleased with his own powers of discernment, Mr Van Dyke concluded all at once that he himself, with Tek Chiu's aid, would study Chinese, and that there was need for an additional Chinese clerk on the estate. He sent for Tek Chiu; and Tek Chiu was forthcoming. The mediating language was English—for Mr Van Dyke knew English well—and the mediating man was Cheng Ann.

'I understand,' said Mr Van Dyke, addressing Tek Chiu, 'that you write well your own language in the character. You will therefore assist Cheng Ann in the work of clerking the estate. Your pay will be according to the average pay of one of the twenty best of the four hundred coolies on the estate. And as I wish to study your language, you must help me. I shall pay you a little extra in consideration of this work at the end of your service here.'

With gratitude deeper than he could possibly show it, Tek Chiu returned thanks to the plantation oracle. Now, more than ever, he would have opportunities to make progress in his knowledge of English.

Tek Chiu's promotion, which took place towards the end of the planter's year, seemed however to be the precursor of several upheavals. Many of the coolies began to think of squaring their accounts, and leaving Deli for China and home. These expectants had a fair amount standing to their credit in the account-books of the estate. But the hour in which the labourer would receive his hire, although impending, had not quite come.

For the coolies themselves it was a time of hope, and for the manager, his tindals, and assistants, it was a time of activity. Tek Chiu, an arbitrary witness of the drama, who had now worked off his debt, and who at the time of his promotion to a clerk's duties was beginning to pile up surplus savings on a small scale, remained free at that time from the special solicitude of the manager and his underlings. Nay, if Tek Chiu had realised the normal expectations entertained regarding him, he would at that stage have joined voluntarily in the efforts that were being made on all sides to find enjoyments for the labouring coolies. But Tek Chiu was an oddity.

It was a pressing problem. Coolies had been kept well-disciplined and industrious throughout the year hitherto. In what way were these coolies to be kept there still? At this point existence itself rather than the *mode* of existence came to be of paramount importance. Voluptuous coolies had already indeed received small money advances from the manager, and in gambling, opium-smoking, and other vices had squandered these advances. At that point of time these four hundred coolies were capable of sub-division according to their monetary circumstances. Some had been spreading their enjoyment over the whole season, and were in debt to their employer, to the limit of what the employer considered safety. Others had the two sides of their account in even poise. Others again had a little, but only a little, to their credit; while a fourth class, the residue, and these a large number—the eligible candidates to return, like Jacob, to their fathers' homesteads—had, as per testimony of the estate books, considerable balances in their favour. They were about to reap the reward of thrift when their overseers, as if by sudden inspiration, insisted on 'means of enjoyment' being put within their reach. Before the exact moment when the accounts would be made up between the employer and the coolies, inducements for another year's engagement had to be forthcoming.

The planter's generosity, that did not grudge advances as a set-off against the cooly's credit balance, was conspicuous at that point. Arrangements were made for theatre shows. The tindals obtained from the gambling farm in Deli a license to conduct a branch business on the estate. Advances in the shape of a loan to each man were liberally bestowed. That artifice secured most of the coolies for another term of service. Planters find it a troublesome and expensive business to import new coolies; for it is advisable that the planter should keep from being under the depôt-keeper's power as much as possible.

'Gambling,' says an eminent planter, 'is no doubt rife wherever bodies of men are gathered. They have no other way to amuse themselves after their day's work; and therefore, in my opinion, as long as men from outside are not admitted, and the play is among themselves, I see no harm in it [it being tolerated by Government on estates in the Straits Settlements], especially as it is admissable in the Native States and over the border.'

'The whole system,' said Tek Chiu to his senior colleague, Cheng Ann, 'levels coolies downwards. The very few who are morally strong survive all these glaring temptations. Many others, although thrifty, and desirous of soon leaving the estate after they have saved a little money, are nevertheless prevented through their own weakness from fulfilling their nobler ambitions; and this weakness of theirs is encouraged and fostered by temptations studiously brought near to them.'

Cheng Ann verbally approved of this sentiment; but he was timid in his approval. Cheng Ann was an official. And Tek Chiu seemed to forget that he was an official too.

This first upheaval after Tek Chiu's promotion to a clerkship and to genteel society in the estate, an upheaval that consisted in a levelling downwards of the credit-balance of thrifty coolies, was succeeded by a second and more palpably serious one. The European markets dealt shamefully with Messrs Mann Peck and Cos'. tobacco leaves, and Messrs Mann Peck & Co. were compelled to suspend payment. Mr Van Dyke had, on behalf of his firm, made many money advances to coolies for the current year, and this ill-advised premature generosity added to the bankruptcy of the bankrupt firm. The estate and its management were soon to pass into other hands.

Tek Chiu's promotion had taken place at the time that marked the crossing between Tek Chiu, unpaid cooly, and Tek Chiu, voluntary labourer. Like the prisoner of Chillon, he had, while as yet he was unpromoted, begun to like the chains of his bondage. Readily therefore had he, installed now as a clerk, consented to work out a second year's term of service. Nobody on the estate knew at that time what the fortunes of the planter's firm were so soon to be. Before the collapse had actually come, however, Mr Van Dyke, and he alone of those on the estate, knew of the wicked fluctuations of tobacco in Europe, and as to the probable consequences for that firm of which he was the managing representative. The coolies had already received advances large enough to chain most of them for another season. The mill would have kept going rightly enough had it not been for the stopping of the big wheel.

It were idle to speculate on what might not have been. Had Messrs Mann Peck & Co. been declared insolvent a fortnight sooner, the Great Dragon Lodge of the Ho Seng branch of the Triad Society might not have been formed. But The Great Dragon, so named by Tek Chiu, came into actual existence; and its organisers were Cheng Ann, Hopeful, and Lin Tek Chiu. In a secluded part of the estate, with insignia sent to Hopeful from Penang, where such societies so abounded as to be co-extensive almost with the entire mass of the Chinese male population, and with such other means of inauguration as the circumstance would possibly allow, in one night two hundred and twenty-three Celestials swore, for the first time in their lives, that they would thenceforth labour to overthrow the Ch'engs (the Manchus) and restore the Bengs (the Mings). They pledged, with their necks beneath gleaming swords, fidelity and honour towards one another and towards all the brethren within the Four Seas.

Although there was a marked absence of the completeness in arrangement characteristic of similar rites as celebrated in Singapore or Penang, the physical surroundings of that great meeting were literally in consonance with the conditions that surrounded the inception, in the reign of the Emperor K'ang Hi, of the Heaven and Earth Society of China. 'In the mountains, for fear of the Ch'ang officials,' the Great Dragon Lodge was inaugurated.

The Lodge had three distinct sub-divisions, at the entrance to each of which a test was applied to those venturing in. There was first the Ang Gate, where stood the executioner to behead traitors, and others whom he might consider unsuitable for the ordeals. Beyond that gate was the Hall of Sincerity and Justice on the door-post of which was the remarkable couplet,

M

embodying the sentiment that goodness is the test and basis of brotherhood—

> 'Though a man be not a relation, if he be just, he is worthy of all honour;
> A friend, if he be found destitute of honour, ought to be repudiated.'

The last of the three important stages was the entrance to the city of Willows. Within was the pavilion, above which was the grand altar, on a level with the master's pulpit. On the altar stood the peck measure containing rice, and a heavy stock of other articles. The Five Ancestors, the Five Tiger Generals, the Five Elements of Nature, the cardinal points of the Compass, the Seasons, Heaven, Earth, Sun, and Moon, had all their flags which, planted in the peck measure of rice, besieged that soil with the frequency of tobacco-plants round a stump. Added to these were other articles that were not flags, such as the Spirit Tablet of the Five Ancestors, a pair of scissors, the 'precious mirror,' and a yellow Drooko. On the outside of the measure itself, inscribed on front, were the four characters of plantain, taro, plum, and orange. Below was the pavilion; and on the east side was the circle of Heaven and Earth with its overarching words—an aspiration for the triumph of righteousness.

> 'Agitate Heaven and Earth and reform the world:
> Let the 'Ming' triumph, and let righteousness prevail throughout the Empire.' ['Ming' is a word that signifies 'Bright']

Hopeful had received from Penang the requisite credentials and furniture—regalia, scrolls, and other symbols of authority, several booklets containing a list of the thirty-six rules as to the conduct of members, and a book treating of the ceremonies of initiation. Tek Chiu had studied all the literature obtainable; and after he himself had rapidly passed through the ceremonies, that were abridged in his case on account of the exigencies of the hour, he was chosen to fill the important office of Vanguard of the new Lodge; while to Hopeful and Cheng Ann were assigned the offices of Master of the Lodge and Executioner respectively. From among the coolies already members of the Triad Society were chosen a suitable number of councillors and district head-men—the latter mentioned of these being commonly designated 'Grass Shoes.' They were sometimes honoured with the more substantial name of 'Iron Planks.'

With queue loosened out, right shoulder and breast made bare, clothes newly washed if not new altogether, these Society men, asserting that their necks were harder than overhanging swords, kept repudiating the Manchus and sighing for the Mings.

Through long and intricate ordeals, Tek Chiu, as the Vanguard of the Great Dragon, led his large army of applicants for membership, Hopeful, as the Master of the Lodge, duly asking questions and receiving the proper answers. Tek Chiu, aided by the book of directions, answered on that night each time he entered the city of Willows three hundred and thirty-three questions. And he survived.

The spirits of the Five Ancestors were worshipped and invoked. The brethren one and all, with the oath of allegiance, mingled and drank their own blood. The 'Traitorous Minister,' whose malicious ingratitude towards the deliverers of his land from troublesome Philistines had made Imperial oppression reach its climax, and had in that way occasioned the inception of the Heaven and Earth Society, was, as represented in a domestic fowl, beheaded once again.

And when at last these heroes of Ang had overcome all their difficulties, having performed their ceremonies of kneeling and kow-towing, they reached the Market of Universal Peace, and entered the Temple of Virtue and Happiness.

These Celestials were far from their native land. Beer bottles and soap-boxes, included in the paraphernalia, served as substitutes for better things, and reminded the heroes that they were in the territory of barbarians.

Tek Chiu, a leader of men, more than any one else in his vast army gave due appreciation to the significance of the rites. Yet all these rites, so imposing and complex and so mysterious, united the hearts of the whole army as the heart of one man. With varying degrees of intelligence—many without intelligence at all, and merely unconsciously breathing the spirit of their nation—these men, in the ceremonies of that night, responded with approbation to the claim which Taoism makes on China. If Confucianism has given practical morality and Buddhism religious enthusiasm to China, Taoism too has its place as appealing to the transcendental instincts of the nation. The Chinese, like other people, have a passion for the mysterious. It is a juvenile stage, a hindrance as well as a help to thought and comprehension. It is at once the Romanism and the Anglicanism of the religious and political life of China.

A 'draught of wind' invaded the meeting and did not seriously affect the proceedings. It was Mr Van Dyke, who, attracted by curiosity to be a spectator, had thereby, according to the laws of the Society, incurred the penalty of losing his head. But the executioner was cheated out of his function. Mr Van Dyke got back to his bungalow without hurt.

'I witnessed some of your proceedings last night,' said the Dutchman to Cheng Ann and Tek Chiu on the following day. 'You Chinese people are very fond of display. What is the benefit to be derived from membership in such a Society?'

'We both get and give substantial benefit,' said the Executioner.

'All members get a respectable burial,' said Tek Chiu, feelingly. 'And then,' continued he, 'disputes amongst members are referred to the elders and amicably settled with little delay.'

'Yes!' said Cheng Ann; 'think of the money that Europeans here and in Penang give yearly to lawyers. We Chinese have no confidence in law-courts.'

'Our imperfect means of dispensing justice in China,' said Tek Chiu, following up his friend's suggestion, ' has given the masses of the people from time immemorial a dread of the Yamen. Our Chinese past has trained us to take for granted that it is a right thing to resist authority. We Chinese have, however, implicit confidence in our seniors when any business of vital importance has to be decided. But we must first have a guarantee that our seniors will act justly, and this guarantee is best supplied us by the ties of brotherhood which are created and fostered by such a Society as that to which we now belong.'

The language difficulty prevented Mr Van Dyke from getting the benefit of Tek Chiu's arguments on behalf of the Society.

'What I have already heard about your Societies is not flattering to those who belong to them. Only a few weeks ago I read in one of the local newspapers about the Chinese Broken Coffin Society and its dark doings. Its professed aim is robbery by means of murder.'

'It is a bad Society,' said Cheng Ann, speaking almost under breath. His new status as executioner did not save him here from trepidation.

'That is the Water Way Peace Society, I presume,' said Tek Chiu. 'You mean the Society that exists for the purpose of robbing people of their valuables on sea voyages by first quietly dropping the owners of the valuables over the ship's side?'

'Yes,' said the Dutchman.

'Membership in our Heaven and Earth Society safeguards us against such calamity as that,' observed Cheng Ann.

The Dutchman was becoming suspicious of these two Chinamen. He had never been particularly famous for trusting any one. But Cheng Ann's matter-of-fact tribute paid to the protective powers of the Society that had come so near to his bungalow was a special warning to the Dutchman.

Tek Chiu, correctly discerning the silent workings of his employer's mind, explained that the members of the Broken Coffin Society were sea pirates of the new generation. The change from the old to the new species of piracy had been brought about by the steam engines of foreigners. It was primarily no fault of the

Chinaman. The pirates of China were compelled to change their methods of operation—otherwise it would follow that their trade would cease to be at all. 'The same holds good in the matter of gambling in English colonies,' continued Tek Chiu. 'Cheng Ann tells me that in Penang the rich man may gamble as much as he likes, while the poor man who gambles is punished. The English law which, as I understand, is usually just, is thwarted by the ingenuity of the European Society-man; while the poor man who, like the pirate now out of date, does his work clumsily is seized and duly punished.'

'But the Broken Coffin Society men are punished,' said Mr Van Dyke.

'Yes, when they are caught,' said Cheng Ann.

'But although our Society has its dangerous and unworthy subsections and cliques, comprising men who use Society privileges for selfish and criminal ends,' said Tek Chiu, '*our* real aims are the highest and the best. And although there are bad men in our membership, the loyalty that we owe to the Society becomes all the greater. We who are free from crime act as a conscience to the blackguards, who, however bad they may be, will on account of the oath that binds them do us no wrong. And on the other hand, we may do them much good in dissuading them from evil courses.'

Mr Van Dyke did not quite admit the force of Tek Chiu's arguments, which, as Tek Chiu himself had stated them, sounded dangerously like sympathy with Broken Coffinism. But such sympathy was far from Tek Chiu's position. His virtual contention was that there was no reason why A should cease altogether to be social simply because B was socially bad.

'Friendly Societies are very good,' said Mr Van Dyke. 'But I am referring to secret and dangerous Societies.'

'These qualifying names are purely arbitrary,' said Tek Chiu. 'All Chinese Societies are professedly good, and they, all of them, are just what members choose to make them. There is no fixed principle according to which you can draw a distinction between those that are exclusively benevolent and friendly, and those that you call secret and dangerous societies.'

'Is the Broken Coffin Society entitled to be called friendly, or is it justly designated secret and dangerous?'

'It is justly designated secret and dangerous. It is the fault of our Triad Society, certainly, that such a dangerous and criminal clique is not exterminated at once. Such bad sets of men are like bad teeth that ought to be pulled out. But because a man has a bad tooth in his head, he should not be prohibited from eating.'

A Chinaman is a social being—a tool rather than a member of his community. If he were to cease living a social life, he would cease to be a Chinaman. The Chinaman abroad lives a large part of his being in the 'hoey.' The hoey unites men more closely even than the sons of one father in a family. So powerful is the bond of this Freemasonry of China, that if two brothers in a family belong to different hoey's their relationship in such a set of circumstances is more distant than is that which subsists between those members of one hoey who are not relatives in the ordinary sense at all.

This bond—that tames Fenians, compelling them to be loyal to their oath—that creates disunion in families, bringing into their midst not peace but a sword—that settles disputes, making brethren bless when otherwise they would curse each other—that insures for those within the elect circle, when occasion serves, a decent burial and the due performance of rites which is the Chinaman's heaven—that professedly enjoins sobriety and morality in conduct—that works and waits and longs for a kingdom which is an everlasting kingdom—that protects and fosters those within it, which is Chinese Calvinism—that potentially includes, too, all men within the Four Seas, which is Chinese Universalism —this bond is essential to Chinese political and moral and religious life, is expressive of that life as it is, and typifies and foreshadows it as it will be.

CHAPTER XVI.

FROM NEW TO OLD.

IN the north-eastern district of Borneo, not many miles south of an imaginary line (please consult the map) from Labuan to Darvel Bay, cutting off, in an equilateral triangle, that part of the island which is now British territory, was a large tract of land designed by Mr Van Dyke's new firm to grow tobacco and to do many other wonderful things. Cheng Ann and Tek Chiu, as trusty lieutenants, had followed their manager to that field of enterprise. But to Tek Chiu's mortification, the Chinese coolies of this new estate were all of them Khehs or mountaineers, speaking a dialect of Chinese quite different from ordinary Fokien. In his study of English, in which he had progressed with amazing rapidity, Tek Chiu had studiously avoided Malay, although the Malay language was really the meeting-ground of the polyglot population of Malaysia—which is modern Babel. Tek Chiu was therefore unable to communicate with these new estate coolies. He could perform, as heretofore, the ordinary duties of clerking; but the work of interpreting was laid entirely on the shoulders of Cheng Ann, who could speak Malay. All Chinese coolies learn sooner or later to speak Malay, so far as to give expression to the common needs of life.

But niceties of thought—and coolies are not without these—have to be either expressed in their own Chinese language or left unexpressed altogether.

Tek Chiu was not to wait long in Borneo. A sojourn of five months would suffice to put the copestone on that building of mind-preparation for future life in Singapore which his experiences, first as cooly and afterwards as clerk, had been constructing. In later days Tek Chiu looked back with wonder that he should have been guided to the largest island of Malaysia. He was never able to give explicit reasons why he had accepted Mr Van Dyke's invitation to go there; for as a free man, he could have elected to go straight from Deli to Singapore. But to Borneo he had gone for a miserable pittance of a wage, but, as the venture subsequently proved, for deeper knowledge and larger views of life than the sunniest days of his Black Rock childhood had given him.

After two months' stay in Borneo, Tek Chiu made a new acquaintance, which in a short time deepened into friendship. A visitor from Siam, who was a European and a Welshman, George Evans by name, in a delicate state of health, had come for a few weeks' holiday to this part of Borneo. He was one afternoon, in company with the Dutch missionary, visiting Mr Van Dyke's coolies, fifty or sixty of whom were Christians by profession. After Divine Service, conducted according to Protestant traditions by Mr Venters, the Dutch missionary, who had a fairly good knowledge of the Hak-ka (Kheh) dialect of Chinese, Tek Chiu, who was on the spot, aired a little of his English by asking the silent foreigner if he could speak the Fokien dialect. Mr Evans replied that the only Eastern language he knew was Siamese. He had been for four years a missionary in Siam.

Cheng Ann, with his fluent English, came to the rescue of Mr Evans and Tek Chiu. He invited the two missionaries to accompany Tek Chiu and himself to the bungalow. The two teachers, wearied with much walking, gladly accepted the invitation and drank tea with their polite hosts.

Cheng Ann's eye glistened with mischief. He had often desired in the presence of Tek Chiu to overhaul Christians, and this longed-for opportunity seemed now to have come. Cheng Ann's powers of dialectic were limited; but such limitations never seemed to hamper him. Tek Chiu and he had often talked and reasoned together in the Fokien dialect; but at a certain point these two friends were almost always compelled to stop. Tek Chiu could not well avoid suitable quotations from the Classics; and Cheng Ann, thus lost in wandering mazes, invariably made his versatile powers of expressing himself in Chinese, Malay, and English compensate for the conspicuous lack of profundity in his thought.

With characteristic hardihood, the young Baba opened the dialogue in English; and Tek Chiu got modified translations of the discourse conceded to him at irregular intervals.

'What kind of Christianity have you come to teach to our fellow-countrymen?' asked Cheng Ann politely, addressing Mr Venters. Even the most anti-foreign of Chinamen—and, much more, Straits-born Chinamen—are deferential in the presence of Europeans and Americans. But the manifest good-nature and homeliness of the two missionaries, and of George Evans especially, seemed to dispel all reserve, and to equip Cheng Ann with exceptional heckling powers.

'There is only one Christianity,' said George Evans. Mr Venters was tired out after his exertions at the open-air service.

'In Penang there are three or four kinds of Christianity,' said Cheng Ann; 'and I have always been at a loss as to which of them ought to be adopted.'

'You mean the different Churches, I suppose,' said Evans.

'Yes!' said Cheng Ann. 'The Roman Catholics will tell you that there is only one Church of Christians. A priest in Penang told me that all the other bodies of so-called Christians are so much counterfeit coin.'

'That priest is a liar!' interposed Mr Venters, who, as a Dutchman and not giving due heed to style of English utterance, spoke as he thought. Turning round and speaking to Evans, he added, 'The arrogance that is common to Popery and Anglicanism is the most potent engine of obstruction to the spread of Christianity that there can possibly be.'

'Remember, friend, that Churchianity is not Christianity!' said Evans, addressing Cheng Ann.

But Cheng Ann was not at that point ready for such a sweeping correction of his assumptions.

'It is very perplexing for us Chinamen to know which body of Christians is to be believed. You differ amongst yourselves on leading points of doctrine. Some Christians worship the Virgin Mary, while others despise her. Some say that a church building is useless as a place for devotion unless it be consecrated by the Bishop, while others condemn consecrated buildings as edifices of superstition and idolatry.'

Cheng Ann had received his early English education at the Roman Catholic Brothers' school in Penang. He had come into contact with Christianity as taught by the Papacy: the arbitrary vestments, rather than the abiding truths of the Christian religion, were therefore supplying the materials for his judgment.

George Evans, continuing the conversation—his Dutch companion had given him full scope—felt the cogency of the Chinaman's arguments with respect to differences amongst Christians. It was the greatest thorn in the side of aggressive Christianity.

Tek Chiu, deeply interested in the dialogue, kept boring Cheng Ann for translations. His knowledge of English was being put to the test, and the subject under review was of vital importance to him. When Cheng Ann's argumentative zeal flagged, Tek Chiu took speech in hand; and the Baba ceased to be a fountain in himself, and became a pipe of communication between Tek Chiu and the foreigner.

'You speak of unity beneath differences in Christianity', said Tek Chiu. 'You assert certain fundamental truths in Christianity, truths which if received make a man a Christian.

'What are these truths?'

'God is our Father, and Jesus Christ is His Eternal Son, and our Saviour. God, as our Father, loves us, and desires that we in return should love Him. Jesus Christ, as the Son of God, is the one Way through whom men gain free access to God. God's Son, as man's Brother, gave Himself up to die on the cross; and His death means forgiveness of sins and life everlasting to all believing in Him. God's Eternal Spirit enables men to appropriate and enjoy these blessings of salvation.'

'The Christianity that you preach is the same that I heard a few years ago in China. A young English teacher about your age told me exactly what you have now told us here.'

Tek Chiu's mind had travelled back in time and space to Even Way Hospital and Henry Bell. But he suddenly bestirred himself out of his reverie.

'I have often wondered with myself what this great doctrine of Christianity can mean,' said Tek Chiu. 'Our Chinese Classics teach us excellent moral precepts, as you must admit.'

'I am not a Chinese scholar,' said Evans, 'but I have carefully read through Dr Legge's large edition of your Classics, and I consider that they are very good.'

'Then,' said Tek Chiu, 'may not the unity that you speak of as binding the different sects together, in spite of manifold diversity, be still wider than you Christians think? Your countrymen, as missionaries in China, are doing works of great benevolence; and I have from my childhood seen and commended these works. I have never once in my life thought or said hard things about your religion. With my whole heart I believe that your countrymen in my native province of China are teaching a large part of the true religion. Nevertheless—and you will pardon me for my thoughts, and teach me wherein I am wrong—I think that there is yet a part of the true religion that the Chinese have from their own sages; and, although I have not as yet argued upon it with any foreigner, I have come to think that the foreigners are less clear upon the matter than we Chinese are.'

George Evans was surprised and delighted to hear a young Chinaman speak in such a way. 'If this young man,' said he in an 'aside' to Mr Venters (and Cheng Ann, the interpreter, heard the remark with mixed feelings), 'if this young man is a representative Chinaman, then the Chinese people are vastly superior to the Siamese.'

With growing desire to encourage Tek Chiu in his earnestness, George Evans asked him to explain himself on the question of the Chinese contribution to the true religion.

'I was thinking especially of filial piety,' said Tek Chiu.

'I cordially admit that each nation of the world has not only its peculiar defects, but also its peculiar excellences,' said Evans. 'You Chinese people can teach a lesson to the world on this subject of filial piety. On that point both of us agree. But it is now your turn to bear with me—the Christian faith approves of every doctrine that enjoins love to God and love to man. Christianity, however, is, first of all, a fact and not a doctrine. Do you comprehend?'

'I think I do. For years past I have silently brooded over this distinction to which you now refer.'

'Have you read our Bible?'

'No; but I have read missionary tracts containing summaries of the Christian religion, and I have seen many references to your Bible there. But of course I could never properly understand these references, not having a Bible myself.'

'If you are learning English, your first duty is to read the English Bible. The Bible is the greatest of our English Classics.'

'It is not an English book at all,' said Cheng Ann. 'It is simply a translation from the Jews and the Greeks.'

'Translation it certainly is,' said the Welshman. 'But it is nevertheless the most English of English books. The English Bible has made the English language what it is. My friend here,' Evans continued, referring to Cheng Ann's display of intelligence as to the original language of the Bible, 'has reminded us that Christianity itself is not English. It is no more English than it is Chinese. For that matter, it is less English than it is Chinese. The East, not the West, is the cradle of Christianity.'

'It is very strange,' remarked Cheng Ann, 'that we here in Asia are exactly where we were before the dawn of Christianity, while almost all Europe has become Christian.'

'Although Mohammedanism, that rules the Arabs and their dependants, is younger than Christianity, your statement is, in the main, true,' said Evans. 'The Founder of Christianity prophesied that the first would be last, while the last would be first. The Chinese had a civilisation when we in the West were a wild, crude, savage people. But the knowledge of Christ the Saviour came to us, and finding us wild, and fierce, and ignorant, changed us. And the Chinese Empire, with decidedly the largest population and almost the oldest civilisation on the surface of the globe—China, the great Turanian people, has during all these centuries stood almost unchanged.'

But it was time for the two missionaries to leave the attap bungalow and find their way back to a Dutch hotel, five miles distant from Mr Van Dyke's plantation.

George Evans was to stay three weeks longer in that region. It is difficult to say whether he or Tek Chiu was the more anxious for further discussion on the topics which the unexpected visit of that afternoon had raised. On taking his leave with Mr Venters, Evans had to give a faithful promise that he would revisit the estate. He volunteered also that next time he came he would bring a Bible. 'Stop a little!' said Evans, turning back after he had left the bungalow; 'I have here,' he said, taking a small volume from his pocket, 'an English Bible presented to me once by a dying friend. I gladly give it to you.'

Handing the book to Tek Chiu, and without waiting for acknowledgment, he hurried to overtake the impatient Dutchman.

On two subsequent occasions during his short stay in Borneo George Evans visited these two Chinamen. Cheng Ann's love of experiment had passed away within the very first hour of his catechising George Evans, but Tek Chiu's zeal had began where Cheng Ann's had left off. The latter therefore most gladly welcomed the subsequent visits of the Welshman.

The third interview—the interview that was to end for ever on earth all fellowship between George Evans and his catechumens—lasted less than an hour. George Evans was in haste to be gone. He had to leave Borneo for Siam on the following day. As the grave difficulties of language had to be overcome, Cheng Ann was, as on previous occasions, indispensable to the last dialogue between the young missionary and Tek Chiu.

'I commend your ambition to go soon to Singapore. There you will have better chances to improve your English, and to study carefully and prayerfully the questions we have been discussing together.'

'If I could only believe that Jesus Christ is a

Person, and that He still is, this world would be a thousand times brighter to me than it is now. And yet my father on his death-bed charged me never to forsake his teaching. He charged me to beware of foreigners.'

'You are not asked to accept foreigners' teaching at the expense of the teaching handed down to you from your father. You are asked to go back far enough through Chinese life and history to the Unity underlying all contrarieties, and to see that that Unity is a Person, a Person hating evil and loving good, a Person living in Chinese thought and sentiment, and leading China onwards towards better things. You are asked to be true to your own ideals of love and goodness, and to feed these ideals so as to keep them living. How is this to be done? You and your fellow-countrymen cannot live to yourselves. Try, as so many have tried before you, to live a self-contained life, and that life will then become death. Your ideals of love and righteousness will then perish with you.

'But as a Chinaman, speaking, as you have spoken, of the true religion and of China's contribution to it—what does this mean? It means that the Kingdom of God is already within you. You cannot avoid looking at yourself and your nation in the light of the Universal. And when the great Chinese nation will have come to look at herself with your eyes—and you are one of her children—then the Christian missionary problem is more than half solved. You as one Chinaman at least cannot go back to the past. When the light of the Universal has once shone through man's mental eye, he can never again do without it. Let me tell you, then, that whether the God-Man Jesus Christ becomes your personal Saviour or not—that is a great practical question which you will also have to settle —you have already ceased to be a heathen.'

'And my venerable father, what about him?'

'He was a Christian if what you tell me of him is true—a Christian in the making.'

'My father loved truth and followed it.'

'Exactly so. And you ought to follow him.'

'And refuse to become a Christian?'

'Become a Christian in profession and practice as you are in theory. You will never know the joy of being a disciple of Christ until you acknowledge Him and live for Him.

'As to following your father, you follow him most by following Christ. The sun brightens from dawn till noon; the plant grows from seed to fruit; spring passes into summer; time itself refuses to stand. If time stood still, it would cease to be. Motion is the fact in the universe. True consistency acknowledges progress, does not contradict it. Therefore be true to your father and follow Christ.'

'God willing,' said Evans, taking leave of the two Chinamen and the bungalow, 'I shall see both of you again. But whether we meet again or no, let me urge upon you to search and find and follow the truth I have declared to you. Remember that this truth is not of my own or of any other man's making. It is given to those who have faith to receive it. It is preached through those who have purity of heart to see it, and grace to reflect it. We who preach this Gospel are mere instruments. The Divine Spirit is the power that comes not from us but from above. To that power I commend you both. Farewell.'

According to arrangement, George Evans was to leave Sandakan *en route* for Bang Kok *via* Singapore on the afternoon of next day. He would therefore have to take leave of Mr Venters' hospitality next morning before dawn. But the Power that George Evans had just magnified willed differently. Within an hour of his departure from Tek Chiu's quarters he arrived at a Chinese village. It was arranged that he should meet Mr Venters there, and Mr Venters had not arrived when Evans reached the place. Evans arrived at the village to find the people much excited. At that moment a gang of coolies armed with hedge-knives were running 'amok' in the village. The young Welshman had no opportunity to see or be afraid. He was struck from behind and killed on the spot. Like maniacs these coolies, five in number, rushed through the village.

In less than half-an-hour Mr Venters, having escaped death, and ignorant of the terrible tragedy, arrived, and found all the village houses and shops closed—everything as calm as though it were midnight. Towards the other end of the village—the appointed spot—Venters looked, but no Welsh guest stood there. What! Was he lying on the ground? had he fainted? My God! The stillness of death and the ugly gash on the crown of the noble head told at once the saddening, gruesome, ghastly tale.

The five members of the murderous gang sat down on the wayside a short distance from the village to eat mangoes. Their brief rest was timely. In a moment they were within the firm grasp of Dutch law. A Dutch garrison, having got the alarm from the manager of the gambier plantation whence the five coolies had escaped, sent out twelve armed policemen. These after some difficulty here encompassed the runaways. Two of the five desperadoes were shot dead while attempting to resist, and the three living captives were brought bound to the garrison.

Tek Chiu reeled and staggered at the news. 'Had it not been for anxiety to discourse with him, he would not have come here, and he would not have been murdered,' said Tek Chiu, as if speaking to himself.

Cheng Ann, overhearing the remark, said: 'He spoke of a Person guiding his footsteps. It seems strange that he was guided to meet such a fearful death.'

Tek Chiu looked intently at the Baba and said nothing.

Both clerks were called by the Dutch resident magistrate to give evidence as to the time when they last saw the deceased.

'I hear that two of the prisoners are Hakkas, while one is a Fokien,' said Cheng Ann to Tek Chiu, as they were on their way to the foreigner's 'Yamen.' An hour's walk from their own estate brought them to the court-house erected for the special convenience of planters. The resident Dutch magistrate was to hold a preliminary trial there.

Tek Chiu and Cheng Ann entered the court-house as the magistrate was taking his seat. A man with a loud voice uttered something in Dutch. It was a call for the prisoners. Heavily chained, and with dejected looks, the three coolies entered the court-house from a side door.

Two of the wretched men were middle-aged, while the third was a young lad. Tek Chiu, sitting with Cheng Ann in the back part of the court-hall, suffered annoyance from the punkah. He could not see plainly the faces of the three culprits.

The charge was first read out in Dutch, and interpreted in the Hakka dialect to the two middle-aged men, who were arraigned together. The young Fokien, whose name the Dutch registrar failed to pronounce correctly, had then the charge interpreted to him in his own dialect. The Chinese interpreter gave the right name and the right tones: 'Tiew Seng Kee.'

Not till the mention of the name did Tek Chiu recognise, to his horror and amazement, the young prisoner's face. It was his old 'chum' of Scholar Wu's coaching class, the school-mate who had taught him to gamble.

As Tek Chiu stood in the witness-box, Seng Kee recognised his old friend, and for the first time since his arrest burst into tears.

The routine of law was proceeded with in due course. The preliminary inquiry and the regular trial took place. These coolies had had a quarrel with their European manager, a Dutchman—who, they said, had been dealing very unjustly with them. Five of them had met together in secret and had resolved to abscond. They partook freely of Chinese whisky, and armed themselves with weapons for purposes of self-defence. Having escaped from the plantation, they lost all control of themselves. One man had been murdered—a European.

Dangerous weapons were found in the possession of each of the three prisoners, as also in the possession of the two coolies who had been shot dead at the time of arrest. At the close of the trial the three prisoners at the bar were sentenced to death.

Two days before the appointed time when Seng Kee with his two fellow-culprits was to expiate George Evans' death by their own, Tek Chiu, through Cheng Ann, told Mr Van Dyke that the Fokien, Seng Kee, was an old school-mate of his, and that he wished to beg the magistrate for an interview with the condemned youth. With little difficulty Mr Van Dyke got for Tek Chiu the permission asked for; and Tek Chiu, armed with a permit, with haste and without hindrance, found his way into the condemned cell. Hard, terribly, had it seemed to Tek Chiu, that his first cup of fellowship with the home-land since the beginning of his exile should have such bitter mixture! Had these two youths met in almost any other possible set of circumstances, what a joy! But this reunion was sorrow upon sorrow. Alas for the wild-fire hopes—the unrealisable happiness of what might have been! Under the shadow of the gallows these two old school-fellows met.

Tek Chiu was anxious to know all from Seng Kee's own lips. How had he reached Borneo, and why had he joined in the murderous gang?

Seng Kee said that he had left China as an unpaid cooly, just as Tek Chiu had done before him. Borneo was not a place of his own choosing, but on that matter a cooly had of course no choice. The 'big dog' on the estate had harboured a spite against him in particular, and had been constantly ill-treating him. He was the only Fokien Chinaman on the estate. He was glad when a chance seemed to present itself to him to run away, and he had therefore joined with the four Hakka coolies to escape without ado. But he had taken too much whisky, like the others. The man who had murdered the foreigner had been shot dead already.

He himself had had no intention to kill any one, and he had not so much as lifted a weapon. He had simply wished to run away; but as he did not know which way to go he had kept beside the others.

A Javanese officer beckoned on Tek Chiu to leave the cell, as the time granted for the interview had expired.

'How exactly similar is Seng Kee's case to what mine was,' thought Tek Chiu, as he communed with himself on leaving the prison. From the complex consequences of the gambling-house tragedy Tek Chiu had made his escape; but for Seng Kee the stern decree of destiny had opened up no such deliverance from the consequences of an ill-starred flight. Tek Chiu was thinking out the matter in his own way. Had he known mathematics, he would have said in so many words that, while both cases were parallel, the difference between Chinese and Western modes of administering justice had made their respective consequences not parallel but rectangular. As it was, Tek Chiu certainly did think of this difference of consequences. But on what principle is it to be explained that Tek Chiu found here no relief in contemplating such a contrast? His heart bled for Seng Kee. He had no room for consolation, on account of crowding griefs.

Was there no balm in Gilead? Poor Tek Chiu's mind experimented, but successively failed at each point. Dutch law had given its irrevocable judgment; and, with all his accumulated education on the subject, that concept was still for Tek Chiu mysterious and unknown. Ignorance made him timid, and paralysed him for interceding with any one on Seng Kee's behalf.

Tek Chiu more than Seng Kee felt the strain of the calamity. Keenness of susceptibility and depth of sympathy made the death-sentence Tek Chiu's affair; comparative bluntness of feeling—not bravery—made Seng Kee suffer much less than his friend.

Tek Chiu had only one statute-book, the Bible, and that book was as yet unexplored. But the murdered missionary had summarised for him the 'great meaning' of law and Gospel.

Between the first visit of Tek Chiu to the condemned youth and the morning of execution there was agony of soul both in the cell and in the attap bungalow. During that period Tek Chiu for the first time in his life prayed in name of a Redeemer to the Father in heaven.

On the day of doom Tek Chiu got special permission to accompany Seng Kee to the gallows. When the three wretched prisoners had been taken out of their cells, Tek Chiu signified that he wished to say a word to the presiding magistrate.

'What do you wish with me at this time?' asked the magistrate in English. Tek Chiu was dressed as a Baba, and he did not feel insulted at that moment that his clothes were being identified with himself.

'I wish to die instead of my friend; and I beseech you to accept my life instead of his.'

The magistrate stood bewildered for a few seconds, and then regaining self-possession, said—

'Your request cannot be granted. That is not in accordance with our law.'

Tek Chiu had been reading of the sacrifice on Calvary. Graven on his mind were the words of Calvary's victim: 'Greater love hath no man than this, that a man lay down his life for his friend.'

Seng Kee, as he was being pinioned—a luckless Celestial receiving his last outfit—spoke aloud to his school-mate, no one forbidding him—

'Your Uncle Peng is dead. . . . Your bride has been given to a Christian preacher. . . . Teacher Wu is in Singapore. . . . He teaches in a school there. . . . He became a Christian because the young foreign teacher died.'

There was no time for commentary. The law that admits no doctrine of substitution had to be speedily magnified and made honourable in that obscure part of Borneo. Seng Kee, once a student, now a cooly and a rascal, who had neither killed a man nor smuggled salt, was compelled to die. The event meant a heavy blow to the planters.

Tek Chiu would speedily quit Borneo and Dutch jurisdiction.

CHAPTER XVII.

THE ODD CHRISTIAN.

LIN TEK CHIU with his personal effects arrived at Singapore, after an absence of nineteen months from that metropolis. These personal effects, which included a modest supply of clothing, consisted of three chief items herewith specified—let curious-minded people take stock and for ever hold their peace—(1) Forty-one guilders; (2) a Chinese-English dictionary, which was a welcome donation received at Deli from Hopeful; and (3) a small English Bible, which was George Evans' gift in Borneo. Add to these possessions yet again a vigorous brain, a tolerably robust body, and an alternately light and heavy heart. Such was Tek Chiu now; for the tragic deaths of George Evans and Seng Kee, to say nothing of Seng Kee's information as to Uncle Peng, had within three weeks added ten years to a still tender age.

Tek Chiu's first concern was to seek out Scholar Wu. In a large city that contained so many thousands of Celestials, how could he discover the whereabouts of his old Professor?

The unfortunate Seng Kee had mentioned that he was teaching in a school. That was a clue.

During the first two days after his landing at

Singapore Tek Chin must have explored the city from one end to the other. Making careful enquiries at different schools, he still failed to find Scholar Wu. Each school he visited taught English as the essential article of instruction. The Chinese language, if taught at all, was taught as a specialty; and yet the crowds of children at these schools, as the features, the loose jacket, and the queue could testify, were of Celestial origin. And the children themselves spoke neither Chinese nor English, but Malay.

At last, in a purely Chinese quarter of the city, in a street swarming with Fokien Chinamen and almost unadulterated by the presence of any other element, in a purely Chinese school, built according to the model of a Chinese Buddhist temple and wearing apron-like a picture of the Buddhist hell at the entrance, Tek Chin met Teacher Wu.

To each of these two wanderers, now to revel in the joy of re-union, the gambling-house tragedy seemed to have taken place but yesterday; and yet almost two years had really passed since that epoch-making event. The experiences of that period had revolutionised the lives of both of them. Even Scholar Wu's matured years had not been able to abide the test of that time.

No rapturous demonstration took place at the meeting between Scholar Wu and his favourite pupil. They met, and kept looking at each other for a while in silence. Effusiveness was foreign to both these natures. Neither of them seemed fluttered; yet each was overjoyed.

Master and pupil exchanged histories, each giving a tale of thrilling Chinese autobiography. Scholar Wu had already been about a year in Singapore. He had been for four months in the employment of a wealthy Straits Chinaman, who loved the cause of Chinese education among his fellow-countrymen, and who, in the almost exclusive support of that educational establishment, gave proof of his love. In this employment Teacher Wu meant to stay.

For eight or nine months prior to his getting that teaching appointment he had made many attempts, but without success, to earn his living by his brains. But he was not quite destitute; for a scholarly Chinaman, deeply versed also in English books, had done a great deal to help him; and such kindness, Wu declared, he could never forget.

Uncle Peng had peacefully passed away. 'The sad news reached me,' said Wu, 'two months after I arrived here. Your uncle was ill when I left; but I did not think that the illness would be fatal.'

Teacher Wu then led Tek Chiu into his sanctum—a place behind, secluded from the gaze of the hundred little Chinamen who, competing with each other in their exercise of lung power, were singing over their lessons, while they all were keeping their eyes directed now towards the visitor, now towards their teacher. For these small boys kept noticing that their old teacher had begun to wear a sort of holiday look. The buzzing sounds were the touches of sweet harmony to Tek Chiu. He felt himself in China once again. Inside the little Bible presented him by the late George Evans, was a leaflet containing words which Tek Chiu understood only imperfectly, but which he had committed to memory. As he stood among these children, far away from his native land, and with recent news of the last representative of his father's house having been called away by death, Tek Chiu thought over his English hymn :—

> 'Oh, touch those chords which long ago
> Gave forth a trembling sound !
> But now, as seasons onward flow,
> Each string is silent found.
> Put forth thy hand, and gently try,
> Call not the effort vain ;
> Deep in the heart's recess they lie :
> Oh ! touch those chords again !'

But Tek Chiu followed Teacher Wu out of the presence of his harmless inquisitors to the little room behind, there to receive his home mail. Uncle Peng had, to the disgust no doubt of the Singapore Post-Office authorities, had they come to know of the matter, entrusted Scholar Wu on his leaving China with a letter for the fugitive nephew. On his arrival at Singapore, Scholar Wu had sought anxiously to fulfil his commission, but his search had been vain ; for Tek Chiu at that time was in Deli in the thick of tobacco-planting. Now at length on this day of meeting Wu discharged his trust. There it was—a letter from Black Rock, written in clumsy penmanship by the hand of dear old Uncle Peng. It bore the red mark—the sign of goodwill and happiness. The writer still spoke in his letter, but he was now in Black Rock no longer. Old Peng would never write again to his brother's boy —the boy whose exile, sustaining his bitter grief, had hastened his death.

The contents of the letter raised questions that drove Scholar Wu back in time to make explanations. Uncle Peng's brief reference to Min Niang implied for Tek Chiu that the foreigners had acted unjustly in giving the bride to another. With Uncle Peng's opinion Scholar Wu said he completely agreed. The foreign missionaries had acted unjustly, but it was, Wu added, an error of judgment on their part.

'It is clear,' said Wu, 'that the lady missionaries and Teacher Richmond thought you to be a profligate. I am no doubt partly to blame for that opinion which they were led to hold regarding you, since I allowed you to accompany me too often to the gambling-house. And again, had Min Niang's uncle, Pun Lun, acted as a man of principle should have acted, he would have represented things to the foreigners in their proper light, and the betrothal to which I was witness before your birth would have been duly honoured. The foreigners have no doubt grievously erred; and all I can think and say about the matter is that many of them, however well-intentioned they are, have neither comprehension nor appreciation of our manners and customs. You have in this matter been deeply wronged; but don't forget that it is decidedly preferable to be wronged by others than to do wrong to them.'

'My heart entirely agrees with what you say,' said Tek Chiu. 'But, teacher, you now speak very mildly about the foreigners. Before I left China you had nothing good to say about them at all.'

Tek Chiu had already described vividly and with approximate completeness his meeting with Seng Kee in Borneo and the touching scene on the scaffold. But he had concealed from Wu the fact that Seng Kee had referred to the subject of his conversion to Christianity. Tek Chiu wished his old teacher to unfold himself on that matter in his own way. Wu's reference to the violated matrimonial affair and the conduct of foreign missionaries in that connection had already convinced Tek Chu that Wu was now no longer the anti-foreign graduate.

It was true that Teacher Wu had now been condemning short-sightedness on the part of foreigners; but a Christian could do that.

The looked-for acknowledgment came at last.

'You are quite right. Formerly I detested foreigners. I thought of them all as devils. A few months before I left China, however, my life passed through a great change. I made friends with a young foreigner—a teacher—who was sojourning for a time in Black Rock. He listened to my arguments with great respect, while I in fairness had in turn to listen to his. In time I came to feel myself pass through a sudden change. It was like the work of an earthquake. I cannot exactly tell you all the reasons why I changed; but I know that I suddenly came to feel the power of a Person leading me like a father leading his child. I stood by the death-bed of young Teacher Bell—I think you met that teacher once or twice yourself—and I felt then, as I have felt ever since, that no one but a personal Saviour and Lord could have made a man die as Teacher Bell died in Black Rock. At that time I truly felt that a Christian has firm grounds for his beliefs. Since coming to Singapore, I have discoursed with a Straits-born Chinaman who refuses to believe in Christianity because of Bible miracles. That Baba refuses, for example, to believe in the virgin-birth of the Saviour Jesus. Well, of course, you know that the miraculous element in the Gospel claim is a comparatively small difficulty to us who are loyal Chinamen. To me, in particular, belief in miracles has been an easy thing. The death of Teacher Bell was a miracle.'

'My case, teacher, coincides in some respects with what you have told me. I met a foreigner in Borneo—the young teacher whom the Hakka coolies murdered. Well, that foreigner reasoned with the Baba clerk and myself. It is so curious, too, to think that he urged me to accept Christianity, not, he said, because a Chinaman ought to be false to his sages, but because he ought to be true to them. The substance of that teacher's argument was that the teachings of other nations are as much necessary to China as the "un" is necessary to the "yang" in our own philosophy. There are, he said, great truths that are independent of space and time. Of such truths are "God is," "God loves," and others similarly fundamental. These truths are as necessary as is the truth that two and two make four. Any religion, therefore, that would stand the test of criticism must be capable of universal application. The whole of the human race, he pointed out, is progressing towards the due recognition of universal truth, and China cannot possibly be an exception to this march of progress. It therefore remained, he added, for the Chinese people either to accept Christianity or to explain it away as false. Teacher Evans' strong and abiding contention was that Christianity is the highest conceivable expression and growth of the world's religious life. The Christian doctrine and the Christian life in their essentials are eternal, and these fulfil and don't destroy the highest and deepest aspirations of the Chinese people.'

'That argument is irresistible,' said Wu. 'By somewhat different roads, both of us have come to see the same bright Light; but I must not conceal from you the gloomier thoughts of my soul. It may be that in this matter also we have passed through kindred experiences. But I fancy that your nature, my boy, if I understand it aright, is to shut your eyes when you traverse dark places. Well, the foreigners of these parts are not like those we were accustomed to meet in China. Here, in Singapore, we of the literary classes are paid back in our own coin. European scholars despise us. They speak of us as though we were curiosities.'

'The civilisation of the Western foreigners is much younger than ours, teacher,' said Tek Chiu. 'I think that their haughtiness—and I have already seen something of it—may be compared to the thoughtless buoyancy of the child or to the antics of the puppy dog.'

Tek Chiu hurriedly sandwiched this remark out of appreciation for Wu's reflections, while he listened attentively as Wu proceeded—

'And then again the large and imposing places of worship where the foreigners congregate contain all the piety that these people seem to have. The teaching of Christ is only nominally followed by the great number of foreigners who are here. And there is a large number of them, too, who never enter a place of worship at all. These people are supposed to miss a regular supply of goodness that there is to be had at these places. But I suspect that the non-attenders are quite as well off as the attenders; for the latter class never take their property with them out of the building.'

'Teacher Evans told me,' said Tek Chiu, after Wu had made a pause, 'that a European in the East either rises or sinks lower, from the place in the scale of morality which he occupied before he came into contact with us Eastern peoples.'

'How did he account for that?' asked Wu, with the docility of an anxious inquirer.

'Every man's life grows either to a flower or to a weed. Men coming from Europe to Asia are, as it were, transplanted; and the growth of character is for Europeans more rapid here than in their native soil. The East, that is perhaps more reluctant to move us that belong to it, makes Europeans thrive with a vengeance. In the East the growth of the individual, in the West the growth of the community, is the more rapid. Teacher Evans named this as the great Law of Compensation.'

Wu listened deferentially and thoughtfully. He resumed his seat in the professor's chair once more.

'I should be much disappointed,' said Wu, 'to think that Europeans in Europe are no better than those here, even although it be the case that growth of character is much slower there. Be the Law of Compensation, as you have stated it, true or not true, another way out of the difficulty is to say that the worst and not the best of Western folks come to the East. Men leave their homes because of failure. That is why we are here, and that is why so many of our fellow-countrymen are here too. I suppose it is the same with our Western neighbours.'

In these remarks Wu gave proof that his changed life combined humility and magnanimity. His was a genuine modesty.

Tek Chiu changed his guilders for Mexican dollars—such was the currency in Singapore at that time—and took up his abode with Wu. He would look about him for a few days, and find a channel for his ambitions. The opportunity soon came. He became teacher of Chinese in an English school, a post which he held for six months, receiving as wages thirty dollars a month. This was a more lucrative post than that which Wu held, that disenfranchised graduate's wage being twenty-five dollars a month. But Wu was never envious of his pupil's success. Tek Chiu's good start in Singapore was the product of his diligence at the study of English in Deli and Dutch Borneo. In his new and more congenial sphere his English grew from day to day. Scholar Wu had as yet learnt no English at all, and he did not mean to learn any. But he picked up a little Malay. This was inevitable.

Wu's Christianity in some important respects had intensified his Chinese conservatism. He had refused to associate himself in regular church membership with any body of Chinese or European Christians as already existent in Singapore. Christian brethren had occasionally visited Wu, and afterwards discussed with one another as to the cause of his antipathy to Church organisation, but these brethren had been unable to induce Wu to become a candidate for baptism. Thus, although Wu was by life and profession a Christian, the members of the different missionary bodies spoke of him as an odd one. A worthy European missionary, who prayed and worked for the peace of Jerusalem in connection with the 'Select Few' body— a body professedly free from all connection with the sects—had several times approached Wu; but to this worthy missionary, as also to the zealous members of his flock, Wu had extended even less encouragement than to anybody else. 'Strange behaviour this on the part of a Christian who condemned all sects, and who had thus appeared so promising,' so thought good Mr

Hanson of the Select Few Mission. Mr Hanson indeed had already found most of the living ornaments for his temple from among those very bodies of people towards whom the 'Select Few' were wont to look alternately with suspicion and pity. That fact, to extenuate, if possible, the faults of these erring human institutions must be gazetted. Heathenism, as so much raw material, gave its contributions grudgingly, it is true, to the sects; and these sects were useful in purging away the coarse dross to produce crude Christians. But the 'Select Few' represented the last and complete stage of refinement. If a Chinaman entered the 'Select Few' congregation, he was fit for Zion. Dipping was indispensable. A well-watered tank between the Select Few and their preacher was the Singapore Jordan.

Teacher Wu brought himself on Tek Chiu's arrival to review his negative position in ecclesiastical polity. He opened up the subject to his quondam pupil. On this important question Wu was not without a conscience.

'I did not seek for admission into the Christian Church at Black Rock, as it was my resolve to leave soon for Singapore. My application in that case might have been misconstrued as a bid for special advantages to be derived by being a Christian down here in a British colony. But my friends in Black Rock well knew what really took place, as I did not conceal anything. On the contrary, it was my duty and privilege to make the truth known so far as I could do so without self-glorification.'

'Did you attend Black Rock church on Sabbath days, teacher?'

'I did.'

'You don't attend church here?'

'No. But I hope ere long to be a humble member of a Chinese Christian Church in Singapore, if God should be pleased to prolong my life.'

Tek Chiu did not seem to understand the remark; nor was it to be expected that he should. The old teacher was conscious that he had propounded an enigma.

'Ere I left China, I felt that the Christian Church there, even with its native agency, was a foreign institution. But the Churches of Fokien province, such as they are—I know nothing of those in the other seventeen provinces—are ten times preferable to what they are here. Here their name is legion, and they are anything but Chinese.

'The truth is,' continued Wu, 'that the vices of European foreigners, including drunkenness (particularly on the part of soldiers and sailors, who seem less anxious than other Europeans to conceal their excesses), and high-handed arrogant treatment of us and of other Eastern races, render it necessary for the Chinese to be more clannish here than in China. Therefore, if the religion of Christ is to be a living force among our fellow-countrymen, as it sooner or later will be, it is highly desirable—nay, for missionary purposes essential —that foreign and accidental elements should be eliminated to the utmost possible extent. Is my meaning plain?'

'Perfectly plain.'

'Personally, though only in some respects, I sacrifice a good deal by keeping aloof from Christian Church organisation at the present time. You and I, Tek-Chiu, could of course understand and appreciate what is praiseworthy in the work of foreign Church Missionary agencies here. But we must think of our poor and ignorant fellow-countrymen who have not had the mental training to separate the wheat from the chaff, the essence from the accidents of true religion. And in other respects, of course, I personally lose nothing whatever by thus keeping aloof from the Churches, to the astonishment of worthy Christian brethren who, I am sure, are suspicious of me and misunderstand me. I positively object to be patronised by foreign bishops, and what else do you call them—*padris?*'

Scholar Wu had to use a Malay word here. He could not well avoid it.

'Be it far from me,' continued Wu, 'to be the cherisher of proud thoughts. But it is clear that all foreigners, including good Christians, have the weakness to despise us Chinamen. They show this attitude in many ways. They seem to think that they honour us by speaking to us. Now, as we owe a duty to the foreigners, I consider that it is the duty of a Chinese Christian to help the foreigners out of their weakness by keeping ourselves manly. This is the law of Christ. No one has a right to look down upon his neighbour.

'And, then, in Church arrangements, there is all this drapery of Western heathenism! In our Buddhism, we Chinese have taken on too much of that Western heathenism already; we wish no more of it. We wish Christianity in its essence and purity. That God is a Spirit and that His selected temple is the human heart, not stone, or brick, or mortar—such is the doctrine and church our countrymen require. China will have this in time, and God speed the day. I pray that China may take a firmer and truer hold of Christ than those Western nations that have in time preceded her. These nations, as Christians, are having their day of Christ's love and life, and they are far from being whole-hearted in their devotion to Him whose name they bear. Will China do better when her day dawns? I hope and pray she may.'

Scholar Wu had never been so communicative before in all his life. Since the days of Henry Bell he had thought a good deal over these matters, but had spoken little. His eloquence, therefore, when he was now in company with an appreciative listener, was the expression of many days' matured thoughts. It reminded Wu himself of the old wine-party. But it was twenty years since then. Much may be added to a man's knowledge and wisdom in that space of time, provided he avoid Rip Van Winkle's mistake.

The national spirit in Teacher Wu would die hard. Pity indeed if it should ever die at all!

CHAPTER XVIII.

THE SOCIAL CANCER.

Scholar Wu's eloquence on the Chinese Christianity of the future has silenced one and all of these our actors for the space of a year. But, at length, in the Chinese heart of Singapore a voice—a woman's voice—is heard. Its tone is distress and despair. It seems to mock, if not to contradict, the bright expectancy of Wu. Is Nature—ay, Nature's God—careful only of the type, while careless of *this* single life? And what of those other single lives that are so thickly studded round this one? Welcome is the hope that the day will yet break, and the shadows surrounding womankind and China's daughters flee away! But the present; the actual present!

Seven thousand of them—a large army. The overwhelming majority are from Canton province. Their ages range from thirteen to twenty-five. This is no Salvation Army. Its mission is twofold—(1) To commit suicide in certain prescribed ways, and make room for new supplies of troops from the Flowery Land—supplies which, because they are new, are always made welcome. Here is a cruel contradiction to Chinese conservatism. The other purpose or effect—systems unlike personalities are less mindful of motives—is (2) to overcrowd prescribed wards of the Singapore hospitals, and—if indeed this mission be not after all threefold rather than twofold—to make medical men swear.

But medical men must either hold their peace or allow their thousand denunciations of vice and their ten thousand denunciations of Exeter Hall to become chemically absorbed in the street rattle of rikishas and gharries. A Cantonese girl speaks here: medical men with their scientific testimony may go their own way.

The words are spoken, not in the Cantonese, but in the Fokien dialect, and with that tolerable amount of fluency which an imperfect knowledge of language and the melancholy of a fallen woman's life will jointly permit.

'And during these long years of your absence I don't suppose you have given me five minutes' thought?' said the voice.

'I have thought about you more than once,' was the answer.

Two people are necessary for a dialogue. The second voice belonged to a young man—a Straits-born Chinaman.

'The sight of you to-night in this dismal place has brought back to me all my misery,' said the woman. 'When first I met you, I was a woman that loved purity. Now I am a devil. I hoped for you to come and ransom me. You, above all others in the world, I trusted. And all these years I have trusted you in vain.'

The woman spoke deliberately and with tones of righteous reproach. She had a conception of goodness and honour, deeply sunken though she was in sin.

'I certainly hoped at that time to do something for

you,' said the Baba, feeling abashed as a felon before his judge. 'But my father hurriedly called me back to Penang, and since then I have worked first in Deli and afterwards in Borneo.'

This Straits Chinaman was Yeo Cheng Ann, not long ago acting in the capacity of a planter's clerk and theological interpreter.

As the cruel Aeneas (not the heroic personality that Virgil makes men believe he is), with excuses of devotion to filial piety and duty, left both his dear wife to the flames of Troy and Queen Dido to despair and death, even so had Cheng Ann four years ago left this Cantonese girl. She was helpless in the hands of her proprietors, when Cheng Ann raised her hopes of release, and then shattered these hopes, and the girl along with them.

Cheng Ann had now found his way back to Singapore. Till this unexpected meeting he had neither thought nor purposed in his heart to meet the girl whom four years before he had helped to launch out into the deeps of ruin. At that time he met a girl of eighteen, beautiful in her crimson blushes. But now the girl is old. Although she styles herself a devil, she refutes such a designation by wearing the looks of a woman. Yet this self-same look refutes arithmetic. As she seems, and as she is, she is no young woman of twenty-two—her life is fifteen or twenty years beyond that point of time.

Recent friendships in Deli and Borneo had helped to quicken Cheng Ann's sensibilities, sensibilities that never at any time could be quickened much, since they scarcely had existence at all. But this woman's words stung him, and brought him to a sudden halt in his mad career. By this interview his memory was forced back to the occasion of four years before. On that earlier occasion, so fraught with evil results for the luckless woman, Cheng Ann, either thinking that the widespread acknowledgment of other people's immorality justified him in his, or—what is more like Cheng Ann,—thinking nothing on the subject at all beyond blind self-gratification, had made friends with the girl's guardian, the procuress. This old hag had both in Hong-Kong and in Singapore registered the girl as a seamstress. The girl was made to begin her infernal profession when Cheng Ann sought her. His animal impulses and the old hag's fiendish persuasions had jointly overcome the unavailing protests of the helpless girl. The exactions of the samsings levied on the institution to which the girl unwittingly belonged had become unusually heavy; and the old procuress, with an eye to lucrative business in the near future, had made Cheng Ann, who was a bright and attractive-looking personage, the special favourite for a special mission of infamy.

'But I shall do what I can for you now,' said Cheng Ann, after a silence. The woman had said nothing in answer to Cheng Ann's self-excuse.

'You have lost your opportunity to do good. My life is now too worthless to be capable of amendment. I am like an old soiled and tattered garment that cannot stand repair. Leave me, and let me never see your face again. Your presence but serves to make me see too clearly my own ruined life.'

Whether the woman in expressing desire never to see Cheng Ann's face again literally meant what she said, or whether she meant merely to awaken the man's conscience, it is difficult to determine. This daughter of Eve, in any case, had already atoned for the sin of her ancestress, who, as one of the agents in leading Adam astray, has handed down a large debit account to be paid in the current coin of ruin by many of her large family of daughters. Surely in this one instance at least the man and the woman of Eden have changed places!

Cheng Ann was guilty, and he knew it. There he stood before that woman, who was stretched on a wooden couch, her head resting on a soiled, grimy pillow, an opium pipe and its belongings at her side. That prostrate woman was for a time a judge—not clad in the regalia of the Queen's Bench, but—poor soiled flower —the beauteous tinge of modesty had almost, yet not wholly, gone. She had spoken as one inspired with a force wafted through that suffocating den from the region of Heaven: an electric current seemed suddenly and instantly to have made her, 'battered' as she was 'with the shocks of doom,' well tempered here to communicate a shock of power. The charge must have come straight from the heart-throbs of the righteous Judge of the oppressed.

And was it not Cheng Ann's work as theological interpreter that had made him 'chargeable' here,— sensitive to the well-aimed shafts, not of Cupid, but of Conscience?

'Whatever I can do shall be done, even although it should cost me a great deal,' said Cheng Ann, as he rushed out from the presence of his monitor, wending clumsily his way through dark passages that abounded with entrances similar to the one he had just quitted. One apartment alone among all these caves of hell had suddenly become—Cheng Ann could not just tell why

—a consecrated building. Ritualistic people would have envied the spot had they only known of it. But Cheng Ann was glad to leave it.

Everything has an end. The long passage leading out of a brothel is no exception to this rule. Cheng Ann saw not the dazzling multitudinous lights that crowded the front entrance to this female cooly-depôt. He saw not even the groups of female children as they played on cymbals, thus working their apprenticeship for darker service behind. Nor did he hear their music. He rushed out into the open street. It was as though soul and sense had become suddenly entombed in a coal-pit. The reproaching woman he had just left had done this—but no! The girl he had met four years ago —it was she. Think again, Cheng Ann! You are not accustomed to think, but essay the task for once, and be a man. The woman was but the occasion—not the cause. The cause was to be found in self—in cruel, selfish sin.

Cheng Ann was a generous, impulsive soul, but withal a weakling. Therefore the conscience wound that hurt him for an uncomfortable hour soon, too soon, found relief in thought that minimised the wrong. ' It is the prevalent and acknowledged practice here; it is publicly recognised! Some one else — perhaps less worthy than I'—O Cheng Ann, Cheng Ann!—'would have initiated her into her trade. The thing was inevitable. People must be of service to the State in some way or another. Poor thing! she certainly does not seem happy.'

Poor Cheng Ann! your reflections sadly lack originality. Your conscience-balm is a medicine well known to young men of different races in the East, young men who have used that medicine extensively.

In the open street, while Cheng Ann ruminated, laying flattering unction to his soul, another voice—this time a man's—spoke to him in beautiful English.

'Cheng Ann! are *you* here?'

'Tek Chiu! I've tried to find your whereabouts, and have hitherto failed. This meeting is most fortunate.'

'When did you come from Borneo?'

'Quite six weeks ago.'

Tek Chiu then told all his recent history, and Cheng Ann told—some of his.

Tek Chiu's diligence in English had not relaxed since his arrival from Borneo. He was now a Fokien interpreter in the Central Police Court.

'In plain English,' said Cheng Ann, 'you are a Government official.'

'Don't I look like one?' asked Tek Chiu.

'No! your absence of swagger shows quite plainly that you are not qualified for your position.'

Beyond a significant smile, Tek Chiu took no notice of that insinuation as to his incompetency.

In the matter of competency, or the want of it, it soon became plain to Cheng Ann that his old pupil in the study of English had far outstripped the teacher. Depth and strength of thought, that had always been the possession of the young cooly, had at last commanded tolerably adequate expression in the English tongue; and Cheng Ann found that now in his own pet subject he was behind one to whom had been denied the privileges of being a Straits-born Chinaman. But Cheng Ann shifted his ground.

'Have you learnt Malay yet?' asked Cheng Ann.

'Not yet. I know only a few words.'

'You are at a great disadvantage in this place if you don't know Malay.'

'Yes, I quite see the force of that. I should have a much better chance of promotion in the Government service if I knew Malay. I mean to learn it leisurely.'

Cheng Ann took pains to impress his friend with the importance of his resolve. He also took pains to make obvious the inference that those possessing a knowledge of Malay were people much to be admired.

Tek Chiu fully ceded to Cheng Ann both his premises and his conclusions. And Cheng Ann feeling the appetite of his consummate vanity somewhat appeased, condescended to tell Tek Chiu a little more of his history. Tek Chiu's deference and generosity elicited the display of what seemed to be homogeneous qualities from the Baba.

'I was here in Singapore four years ago,' said Cheng Ann, 'and at that time I was a special chum of three Babas, who were the sons of wealthy merchants here. I had many jollifications with them. The four of us used to visit a house in Tent Street. It was not one of those low houses to which the coolies go, you know; but a stylish place,—a place where a great deal of money was always freely spent. The old woman who kept the establishment had four beautiful girls whom she had brought down from Hong-Kong, and who had cost her, as she said, altogether a thousand dollars. Of these four girls each of us four chums got one. The one given to me was really a good girl, and I got to like her very much. With difficulty, I have now after my absence found out where she is. My meaning is to help her by rescuing her if possible from the destructive life she is now leading.'

In his recital Cheng Ann at first had spoken in tones of a penitent person, but in this latest passage about straining himself to find out the girl with a view to rescuing her, he felt the wings of an angel growing upon him. Nothing short of the wondrous transformations recorded in that historic work 'Grimm's Tales' could here supply the parallelism to Cheng Ann's beautifully transformed character.

'Where did you find her?' asked Tek Chiu.

'After a painful search,' said Cheng Ann, 'I found her in Thorn Street. It is a much lower-class place than the house she used to occupy in Tent Street.'

'But does she really wish to lead a better life?' asked Tek Chiu. 'I suppose you know,' added this police court interpreter, 'that many of these women desire liberty from the hands of their proprietors simply to make extra money, and then when they have cheated their owners they return to their old life. British law respects the liberty of the individual subject. A great many of these women, therefore, take advantage of this order of things not to enjoy the blessings which such liberty surely confers, but simply to squander money, and make void the work of those who had taken a great deal of trouble to redeem them. That is the official view of the matter.'

'The girl has always desired to live a good life,' said Cheng Ann. This was the truth, although Cheng Ann had some timidity in expressing it. Regaining confidence, he asked Tek Chiu a question in return—

'Is the official view of the matter identical with yours?'

'I owe a duty to my office,' said Tek Chiu. 'But,'

he added with decision, clapping Cheng Ann on the shoulder to signify his gratitude for noble discrimination, 'I hope I am a man and a Chinaman before I am anything else. Those women who, as girls, have been imported from China, and who are coerced into leading an abandoned life here, have a right to be heard; and it matters not what stage in their sad career they may have reached. If I can help you in this matter, let me know. I have to meet my brother-officials of the hoey to-morrow.'

Tek Chiu spoke from a sense of the dignity of his position, not as a Government official, but as a Society man. The merits of the case alone, much more when contemplated along with Cheng Ann's anxiety, were calculated to make Tek Chiu energetic.

'Our hoey levies a heavy tax on that very house,' said Cheng Ann.

'I am no party to that sort of thing. And those who encourage such a business are enemies of the hoey, although professedly members of it. The vicious practices in which many cliques within our Society indulge will some day bring the wrath of Government down upon the heads of one and all of us. Two courses are now plainly before our Society organisation in the Straits—reformation from within or suppression from without. As matters stand, we may extend protection to individuals. Our Society is not quite so bad as to deny *that*. Have you taken the number of the house in which the woman resides?'

'Yes.' Cheng Ann consulted his pocket-book, and mentioned the legalised government number of the house in Thorn Street.

'And the name? I suppose you know the name

too,' said Tek Chiu, as he critically scanned Cheng Ann's face.

'Ah Ho,' said Cheng Ann.

'Ah Ho!' repeated Tek Chiu, giving the Fokien tones with a distinctness quite beyond the power of a Straits-born Chinaman to give. 'Let me see the characters; yes!'

Cheng Ann was puzzled and confused at his friend's cross-examination and evident excitement.

'Do you know the girl's age?' asked Tek Chiu softly. He had given Cheng Ann a long, silent stare, and had become calm and deliberate in the process.

'She is twenty-two.'

'Where are your three Baba friends, and what about the other three girls?'

Tek Chiu was asking too much at once. But in course of time he was told that as to the other three girls, Cheng Ann naturally enough knew nothing about them, while two of the three Babas had hurried themselves to their graves in the express train of dissipation. Straits-born Chinamen loved this mode of travelling. For them life's journey did not occupy much time. The other Baba was still in Singapore, killing himself rapidly, but the work was as yet unfinished. He had an iron constitution. With him Cheng Ann was not now on such terms of intimacy as formerly.

Cheng Ann, as an Euthyphron before his Socrates, found that at that moment he had a pressing engagement. Cheng Ann, generous man, had a mind to save Ah Ho. That fact was evident, else he would not have raised the question by way of enlisting Tek Chiu's co-operation. But Cheng Ann was not prepared to purchase that girl's redemption at the cost of too rigid scrutiny as to the exact causes and circumstances of things, involving as these seemed to do the possibility of earning Tek Chiu's contempt for one who always felt himself in the position of a superior.

Men there are who will do good when it will add to good reputation—who also will refrain from doing good when good reputation is to be reckoned up along with the minus quantity of hitherto concealed wrongdoing. Reputation rather than character is marketable, and as such it readily fluctuates in price. Traders who make that article a specialty always welcome a rise, but can never tolerate a fall in its marketable value.

In his desire, such as it was, to do good, Cheng Ann found a conflict of interests. Unwilling to sound the depths of his own past conduct—unwilling, too, to let others do that for him—he yet desired to act nobly, and he was in these conditions finding his task a hard one. A temporary arrangement, therefore, seemed proper at that crisis. He bade Tek Chiu 'Good-bye.'

But Tek Chiu ran after his old superior to ask one more question—

'Does that girl Ah Ho speak Fokien?'

'Yes; she speaks Fokien fairly well.'

A second good-bye was exchanged—the last for a long time. Cheng Ann left next day for Penang. His father had again suddenly called him there, and Cheng Ann was filial.

Hastily and gloomily Tek Chiu walked through the crowded streets, all insensible to the attractions of a wild beast show and a switchback railway—two European enterprises that had come to cause nine days' excitement in the breasts of those having leisure for such a condition of mind. When he found his way to his home, he told Wu of the facts which Cheng Ann had disclosed, and of his own suspicions that the girl was none other than the companion of Min Niang. What was to be done?

Cheng Ann, although he had now forsaken his angelic mission, had done good. The burden of responsibility had not fallen to the ground. It rested safely on the shoulders of Tek Chiu.

His new responsibility bulked considerably in the young man's mind. His humanity, breathing through the channel of nationality, made him think out and devise measures for a girl compelled to live an abandoned life, but evidently desirous of better things; his gratitude for past kindness extended to him by Cheng Ann, at whose request the measures for the girl's redemption were to be taken, and the nearness (as his suspicions indicated) of the affair to the home of his childhood, were also strong motive forces. Of these, the last-mentioned was the spur that 'pricked the side' of his intent.

'The hoey will not help you much on a matter of that sort, I fear,' said Wu. 'The other members will not feel as you do the need for redeeming a fallen woman. "She is already fallen," they will say; "it is her destiny." They will maintain that to buy her off from the procuress without giving her a husband would be spending money in vain.'

'I think I understand the difficulty,' said Tek Chiu. 'The individual rights of woman have not yet been sufficiently emphasised by the people of our nation. That fact marks a serious defect in our national life, and the new faith of Christ's Gospel will rectify it. I have been hoping, however, that I might induce some of the members of our hoey to see the matter as we see it. My curiosity to know if this girl is really the Ah Ho whom Pun Kwi lost lends perplexity and urgency to the matter.'

'You can soon find that out,' said Wu.

'I could not enter one of these places, nor do I suppose that you would care to do so.'

'No; neither of us can enter the den. But there is in Singapore a noble lady missionary, to whom I think we could entrust this matter. She would learn the girl's story; and we could then know for a certainty whether our suspicions are well grounded or not.'

'Do you mean any one of the Roman Catholic sisters?'

'No! no! These Roman Catholics do some useful work in connection with this social evil, it is true. They receive into their convent the helpless babes of lost women—of those who have just begun their abandoned life. Seventy of these infants died last year in the sisters' convent. How many survive I don't know. To take care of these infants is benevolent work. But the Roman Catholic Church treats everybody not as a person but as a thing. I have no faith in this Western Paganism. I think we'd better ask Mrs Watt to find out particulars about the girl.'

'All right,' said Tek Chiu.

'Mrs Watt has a Fokien Bible-woman who can accompany her. But where is Cheng Ann?'

'I'll try to meet him again to-morrow. He did not seem to like my questioning him about the matter which he himself had raised, although he seemed anxious to help the girl. I fear that poor Cheng Ann's life is on a level with those around him in this place.'

Tek Chiu tried to find out Cheng Ann and failed.

But he consulted with the Chinese Christian preachers belonging to Mrs Watt's Mission, and the preacher in turn made known to Mrs Watt Tek Chiu's request.

It was indeed Ah Ho. Cantonese boatmen had stolen her from Pun Kwi, and upset that merchant's calculations. Contrary to that Chinese propriety, which is observed more faithfully by Fokiens than by Cantonese, a young man—a member of the crew of a junk—made love to Ah Ho, won her confidence, and induced her to accompany him to Canton. The old captain of the junk agreed to the arrangement, and admitted the confiding Ah Ho into his ship. But he studied, business man that he was, to suddenly quit the Black Rock landing-place and obey the tide, leaving the lad behind him, and escaping with the prize. The lovers had simply exchanged places; and Ah Ho on board the junk was treated with the jealous care and attention given by a grandfather to his grandchild. In course of time Ah Ho was successfully conveyed to Hong-Kong. On the voyage she was pacified by the assurance that she would see her mother at the end of her journey, and also get a kind and gentle husband at the end of her sorrows. The lad who had decoyed her away, said the old man, was married already. He was a useless, good-for-nothing fellow.

'Out of regard for your welfare,' said the old man, 'I left your useless lover behind in Black Rock.'

Ah Ho was so far satisfied. The young man had held out golden prospects to her. Her own folly had induced her to take one rash step, and she seemed to be faring better than people might think she deserved. Kind Pun Kwi had lost his money. Ah Ho, by her own action, had transferred the benefit of the speculation from the rightful person to the old captain of the junk. And Ah Ho had lost dear Min Niang. Yet such a loss was sooner or later inevitable. A husband was in the question.

Ah Ho never met her mother. Nor was she married to a husband. She was sold for the round sum of two hundred and fifty dollars to the old procuress, who treated her with all the tenderness that a girl of tender years could wish. Falsehood on an extensive scale made Ah Ho contented with her lot. She would go with her new 'mother' to Singapore as a seamstress. There were grander husbands to be had in Singapore than in Canton or Hong-Kong. At Hong-Kong the foreign officials—these wild, savage men—had asked her questions; but her dear 'mother' had taught her what answers to give them. These foreigners meant mischief by their questions.

Western Individualism, the glory of European civilization, that vindicates as the differentia of Christian ethics the supreme worth of a single soul, meets at this point, not beneficially but injuriously, the Socialism of China. It is the sun which, while softening the wax of many other national systems, hardens the Chinese clay.

Individualism in the European colonies of Macao and Hong-Kong makes girls obtainable at these places. At Chinese Canton such girls are practically expensive and theoretically unobtainable altogether. In the European settlements the individualistic idea rules legislation; in China proper Chinese socialism is thoroughgoing; there the saving bond of the family is supreme. Hence it is that the large army of Chinese fallen women in Singapore makes visible a cancer that has been brought into special prominence by the 'constant irritation' of two entirely different systems meeting.

The Chinese Protectorate established in Singapore to vindicate—such is the praiseworthy spirit of its foundation and operation—the liberty of the individual, and to vindicate, too, to some extent at least, the worth of womanhood, offers salvation to these girls when salvation, because offered too late, is impracticable. Western civilization has brought the Chinese prostitute to Singapore; and the Protectorate is the attempt of Western civilization to heal the wound which that civilization itself has made.

In Singapore, and in other places that in the main resemble the Liverpool of the East, where there are different races that make up, with space eliminated, a miniature world, the absence of that family life which is China's glory has added to the size and hideousness of the Social Cancer. There, in such places—the adopted lands of the Chinamen abroad—East and West have met, but have not yet kissed each other. The different elements have been merged together in a common element—the water of concourse—and the result so far has been much effervescence and much waste.

'And to what purpose is this waste?'

'Humanity cannot do without its cesspools and jaw-boxes,' says the self-styled scientist. 'The cancer cannot be cut clean away. The next best thing is, recognising that it exists, to satisfy the requirements of the evil.'

'But what about Ah Ho and her hopes of a good and kind husband? And what about Ah Ho's seven thousand sisters?'

These are vain questions; for men ought to know that the scientist never had a sister. Nor can his scientific analysis condescend either to the connotation or to the denotation of that homely term. His kind of science, like a peculiar kind of prodigal, thrives best when it keeps away from home.

CHAPTER XIX.

REDEMPTION.

MR and Mrs Dimpleton ought to have been the very heads of European society in Singapore. They were admirably fitted for such a lofty function. But an obtuse-minded community could not think of the Dimpletons as members of the inmost circle, the circumference of which the honest and well-to-do Dimpletons merely touched from the outside.

Nevertheless, Mr and Mrs Dimpleton—for no one dared speak of Mr Dimpleton without coupling with his name the toast of Mrs Dimpleton—were centres, and this fact Mr and Mrs Dimpleton themselves well knew. Such was their mathematical standing.

Now Mrs Dimpleton was a woman who could like people much, and dislike people more. After a close friendship had sprung up between herself and Mrs Dickinson, and when such friendship stopped—as all Mrs Dimpleton's friendships sooner or later did—Mrs Samson became valuable by stepping in to fill Mrs Dickinson's place. But Mrs Samson, like a set of Cabinet Ministers, had no more than her share of Mrs Dimpleton's royal favour. The favour was very intense so long as it lasted. But everything has an end.

The rifle-fire of Mrs Dimpleton's displeasure ceased

when Mrs Dimpleton's cannon-shot was suddenly directed against Mrs Samson, and, on the basis of this heavier and later warfare, Mrs Dimpleton embraced Mrs Dickinson. The most advantageous time to come to terms with Mrs Dimpleton—for one had to be a friend or a foe — was when she was in her most belligerent mood. Any afternoon call would almost ensure success, provided that the caller should be somebody else than Mrs Samson. Thus it was that Mrs Jones, who studied to be a neutral sort of person between the afore-mentioned parties, shared with Mrs Dickinson at the point in our story the felicity of Mrs Dimpleton's regard. It was quite enough for Mrs Jones to listen silently, and nod her head occasionally, to the eloquent Mrs Dimpleton, whose most touching passages were delivered on Mrs Samson. And who could blame Mrs Jones? She simply shared in the self-sustaining impulse of all Nature's living things. Tacit approbation of all that Mrs Dimpleton said was the only fireproof coat of mail that Mrs Jones could wear.

Basil Dimpleton found it no small task to follow his worthy spouse throughout the sudden, jerky turns of her fancies. He had to hate and love in turn, as per instruction; for Mrs Dimpleton kept the keys not only of the larder, but also of the household disposition. But Basil, though oftentimes sorely taxed, never failed. As for the children, the 'Ayah' looked after them. Mrs Dimpleton had a great deal more to do than to trouble her mind with children in a tropical climate. Her husband required attention—sometimes firm, sometimes delicate handling—as did also the rank and file of that contingent of European society of which she (for Mr Dimpleton was only nominally joint-head) was the self-elected chief, and which she with becoming dignity adorned.

It fell out that Mrs Samson's husband, a man of such vast knowledge that he knew everything, was an uncompromising opponent of missions. His oracular utterances, of which he delivered himself at tiffin or at dinner, were usually made in the hearing of those not competent to give to these utterances the important attention and consideration they deserved. But the eye-glasses which he wore, and to which he was wont to speak as he poured out his anathemata against Exeter Hall and all the motley crew of missionaries, if they did not make Samson see better, served as so much valuable compensation for the incompetency of favoured, ungrateful listeners. So long as Samson's glasses were on him, the flower of his genius did not seem to be losing its innate beauty or wasting its sweetness. And when, therefore, the spell of the Dimpleton-Samson friendship was broken, and when anger sat enthroned on the seat which love had left, Mrs Dimpleton discovered several objectionable things in the Samson family. She had always, she said, discerned Samson's bumptiousness and vanity, although hitherto she had generously refrained from commenting on the subject.

A catastrophe took place one afternoon. By cruel accident, Mrs Dimpleton and Mrs Samson, sworn foes, met in the drawing-room of meek Mrs Jones. Now, if the truth must be told, Mrs Dimpleton, like Menelaus at the sight of Paris on the battlefield, rejoiced to meet her enemy. Whatever Mrs Samson might have done, Mrs Dimpleton was sure of her own course. With the necessary ostentation, without which Mrs Dimpleton's *Society Gazette* for the current week would have been a rather barren affair, this lady publicly snubbed Mrs Samson by turning her back towards her. And when the company of seven or eight ladies, in due council assembled, were listening to remarks that were being made by a missionary lady who had just joined the company, Mrs Dimpleton completed the discomfiture of Mrs Samson by favouring missions. The missionary lady was Mrs Watt, a lady known to most of that drawing-room assembly as an earnest missionary worker and a good beggar. Mrs Watt was a woman full of good works and alms-asking.

There were those in Singapore who kept alleging that this lady, in consideration of her skill in soliciting money-subscriptions, was, however much she herself might deny it, secretly and at heart a Methodist. Mrs Watt certainly had all the boldness necessary to warrant such suspicions; but the matter was never quite fathomed.

On that afternoon Mrs Watt was bringing home to the company, with the pathos that the subject-matter itself could command, the story of Ah Ho. And as to the steps desirable for that poor girl's rescue, these could not be taken without a sum of money. Mrs Watt was esteemed as a lady by 'society,' and disliked as a missionary by that same august body. Two of Mrs Jones' drawing-room visitors, members of the very inmost circle of Singapore dignitaries, standing high on the lists of Government House, remained silent as befitted their lofty station.

But Mrs Dimpleton, a House Ruler, remarked at a fitting opportunity when silence reigned—

'I shall do what I can for you, Mrs Watt.'

'Thank you very much, dear Mrs Dimpleton! It is so good of you.'

Mrs Dimpleton was more than rewarded by this public acknowledgment. To be avenged of her adversaries was worth the redemption of a dozen slave-girls.

Mrs Watt retired early from that afternoon assembly of ladies, who, thus abandoned, fell to zealously discussing the coming military ball, a subject on which the hitherto silent 'society' ladies suddenly burst forth into eloquence. The company had wakened up from their apathy. They breathed more freely in their native element.

Mrs Dimpleton also left early. Albeit this lady had wounded the feelings of Mrs Samson in the abovementioned twofold manner, as she rose to leave the room she consistently followed out her wound-inflicting policy. She made a remark that was professedly addressed to the hostess, yet really intended for the ear of Mrs Samson, who was close at hand.

'You are not looking so bright to-day, Mrs Dimpleton,' Mrs Jones had said.

'No, indeed, Mrs Jones. I suffer a very great deal in mind and body.'

It was Mrs Dimpleton's habit to speak of herself as a martyr when she quarrelled with anybody. And Mrs Dimpleton's quarrels were perennial. Mrs Dimpleton's enemies changed with changing time, but Mrs Dimpleton herself never changed.

And Mrs Dimpleton was continually doing acts of kindness. If resentment against her latest adversaries was the warp, kind thoughtfulness for the happiness of others was the woof, of her character. Of such is the complex life of humanity, inclusive of womankind. For, indeed, whatever adoring husbands or infatuated lovers may say, it is a scientific fact that the genus womankind includes as species neither angels nor fiends. Woman stands somewhere between these two sets of beings. And, for that matter also, brother man stands there too. No one ever ventured to teach Basil Dimpleton this scientific fact. People either indolently assumed that he knew it already, or they anticipated and passively endorsed Mrs Dimpleton's objections to her husband's studying science.

Mrs Dimpleton will live in history chiefly because of her kindness in offering to stand behind Mrs Watt, and succour Ah Ho. Mrs Watt had sought and found Ah Ho, and had spoken to her of release from her dungeon of death. In her attitude to Mrs Watt, Ah Ho, for obvious reasons, was more responsive and less terrible than she had been in her attitude to Cheng Ann. The poor woman seemed to appreciate the assurance that the smoking flax of her life was not wholly quenched. Mrs Watt had devised measures for her.

After her release from the brothel, the girl would be kept for a few months on probation at a house of refuge for such girls, under the supervision of Mrs Watt; and an honourable calling would afterwards be obtained for her. Mrs Dimpleton's kind offer of assistance would sooner or later be taken advantage of. Meanwhile it was for Mrs Watt to arrange with the Protectorate as to Ah Ho's release.

Rightly enough, the British Government ignores the infamous contracts made between the brothel-keeper and the wretched women. If a woman desires freedom:

from a bad life, British law demands that she shall be free. Each registered woman in a licensed brothel receives from the Protectorate, at the time of the registration that implies the woman's own willingness to live an abandoned life, a ticket which guarantees for herself freedom at any time, provided a man be found willing to take care of her. Such a man, when he is found, acts the part of a saviour. He receives from the woman of his choice her ticket, and presents it at the Protectorate; yet, along with the ticket, if such presentation is to be effectual, he must present satisfactory credentials as to his competency to support the woman he would release. Occasional inspections of brothels by officials are calculated to ensure that each inmate has her liberty ticket in her possession.

When Mrs Watt visited Ah Ho in Thorn Street, the main thing to be ascertained was whether Ah Ho was willing to leave that place or not. The 'mother-superior' of that institution had Ah Ho's ticket in her safe possession. The Cantonese official in Government service who inspected the place at intervals was not fastidious. In the possession of the 'mother-superior,' the ticket would not soil so readily. On that occasion, at all events, neither Ah Ho nor Mrs Watt was sensible of the importance of the ticket.

When, therefore, the lady missionary, after a casual yet memorable visit to the house of Mrs Jones—where she had recounted the tale as known to her partly through Tek Chiu and partly from Ah Ho herself—called in connection with the matter at the Protectorate, the gentleman there courteously and willingly declared that Mrs Watt's mission of mercy would be speedily fulfilled on receipt of the ticket. And when Mrs Watt sought to fulfil this simple condition, having repaired a second time to the den, Ah Ho was gone. The managing woman, assuming the attitude of an accuser, bewailed the loss of the 'dear girl.' It was all Mrs Watt's fault. The girl had no desire whatever, said this 'old parliamentary hand,' to live a life different from that into which she of her own free choice had entered.

'She has escaped,' said the woman, 'and I am in great perplexity as to where she is. The head manager of this place, a very exacting man, will hold me responsible for the loss of the girl; and the people at the Protectorate will punish me. What am I to do?'

The old woman stamped her foot and scolded, while Mrs Watt looked on. The words were Malay, a language which Mrs Watt knew well.

Back went Mrs Watt to the Protectorate. The gentleman whom Mrs Watt had interviewed quite sympathised with that lady's aim; but it was difficult, as he pointed out, to make any practical suggestion on the matter. He would consult his superior and let Mrs Watt know next day.

On the same afternoon King Solomon was consulted. King Solomon agreed with his assistant that it was desirable to seek out and, if possible, find the girl. The brothel-keeper had no right to allow the girl to escape. The brothel-keeper would be held responsible.

In the evening King Solomon dined with Mr Samson, to whom the matter was casually mentioned.

'It is just what one would expect from these fussy Exeter-Hall people,' said Mrs Samson.

The remark was the beginning of a long and well-sustained speech of denunciation. On that evening poor Mrs Watt's well-meant but abortive endeavour proved, like Kant's ideal act of morality, capable of being universalised. It was a fair specimen, said Mr Samson, of evangelical stupidity, that interfered with the ordinary operation of righteous legislation, and bungled it. There, at a point circumscribed by the circle of William Samson's devoted head, equidistant between the fringes of a flapping punkah above and a cup of burning after-dinner coffee beneath, the irrevocable judgment of wisdom was given. From behind these all-seeing spectacles, Mrs Watt's conduct was descried in all its ugly nakedness. The puffing of a choice Manilla not only shared honours with the fulminated, trenchant sentences that escaped Mr Samson's lips, but also bestowed on their delivery all the solemnity and majesty of law.

Mr Samson's arguments were unanswerable.

Mrs Watt sorrowfully told the mission preacher to convey to Tek Chiu intelligence as to the failure of her efforts. So far Mrs Watt's kindness had missed a well-directed aim, and—whether Mrs Samson's husband or the crafty brothel-keeper was to blame remained an open question—Mrs Dimpleton's benevolence kept hanging fire.

'I don't believe that the girl has run off voluntarily,' said Wu.

'Nor I,' said Tek Chiu.

The old teacher and his pupil were talking together in the quiet of their lodging. For the sake of humanity and tender memories, both these friends resolved that they would take pains to discover Ah Ho's whereabouts. As the matter stood, it was a case of trying to find a needle in a haystack. Ah Ho had for a moment become visible above the surface of the great Prostitution sea, and then disappeared. But Tek Chiu was a good diver.

The Vanguard of the Great Dragon Lodge instituted in Deli had since his arrival in Singapore commanded a respectable place in the Ghee Hin Society. Most of the head-men of that Society Tek Chiu knew personally. And he was not long in discovering the clique that levied the tax on the den lately inhabited by Ah Ho. Tek Chiu constantly and bitterly bewailed the darker doings of his hoey; and his increasing knowledge of details increased his sorrow. The head official of the Ghee Hin Society in Singapore was receiving from the Opium Farm in lieu of 'good-will' a monthly sum of two hundred dollars. Subordinate officials were also regularly receiving from that same quarter smaller yet substantial sums.

It was a question of sacrifice that presented itself to Tek Chiu. Ah Ho's release might cost a good deal. But had not Tek Chiu been industrious? He had already saved a hundred and twenty dollars. From that reserve fund he was prepared to risk a good deal, if only Ah Ho were rescued. Cheng Ann was not to be found—but that difficulty did not free Tek Chiu from responsibility.

Thirty dollars sufficed to secure the necessary information. In a house, that was a brothel and notorious gambling den in one—in a dark corner of Swine Street—Ah Ho had found her new environment. Into this den Tek Chiu would not venture alone. He would first consult with Teacher Wu.

'It is desirable,' said Tek Chiu to Wu, 'that we should first make sure of the woman's anxiety to be free. In our own minds we are of course satisfied on this point, but we must be able to convince Mrs Watt and those assisting her in the task of management. Cheng Ann has already given me sufficient assurance, that the girl desires to escape. I well know that Cheng Ann is not the most trustworthy of men. But I know when Cheng Ann speaks truth and when he speaks falsehood. He gave me distinctly to understand that the girl has from the first been forced to live that dreadful life, and that she would welcome redemption. And if we could once succeed in releasing her, I am sure Mrs Watt would care for her, and give her a chance to do better, late as the chance is in coming.'

'My pupil has spoken like a man,' said Professor Wu. 'My own worthless life has been accepted by a seeking Saviour. Why should we despair of a fallen woman? She will rise again.'

'Suggest a plan of action, teacher. We really must see the girl ourselves; yet we cannot enter that place along with Mrs Watt.'

Tek Chiu had here applied to Wu for counsel. And Wu was not without a resource.

'The place in which the woman now resides is also a gambling den, didn't you say? Well, I think I have a plan. That Cantonese man who acts as assistant to the European gambling detective will help us for a small consideration. We shall act as informers against that house, and we can then accompany the European to the den, guarded by him, his Cantonese assistant, and his other "ghosts."'

The 'ghosts' were Malays, whose work it was to follow the detective, and lay bare the wicked devices of gambling,—seize the cups, cards, buttons, and cash, and tie together and hold at their joined extremities the pig-tails of Celestial culprits. Then, following their trophies, these 'ghosts,' whose physical strength constituted but a small part of that of their captives, were wont to be dragged to jail. The 'ghosts,' not their victims, were passive. The victims, having been seized *in flagrante delicto*, and submitting to misfortune with manifest eagerness for punishment, were in this way accustomed to drag the 'ghosts' behind them.

The glory of the 'ghosts' lay not indeed in their physical strength, but rather in their swiftness of foot. Alighting upon a gambling den constructed like a rabbit's burrow, these 'ghosts' would strategically give most attention to the back parts of the building, eagerly scanning and overhauling sky-lights and false walls, disappointed occasionally by stubbornly resisting trap-doors. In this work these 'ghosts' excelled, except when the ingenuity of Celestials outdid them by such invincible measures as that of keeping a watchman to dog the footsteps of the detective's party throughout the city, and duly report when the troublesome limbs of the law were in the immediate vicinity of the den.

Carey, the Cantonese Chinaman and chief informer, was Detective Renshaw's right-hand man. Carey had been a desperate criminal in his own time; but having on one occasion turned Queen's Evidence in a robbery and murder case in which he was directly interested, he was now in substantial fashion showing his gratitude to Her Majesty for her leniency with him. He was now earning a salary of ten dollars monthly as gambling-informer. His services were invaluable. He knew the 'lie of the land.'

By means of such competent weapons Wu's scheme was tolerably if not eminently successful. Ah Ho was alone in the seventh room of the burrow, which the arresting party, with the exception of 'ghost' doorguards, duly entered. Male prisoners had already been arrested in batches, while the residue of them had succeeded in escaping. Ah Ho's was the thirteenth female face which Wu and Tek Chiu eagerly scanned. Detective Renshaw and his ghosts did not think of arresting women. These women were mere children in respect of gambling responsibility. But when the party entered the room in which Woman Number Thirteen was alone, the ghosts kept rummaging shelves, drawers, and boxes, and shaking mats and mosquito curtains, while Tek Chiu, with a hurried remark to Wu—'This is the woman'—addressed Ah Ho.

Dreamily the girl looked up from the couch on which she was resting. She was pale and sickly-looking. She had just intoxicated herself with opium, as was evident from her own condition and the condition of the bamboo pipe and its belongings.

'Ah Ho!' said Tek Chiu.

The girl started as if awaking from a dream, looked at the graduate's son, recognised him, and burst into tears. She was unable to speak. The opium fiend had put a veil between her and reason. But Tek Chiu knew that Ah Ho recognised him. The opium had stupefied her a good deal; yet it seemed as though intoxication had given wings to Memory. Ah Ho was crying like a little girl when Detective Renshaw and his party, Wu and Tek Chiu among them, left No. 7 to explore compartment No. 8. Mechanically these two men continued their gambling hunt. It was an uncongenial quest for those who had no appetite for prey.

'The woman is completely lost,' said Wu to Tek Chiu, when sitting in a room respectably distant from Swine Street. 'The thought of her being an opium-smoker did not previously enter my mind.'

'It is terrible,' said Tek Chiu. 'What *can* be done?'

'I am afraid that nothing can be done,' said Wu solemnly. He added, 'I ought to have known that all these women are sooner or later trained to smoke opium. That habit rivets them to their den, and makes them more vicious. Opium has upset all calculations about that poor girl's redemption.'

'Yes, opium has done much harm to our nation; and it will do much harm still,' said Tek Chiu. 'The European to whom I teach Fokien in the mornings constantly asks me questions about opium-smoking. I am afraid he is not quite satisfied with the answers I give him.'

'I dare say not. If he is an average European here, he cannot well enjoy the unvarnished truth. Men who shut their eyes to the curse are continually questioning those who know about the matter. I suppose they assume that questioning will make the evil less than it is. But you might tell me as explicitly as you can the foreigner's opinion on the subject.'

The foreigner was Mr Samson, who, still a young man, aspired to know the language of a people whom he despised. And Tek Chiu had become his private 'coach.'

'Well, first of all,' said Tek Chiu, 'he denies that England forced opium on China; and he denounces English Christian teachers for making such an admission.'

'Well, what next?'

'Second, he maintains that alcohol does more harm among Western peoples than opium does among the Chinese, and that the moderate use of opium is beneficial and not harmful.'

This second part of Mr Samson's creed, as Tek Chiu stated it, was evidently too much for Wu. He had to lean back in his chair and draw a long breath. Wu used to hold foreigners in utter contempt, and at that point he had almost become a backslider. But no! Wu sat up again in his chair, prepared to hear anything now.

'Third, if the Chinese don't get their opium, they'll become drunkards, and then kill each other. Mr Samson thinks too much of us Chinese to allow us to do that. Therefore, he adds, our opium has been and is a great benefit to us.'

Teacher Wu gave expression to his feelings in a loud heathen oath. That heathen oath he had really used as a Christian weapon, although, as Wu himself admitted, it would be better not to use it again.

'These are the prevalent notions about opium and opium-smoking in Singapore,' said Wu, speaking at last in more resigned and subdued tones. 'Only yesterday I mentioned to a wealthy Straits-born Chinaman that I had got bad news from China about my younger brother's opium-smoking, and he expressed personally his deep sympathy with me. But when we began to speak about the opium habit here in Singapore, and the urgency for every Chinaman to do his best to stamp out the evil, he remarked that to speak about stopping the opium trade was utter nonsense. Straits-born Chinamen are evidently British citizens first and Chinamen afterwards. If the opium revenue were to cease, this colony of the Strait Settlements would be bankrupt. It seems that this great financial difficulty is the root of all the childish and extravagant statements made about the harmlessness of opium.'

'It is a strange inversion of things which most Europeans here seem to accept when they allege that the opium-smoker is quite able to stop the habit, while they assert at the same time that the trade itself cannot possibly be stopped. As for many Babas here, their position, on account of their deeper and wider knowledge, is less excusable. They well know that smoking opium in moderation is a contradiction in terms, and yet they defend the trade. But the influence of Europeans and the practical question of revenue, no doubt, have landed many Babas in this strange position. Well, teacher, I think it would be wrong of us to give up renewing attempts to save Ah Ho. She is a woman whose conduct, more readily than that of a man, can be controlled. Those taking care of her can forcibly deprive her of opium. I saw the other day in a Hong-Hong English newspaper that a medical man there —an Englishman—has for several years made interesting experiments on prisoners. In prison, as you know, men are forced to do without opium, excepting, of course, persons who are wealthy, and who no doubt succeed in bribing the warders. Therefore I think that Ah Ho on her release from her present den could be treated as an imbecile, and forcibly deprived of the drug. That she is a woman and not a man—an article, and not a free agent—is the last thread by which her salvation hangs.'

'You are right,' said Wu. 'That Hong-Kong doctor

to whom you have just referred has said that opium-smoking does no harm either physically or mentally. Would to God his words were true! My poor brother!

Teacher Wu broke down at this point. The picture of his younger brother—a graduate, a member too of the old wine-party—now a skeleton and a devil, with a helpless wife and children, in Even Way city, stood before his mind's eye.

'It is quite easy to understand that doctor's meaning,' said Tek Chiu, whose mind was not in Even Way but in Hong-Kong jail. 'He has forcibly deprived prisoners of opium, and then, having kept the drug away from them, he has declared that the *absence* of opium, not the *presence* of it, is harmless.'

'Then,' rejoined Wu, 'inasmuch as that doctor supports a prison-policy, are we to understand that he favours total suppression of the trade altogether?'

'That is evident,' said Tek Chiu. 'The anti-opiumists wish to make the whole community a prison on a large scale.'

'But you must remember,' said Wu, 'that that doctor speaks of opium as harmless.'

'It is rather odd,' said Tek Chiu. 'I suppose, then, that the prisoners in Hong-Kong don't get opium simply because the article is expensive. This question of expense has made the Hong-Kong doctor an anti-opiumist. Men reach the same goal by different ways.'

Both Wu and Tek Chiu were anti-opiumists; and Mr Samson, a pro-opiumist, had tackled Tek Chiu one morning in order to elicit information on the subject of opium-smoking among the Chinese. Singapore Babas in positions of subordination to Europeans generally feel honoured when Europeans appear to give weight to their opinions. These Babas, therefore, not particularly anxious to do violence to the pet notions of Britishers, on such occasions 'tell a few lies to comfort the questioner's heart.' And the questioner feels strong from his having consulted Chinese opinion.

Now Mr Samson, in his dealings with Tek Chiu, patronising him and reasoning with him alternately, was not a little astonished to find, for the first time during his ten years' sojourn in the East, that an Oriental had taken leave to differ from him.

'You say it will be a great hardship to the Chinese if the British Government forcibly stop the import of Indian opium to China,' Tek Chiu had said to Mr Samson. 'Such a course would be the only consistent and honourable course to adopt, seeing that opium was really forced on China. Western nations have taught the Chinese to like opium, and they should now teach them to dislike it. It is the only way in which these nations can redeem their honour, if indeed their honour can be redeemed at all.'

Tek Chiu's words had raised the whole question as to Britain's past dealings with China.

CHAPTER XX.

RESPONSIBILITY.

ONLY a few days subsequent to the night when he followed the ghosts through the dark recesses of Swine Street, Tek Chiu met Ah Ho in the open thoroughfare. Ah Ho was driving in a rikisha, in company with another girl who was holding the same social rank with herself. It was late in the afternoon, a time when all classes of the community, except shopkeepers, were supposed to have leisure for the recreation of walking or driving. Tek Chiu would have walked past the rikisha without attempting to look inside had Ah Ho not beckoned to him. The Fokien puller, drowned in perspiration, was glad to lower his 'carriage' shafts, and rub his face and shoulders with a lamp duster that also did the work of a bath-towel.

'The lady missionary told me of your being here, and also of your being anxious for my release,' said Ah Ho. 'How shall I repay your kindness? If I thought my dear Min Niang would receive me, I would steal away to her and implore her to forgive me.'

'You would require to go back to China if you wished *that*,' said Tek Chiu.

Few words passed between Tek Chiu and the inside of the rikisha. Ah Ho declared solemnly and in bitter tones that she had been cruelly deceived. She was very unhappy in the place to which she had forcibly been taken.

'Did you not go of your own accord to Swine Street?'

If Tek Chiu had at that moment looked at Ah Ho he would have seen the girl blush and drop tears successively. But Tek Chiu had his face turned sideways, as though the rikisha hurt his eyesight.

'How could I act of my own accord?' asked Ah Ho, with a slight degree of reproach in her tones. 'Except for a short half-hour of the day, during which time you now have met me, I am an absolute prisoner. Whither could I go? Tell me if you think I could now escape.'

Tek Chiu was silent. The companion in the rikisha was a Cantonese girl, not accomplished as Ah Ho was in a knowledge of Fokien. As she could not follow the conversation, she was merely sitting looking with admiration at the tall young lad with the large eyes.

For a moment Tek Chiu took courage and looked into Ah Ho's face. 'Answer me two questions,' he said.

'I'll try,' said Ah Ho playfully.

'Were you taken by force from Thorn Street to Swine Street?'

'Yes; by sheer brute force. I had hoped for release; but the old woman was advised by her superiors of the house to convey me away to a different place. The chance of again speaking with the English lady was therefore denied to me.'

'And are you anxious now for release?'

'By Kong, yes! All these years I have sighed to be delivered from the hands of these people, but my chance has never come. Now that my chance has come, I feel that I am a useless and ruined girl.'

'Why didn't you claim freedom when you appeared before the foreign officials?'

'Oh, I was always afraid of these people.'

'I must now go,' said Tek Chiu. 'I'll take steps for your immediate release. But you must not tell anyone that such steps are being taken.'

'Surely not,' said Ah Ho. 'This girl does not know our dialect. Besides, even if she did, the poor thing would do me no harm.'

'Slowly, slowly, walk!' said Tek Chiu—the idiomatic Chinese for 'Take care of yourself; good people are scarce.'

The rikisha shafts were horizontal once again. The Fokien puller was off at a furious rate, heedless of the literal significance of the parting words addressed by Tek Chiu to the two customers. A bullock-cart was in close vicinity; and Ah Ho's rikisha would have suddenly come into disastrous collision with that engine of obstruction but for the clever cooly, who was as wide-awake as he was furious in his career.

Tek Chiu's latest plan succeeded. Thorn Street institution, from which Ah Ho had been forcibly conveyed, was interdicted for a fortnight. The keeper's licence was suspended for that period of time by an avenging Protectorate. If a brothel-keeper loses a girl, the Protectorate asks, 'Where is she?' And woe betide that keeper if the transfer of the girl is found to have been a shady business! If again a brothel-keeper forces a girl to stay, the girl herself being anxious to leave, woe betide that keeper who tries to checkmate the doctrine of personal liberty. Such is the law. But the practical application of it bristles with difficulties. The desirability of keeping girls, who, being prostitutes once are prostitutes always—such is the practical view — as inmates of certain prescribed licensed houses, is a strong force that counteracts and even vitiates the healthy forces that work in the direction of the personal liberty and dignity of Chinese womanhood in Singapore.

Ah Ho was released from Swine Street and from her infamous calling. She was received into a house of refuge, where Mrs Watt took special pains to tend and gladden her. In six months' time, a period of probation through which Ah Ho nobly passed, a comfortable situation was found for her as nurse to the family of an English lady in Johor. Johor, the most southern part of the Malay Peninsula and of the mainland of Asia, permits gambling and many other Chinese institutions, and owns an opium factory and a Malay Sultan. In this region Ah Ho was happy. The English lady treated her with great kindness, and she herself proved to be a faithful servant.

During that period of six months' probation Ah Ho was in certain important respects quite as much a prisoner as she had been within the confines of the three houses of Tent Street, Thorn Street, and Swine Street. In Tent Street she had smoked opium for the first time in her life. In that aristocratic place she passed through the playing stage of the smoking habit. Here she was chiefly engaged in preparing pipes for others—for members of the opposite sex. In Thorn Street Ah Ho practised the habit more systematically for herself; and at a certain point in the line of that intermediate stage Ah Ho ceased to be morally responsible. Development in the opium-smoking habit had become incapable of arrest. Swine Street was the period of Ah Ho's perdition. Then it was that she was rescued and made a prisoner in a new sphere—the house of refuge, vigilantly circumscribed by the attentions of Mrs Watt and those assisting her. Imprisonment, in the sense of forced separation of Ah Ho from her opium-pipe, was the homœopathic cure—the only possible cure—for Ah Ho's darker, deadlier bondage. Opium-smoking cleverly bridges the gulf between the physical and the psychical world. It ignores a distinction between body and soul. Responsibility in an opium-smoker ceases to be. Everything is engulfed in the category of necessity. Everything that constitutes an opium-smoker's being surrenders to the craving for the drug. The coercive intervention of others is the only hope for the opium-smoker who has come at last to wallow in the slough of the perdition stage. It had been thus with poor Ah Ho in Swine Street.

If there is such a thing as the law of growth in the universe, the opium-smoking habit exhibits that law. The genus growth includes, with inexorable realism, as its species the opium-smoking habit. Both actually and potentially there is a moderate use of alcohol; although, as a caveat, men are reminded every day of actual facts which deny in the case of those endowed with an intense temperament that prevention from excess in alcohol is necessarily guaranteed. Only actually, and not potentially, is there such a thing as a moderate use of opium. Except in such limiting conditions as those of a prison, where development in the habit is summarily and externally arrested, the use of opium passes necessarily into its abuse.

This terrible law of growth is valid even quite apart from the separate question as to whether opium-smoking at any time is indulged in except for purposes of intoxication. In any case there is doubtless a playing stage in opium-smoking. And the playing stage is part only of a larger whole. For if the days and weeks of a man's life are contemplated as isolated things, then the atomism of an abortive science 'that murders in order to dissect' holds the field. In that case the use of opium and its abuse are different things. But if, on the other hand, a man's life be contemplated as a whole, as a thing rounded and complete, then the use of opium whether as eaten or smoked is its abuse.

These six months sorely tried the poor girl. When she would do good, evil was present with her. Old impulses were strong and assertive; but the saving power of those guardians who loved her and prayed for her proved stronger. And when Ah Ho had already survived her first three months of probation, she had begun to apprehend that goodness and moral power of which she had been apprehended. Mrs Watt gave Ah Ho to know that the power that was saving her was no human, temporal power. It was God's love in a Saviour and Redeemer, Jesus Christ, whose heart throbbed to raise the fallen and save the lost.

And in time Ah Ho was transferred to Johor. As she is under the guardianship of a good lady there, those hitherto interested in her may return to Singapore. Scores of sampans ply between Edinburgh and Kranjie piers: and a sufficient number of 'buses and rikishas take up the fourteen miles' belt between Kranjie and Singapore city. The electric railway and the steam launch back to Ah Ho in that region ruled by a humane Sultan and his Datos, form a dream of the future. If Ah Ho herself comes back to Singapore at all, it will be in a rikisha.

Teacher Wu and Tek Chiu remained in Singapore. And Mr Samson remained there too. In addition to his regular duties as Fokien interpreter at court, Tek Chiu had continued to tutor Mr Samson for two mornings in the week. Mr Samson was a man of method and constancy. He had therefore already made tolerably good headway in an elementary knowledge of Fokien Chinese.

The name of Samson had long since risen to fame as a pro-opiumist and a man of practical common sense, who could diagnose all missionaries and their doings. During these months Samson had maintained and enlarged the area of his power. His articles on the opium controversy were greedily received by the editor of one of the local Singapore Dailies, a man who had an unbounded stomach and who loved Samson. When readers of the *Singapore Daily Spectator* saw an article with the heading 'Another Blow to the Anti-Opium Agitation,' these clear-headed people—for all Singapore people, and, most of all, readers of the *Singapore Spectator*, are people of discernment—knew at once that Mr Samson had either himself written the article or had been the means of unearthing it from the pit of Indian official journalism. These people would at once read the article aloud, look at each other, and remark slowly and sagely, 'Samson's the coming man.' And people were right. Samson's habit was, having finished his own article, or having alighted upon another article almost as valuable, and written by somebody else on the same subject, to despatch his 'tamby' with all speed to the *Spectator* office. Addison, the editor, seeing the chit-book, and establishing the identity of the sender, would do little more than open the Samsonian envelope. Only one slight alteration was habitually made by an otherwise exacting editor, who was so indulgent with Samson's manuscript. Samson's practice was to underline the words 'Another Blow,' and Addison didn't approve of it. But in time Addison made an arrangement with his compositor to ignore Mr Samson's mark of emphasis, and to make the forcible words 'Another Blow' quite normal in type. That arrangement having been satisfactorily made, Mr Addison would pass the contribution unopened to his compositor. In such wise did Mr Samson's star shine brighter and brighter. It was a sore point with good Mrs Dimpleton and her spouse.

From the first week when Tek Chiu had begun to teach Mr Samson the rudiments of the Chinese language, and the rudiments too, on Mr Samson's own invitation, of Chinese history in relation to Western powers and opium, Mr Samson had left history alone and confined himself to language. But one morning after seven or eight months of tuition, when Samson's duties as a public man had now become too onerous for his having farther time to devote himself to study Chinese, and when Samson was about to part with his teacher, being strengthened by an extra dose of pro-opium literature from a London journal, Samson became vigorously aggressive. Nor was he unjust; for he first of all asked the young Chinaman to state summarily the history of opium-smoking in China, and to state also Britain's attitude to opium, as the Chinaman interpreted it. Samson would be generous. He would give Tek Chiu full scope, and then with the sledge-hammer of criticism he would flatten the Chinaman.

Samson was sitting at morning coffee in his verandah. Tek Chiu was sitting at some little distance from the small table, which groaned beneath Samson's coffee, bread, fruit, and whisky. On that particular morning Tek Chiu had been somewhat distracted before receiving Mr Samson's invitation to recite history. He had been looking at a solid phalanx of black ants moving upwards from one of the legs of the table. This black host was really one of two hosts. White ants, lovers of darkness, were rapidly eating two legs of the pro-opiumist's valuable and indispensable article of furniture. Of the existence of these white ants, who had already successfully turned two of these table legs into shells, neither Tek Chiu nor Mr Samson knew anything. Before that afternoon Samson's table would fall. Meanwhile Tek Chiu had been looking —having a keener eye than the proprietor himself, whose spectacles were an obstacle— at the extraordinary activity of the 'black squad' who had been making a combined assault on the 'whites,' their sworn foes, and who, loving the light and cognisant doubtless of Samson's bread and butter, were now giving themselves an interval for refreshment. Tek Chiu began his recital as the hungry ants were blackening the bottom rim of Samson's bread-plate. And as the young Chinaman proceeded, the Englishman tried to do two things at once—to eat and to ruminate. And he succeeded—not, however, without exceeding his intention. The bridge of black ants was continued far beyond the entrance to Mr Samson's œsophagus—had Mrs Dimpleton and her household only known of this! —and Tek Chiu was now absorbed in his own theme.

The distraction caused by the bridge of ants had passed away from the young Chinaman's mind. Mr Samson crunched on; and Tek Chiu summarised in good English his version of history. He now knew well the English language, and in some important respects he knew English politics too.

Tek Chiu was very foolish. He ought to have known that Samson was 'the coming man,' and that it was bad policy to contradict the weighty opinions of such a dignitary. But Tek Chiu was a reproduction of Teacher Wu, although, in contrast with Wu, he could say hard things of foreigners in a more musical and palatable fashion. Tek Chiu's recital was an attempted comprehensive survey.

At the close of the seventeenth century the Chinaman abroad—in Java—learned to smoke opium In this way the habit was introduced into China. Emigrants from the southern part of the Fokien Province, returning to their native towns and villages with their newly acquired habit, acted as potent missionaries to their fellow-countrymen. The results of the labours of these zealous smokers are manifest at the present time in the millions of the Chinese people who are confirmed opium smokers.

The history of opium-smoking as amongst the Chinese is like the course of a great river. To begin at the source, it was contact with the foreigner which gave opium-smoking a footing in China. Further down the stream, and flowing into it as tributaries, are the earlier Portuguese, Spanish, and Dutch branches of commerce, as carried on at Canton and other parts of China. In this way more than a century ago the opium trade with China was encouraged and fostered. But it remained for the East India Company, and afterwards for its sedulous guardian the British Government, to do the lion's share in the work of bringing opium to the Flowery Land.

For revenue's if not for conscience' sake it is maintained by the defenders of the *status quo* that (1) had the East India Company or even the British Government never existed, the Chinese would all the same be quite as bad as, if not worse than, they now are in this matter of smoking opium. It is averred that what Britain did for China was to put an end to wholesale smuggling, and make a bad trade as respectable as respectability could possibly make it. Those who argue in this way point out further (2) that Britain's first war with China (1838-1842) was waged not on behalf of opium merely, but on behalf of commerce generally, and of humanity as against Chinese arrogance and exclusiveness, which were a standing menace to civilization. That war, it is maintained, is therefore falsely called the Opium War, since the opium traffic was merely an incident in, and not the main cause of, the war. Such is the attempt of the British people to explain their own dealings with China; and such an attempt deserves well of British patriotism. But the Chinese student cannot reasonably adopt such a reading of history.

Beyond the obvious declaration that 'two blacks don't make a white,' the answer to the first of these contentions is involved in the answer to the second. The opium traffic was not a mere incident in the war of 1838-42. The opium traffic was the primary and efficient cause of that war, since (*a*) it had already done much during immediately preceding generations (in which the habit of opium-smoking had assumed alarming proportions) to *create* among the Chinese people and their rulers the very anti-foreign exclusive feeling which formed the pretext for that war, and subsequent wars with China; and (*b*) the results, direct and indirect, of the war of 1838-42, comprising among other things the inconsistency of the British Government in first, through Captain Elliot, condemning openly the opium traffic, and subsequently, through the treaty of Nankin, compelling the Chinese to pay an indemnity of six million taels for the loss of the opium which Commissioner Lin had destroyed—such results speak much more of opium as a cause than as a contingency of the war.

This rightly-named Opium War has leavened all Britain's subsequent dealings with China. The rules as to the opium tariff in the treaty of the Cheefoo Convention, drawn out in 1876, but not ratified till almost ten years later, show how hard it is for even the most high-minded of Christian statesmen to break away entirely from the iniquitous demands which the opium traffic has entailed upon the Chinese nation. The legislation on the question of tariff consisted in the British Government's refusing on behalf of the Indian Government (which, Shylock-like, demanded literal fulfilment of the terms of previous treaties) to allow the Chinese to put their own tariff on opium passing from treaty ports into the interior. Ultimately, in 1886, the British Government, as claimed by Marquis Tseng, as conceded previously by Sir Thomas Wade, and finally as agitated for by anti-opiumists in England, gave large concessions to the Chinese Government in the matter of tariff; holding firmly at the same time to the principle of compelling the Chinese to be, as regards opium in their own interior, 'free traders.' For if the Chinese were allowed to put such a tariff on their own opium as they themselves deemed proper, the trade of the opium merchants, to say nothing of the Indian revenue, would thereby suffer.

Throughout the various important stages of Britain's dealings with China, China has been in the position of a man fighting with his hands tied behind his back. First of all, the Chinese Government really, as well as professedly, abhorred the opium traffic. And when first the Chinese encouraged the growth of the poppy in their own country, it was exclusively to protect their own legitimate interests in a twofold way: (1) by preventing Chinese silver going away out of the country to foreign countries; and (2) by mixing opium as prepared from the Chinese poppy with Indian opium, thus making the opium, as purchasable by victims, less virulent in its physical effects. But now the Chinese as a people, taught to love the drug, grow opium simply because they have the terrible appetite for it. China's policy of self-protection has passed into a policy of self-destruction. Chinese Self-protection is the mother and Chinese Self-destruction is the offspring. And the father of this offspring is the imperial and mercenary policy of a Western nation.

Only lately a British Minister of State declared *ex cathedrâ* that Britain would never again shed the blood of a single human being in defence of the opium trade. The declaration sounds well, but it practically means little. This Chinese child of dishonour named Self-destruction has already been born and cradled. The Chinese mother, whose name is Self-protection, is too weak and careless for the present and even for the future. But she looks back with regret to her purer and brighter past. And she alternately loves and loathes her child.

But the father as well as the mother of a child has a responsibility—a responsibility which in this case is best fulfilled by strangling the hideous offspring. Once, if not now, the mother would have done that, but could not. Now, if pro-opiumists are to be believed, she has neither the power nor the will. As for the father—he has always had the power, which he has however been unwilling to use. Power he certainly has used—power that has protected and fattened the monster. He might yet save the poor mother and retrieve his own honour—but it won't pay; and this is a practical world. New Ministers of State may come and go; but their nephews and first and second cousins have official posts in India, and in other parts of the favoured East, and they know everything. And thus is sung from year to year the same old song—' This is a practical world.'

It must be admitted that Mr Samson had here shown marvellous patience in listening to the young Chinaman's view of the Opium question. He required time to think over what he had heard. And, moreover, it was time for him to go to his godown and for Tek Chiu to go to his duties at the Supreme Court, where he was to be busily engaged that day.

If the ants were making havoc inside, the rain was doing a corresponding work outside. Singapore is a veritable city of destruction. Malay children were swimming in the streets; Klings, remaining in their flooded houses, unclothed lest their neighbours might taunt them with aping aristocracy, were shivering in the cold; young European gents in gharries, turned into square, flat-bottomed boats on account of the flood, were saying nasty things about Municipal Commissioners. These public dignitaries had made themselves disliked because they had failed both to make scupper-holes in the streets and to ward off the boisterous weather by previous contract. In the midst of such things Tek Chiu chanced upon a rikisha. And in the depths of one of these floods he was suddenly held fast. The rikisha-puller, an old hand at his trade, an opium dross eater, had not strength enough at that crisis to pull or push his rikisha. But help came, though tardily. Dross, indeed, had caused the delay. Chinese coolies, including those of the rikisha-pulling order, are not married men; yet they must have opium in some form or another. Hence the use of opium dross, which is opium in its cheapest and deadliest form. An opium victim won't degenerate to deadly dross if he can get the poison in a more palatable form. For such reasons the opium-habit tells most heavily on the cooly classes, not only making rikishas stick in the flood, as Pharaoh's chariots in the Red Sea, but also overthrowing the 'horses,' making them sink heavily and rapidly in a gulf of misery and death. But opium apologists think little of opium dross, and less of the rikisha cooly. Two more dross-eating coolies came on the scene and extricated Tek Chiu. One non-dross-eater could have done the work quite well.

It was the second day of the Assizes. The Court was to open at eleven, and Tek Chiu, despite the floods, had arrived almost an hour before the time. Celestials were thronging the archways that formed the entrance to the Supreme Court halls. A thin and delicate one among the number was standing in dejected, forlorn-looking fashion. He was about to ask Tek Chiu a question, but he suddenly shrank back. Tek Chiu's was a familiar face. Yet the slim Chinaman could not well disappear in the crowd. He felt compelled to speak.

'You are Lin Tek Chiu, I think.'

'Yes. Are you a Black Rock man ? I think somehow I've seen you before.'

'Yes; we have met before. I am not exactly a Black Rock man, but I lived for a long time there. I was first engaged there doing a merchant's business in a small way, and I was Black Rock Christian preacher when I met you.'

'Oh yes, yes. I well remember you now.'

It was Yew Lay. He had arrived from China some time before, having come for a time to these parts in hopes of recovering his health. He had, before leaving China, been vomiting blood; and now, as he stood at the entrance to Singapore Supreme Court, he was the very picture of physical infirmity. He had a sallow, sunken look.

Tek Chiu was still in ignorance as to the Chinese preacher who had been used as the weapon to deprive him of his betrothed. Yew Lay, on the other hand, cognisant of the fact that Min Niang had previously been intended for the Black Rock gambler and prodigal, could not well possess or display much spirit at this unexpected meeting. Nor had Yew Lay time to be conscious of his own particular feelings. What puzzled him was Tek Chiu's cordiality. Chinese politeness is supposed to be used indiscriminately as a genuine means of expressing sentiment and as a cloak of hypocrisy. But Chinamen, in the company of one another, can readily discern sincerity when they meet it. And sincerity was here, which fact added to Yew Lay's discomfort. For Yew Lay assumed, as a matter of course, that Tek Chiu knew what he really did not know—that Min Niang, formerly betrothed to Tek Chiu, was the wife of Yew Lay. Neither of these two young men referred to that subject on their meeting.

'How long have you been in Singapore?' asked Tek Chiu.

'Six weeks. I came down in that cholera ship.'

'Indeed! I know of that affair. Were you a witness at the Magistrate's Court—I mean in that large building over there?'

Tek Chiu pointed as he spoke in the direction of the 'Central.'

'Yes. And I am to appear again as a witness to-day. I would much rather not appear, but I am summoned, and must do so.'

'You will not be asked many questions. There are European witnesses, and these will be heard first. The prisoner is a European, I suppose.'

'Yes, the captain of the ship.'

'The mandarin who is to try the case is a wonderful man. I wish you knew English—you would then understand and appreciate that mandarin's keen and clear insight into everything. I think he is really the greatest man in this part of the world.'

'I am very sorry for the captain,' said Yew Lay.

'And so am I,' said Tek Chiu. 'But you know more of the matter than I do—what do you think of the captain?'

'He did everything that a man could do to heal the sick people on board. He offered medicine to many people, and those who would not take it died.'

'Yet the authorities,' said Tek Chiu, 'condemn the captain, first for not putting up his quarantine flag, and then for wrongly reporting the number of those who died. How many died?'

'A good many. But it is very difficult to say how many. Had Doctor Gordon or some other competent doctor been on board the ship, he might have prevented every single death. Everybody on board had diarrhœa, as most people in China have at a certain part of the year.'

'I fear,' said Tek Chiu, 'that it will go hard against the captain to-day. People here are much afraid of cholera, although medical men are not very plain on the question as to what is contagious and infectious cholera, and what cholera is, as most people living in China have it during the hot season of the year. The captain did wrong, but no doubt his Chinese chinchew advised him to take the course he did. The British people often fail to appreciate Chinese virtues, and just as often they fail to recognise and rightly interpret Chinese vices. They are treating their own countrymen very unjustly in this matter, although, of course, the mandarin to-day can do nothing but give due application to the law as it is.'

'I don't understand the matter at all,' said Yew Lay.

'It is not difficult to understand,' said Tek Chiu. 'Here is an Englishman, a captain of a Chinese-owned ship. The ship is registered as a British ship, in order to escape the responsibilities attached to Chinese ships at Chinese ports. The regulation of the ship internally is entirely according to Chinese ideas. According to British law, the captain is a free agent. But such freedom is merely nominal. In such circumstances he has a great deal more than the ordinary responsibilities and a great deal less than the ordinary privileges of a British seaman. And to-day the law will come down on him and not spare him, while the Chinese chinchew goes absolutely free. It may be law, but it is not justice. The greatest of their own statesmen, Mr Gladstone, has said, "Laws should be so framed as to be—so far as right itself will allow of it—easy to keep and difficult to break." But in this case the law is so framed that circumstances make it for the English captain very easy to break, and very difficult to keep. Yet everybody whom I have heard speak of the matter says, "The captain had no right to listen to the chinchew, who was influenced doubtless by monetary considerations. To escape quarantine would save money to the owners. The captain is therefore to blame." Well, so far as I can see, the captain is much more a victim than a malefactor. Many others in his position have sinned in the same way with impunity. His misfortune is the result chiefly of the collision of two entirely different systems. One past misfortune in my own life—the loss of my wife—is due to a similar cause.'

Yew Lay shrank back a second time.

'The simple fact is,' continued Tek Chiu, as he was about to separate with Yew Lay at the entrance to the Court-hall upstairs, 'that the English people, who are so slow to recognise their real responsibility as a people on some of the great social questions affecting Eastern races, and Chinese in particular, occasionally make scapegoats among themselves. The captain of your ship will be sent to prison. We shall hear a great deal in Court to-day about his responsibility. Nations can sin with impunity, but individuals dare not. In the multitude of sinners there is safety.'

CHAPTER XXI.

HOMEWARD BOUND.

'Don't go,' said Samson to Addison. The two men were discoursing together, and the two monosyllables were uttered in coaxing, imploring strains. Addison was speaking of leaving for Europe. Yes, it had come to that.

By the latest home-mail there had reached Singapore news of a little girl having died of cold and starvation in London, and Addison had reasoned with himself that he too ought to be in that great metropolis to succour other little girls who but for him might share the same sad fate. Addison's was a noble resolve; but Samson—to his discredit be it said—was here trying to quench the flame of the great editor's philanthropy.

'Who would take your place here?' said Samson, who seemed to have turned into wicked Delilah, the goddess of Philistine mammon. 'The tin mines would cease yielding tin. Chinese coolies would cease to have their opium. Bethink you, dear friend, and stay where you are. We cannot afford to lose such as you. And again, think of the Government here, and the unjust military exaction made on this poor Colony by an iniquitous Imperial Government. Think on all these things, and don't desert us.'

And Samson talked Addison over. The P. & O. time-table was relegated to a remote pigeon-hole in the editorial shrine, not, however, without Addison's casting lingering looks at his fetich as he grudgingly stowed it away. But he recovered himself and looked at Samson.

'Then do you really think I may be able to do good work here yet?' asked Addison anxiously.

'I am quite sure of that,' said Samson. And Samson gave emphasis to the assurance. He struck the editor's table. It was another blow dealt by Samson, not with his brain, but with his fist. And the spectacles almost dropped off.

To differentiate Addison and Samson is a task that would result in Addison's favour. These two bosom friends had been talking together, and as no missionary was present, they had both of them with equal warmth been attacking missions. And Addison's logic had been at work. Addison's father, who had been born before his distinguished son, had been gifted with a good head—hence Addison's logic. And hence the proposal to shut up the *Spectator* office.

The crisis that Samson's coaxing and imploring genius averted had come about in this way.

'The penny-in-the-slot subscriptions that are sent out here from England for the upkeep of missionary "labourers" might in all conscience be put to better uses,' said Samson to his friend.

'Amen,' said Addison, who had some knowledge of the Classics.

'Missions in the East are a complete failure and ought not to exist,' continued Samson.

But dull uniformity among kindred spirits was at

that time, as Addison rightly discerned, undesirable. An internal conflict of opposites would give scope for the dialectic powers of a man who was situated, as Addison was, in the position of leader and patron to the community and to the Government.

'My dear Samson,' the editor began, 'you are no doubt right in saying that missions are a failure. But England must rule the several parts of her great Empire by English ideas. She must give education to the Asiatic races, and even in the matter of religion'— it was clear that Addison was condescending here— 'England can scarcely avoid making her influence felt among these races. Yet although I am an Imperialist born and bred, I must confess that the social conditions of human life at home are very perplexing. Think of the benefits we are conferring on these Eastern peoples by our presence here, Samson, and then think of the tens of thousands of poor and outcast at home. Along with missionaries, Samson, you and I are in the wrong place out here. I must tell you now, Samson, what I have for some time had in my mind—and mark you, Samson, I'm serious.'

Addison then concluded his speech in a lower tone, speaking slowly and with dramatic diction: 'I am carefully reconsidering my position.'

There was silence for a few moments, during which time Addison sought and found the time-table. Then followed Samson with his remonstrances, persuasions, and prayers; and all sections of the community and the Government breathed freely once again. The slums of London, Liverpool, and Glasgow, and the 'Dives' of New York had to remain in darkness, a darkness which, nevertheless, was always made visible by Addison when, in his *Spectator*, he dealt with missions. Such references to misery at home Addison invariably made as an atonement for his sin in yielding to Samson and shelving the time-table.

It was quite clear that Addison had a conscience, and quite as clear that Samson hadn't one. In this respect these two men, otherwise sworn brothers, were divided. When Samson referred to mission work among Asiatic races, he simply growled. When Addison dealt with the same unsavoury subject, his was the attitude of a grandmother, now pitying, now scolding her naughty, foolish grandchildren. Addison always spoke of a sympathy with Christian mission work, which he was very sorry to deny to missionaries. And thus the poor missionaries and all their doings were repudiated.

But so far as eloquence on matters missionary was concerned, Addison had to hide his diminished head in presence of Samson. It was Samson's work to speak, not to listen to Addison. Samson, although quite destitute of a conscience and blind to moral discernment, was peculiarly sensitive to pleasure whenever he felt that he had done anything. Leaving Addison's office, Samson felt that, in dissuading the editor from his logic, he had done signal service to Eastern society. By a pill, the constituent elements of which were native States tin, Indian opium, and military contribution gunpowder, Samson had for a time cured Addison of his home-sickness.

In the enjoyment of such self-satisfaction Samson met his Chinese 'coach.' Tek Chiu was ascending the *Spectator* stairs as Samson was descending them.

'Well, what business have *you* here at an English newspaper office? I should imagine, judging from your eloquent remarks on opium the other morning, that you study to have as little to do with us Europeans as you possibly can.'

'You judge wrongly then,' said Tek Chiu. 'I highly esteem English civilization and English people. I neither worship them nor swear at them. Through your nation I have become a Christian—that is one reason why I cannot be quite anti-foreign.'

'A Christian!' sneered Samson in surprise.

'Yes! a Christian,' repeated Tek Chiu without the slightest appearance of discomfiture. 'Through Christianity I have been taught to read history aright. And I condemn you English people not because of your Christianity but because of your want of it.'

Tek Chiu warmed in his words, while Samson, spectacles and all, stood looking at him. It was the first time, felt Samson, that a Chinaman had quarrelled with him. Tek Chiu had previously presumed to differ from Samson. But now he was presumption incarnate.

'Europeans here of your type are the enemies of your own race and of Christianity. To go no further than your own worthy self, let me illustrate my meaning. You are nominally a Christian—an adherent, on your own profession, of the Church of England. And you sneer, forsooth, when you meet an Asiatic who professes Christianity. Yours is an absurd position. The religion of Christ would be worthless, since it would not then be what it professes to be if it is not capable of becoming the religion of all nations of the world. And it is just because it has the germs of universality in it that it is true.'

'The Christian Chinamen whom I have hitherto met

are not so zealous as you seem to me to be,' 'said Samson in sneering tones, yet compelled to be respectful.

'I don't wonder at that. There is very little Christian life among your people to help them or to give them zeal. I read regularly your *Spectator* articles, and I am compelled to pass my own judgment upon them as to their value.'

The first part of this last sentence, which stated that Tek Chiu regularly read Samson's articles, pleased Samson well enough. But the closing part of his sentence put Tek Chiu completely out of court. It was bad policy of Tek Chiu to pass reflections on Samson's articles. That was a tender subject with an otherwise invulnerable man.

'You will pardon me for saying,' continued Tek Chiu, 'that I think your great ability might be better employed than in sneering at men who are striving to serve their Master and to make valid your own professed faith.'

Tek Chiu's politic tribute to Samson's ability had a slightly softening effect. But Samson was still in fighting form. When Samson felt that he had a blow to deal, he was particularly anxious not to miss his opportunity. Although he had some business on hand, he waited to take his revenge out of the young Chinaman with whom he had not had a discussion since the morning of the ants and the rain. And that discussion had been rather one-sided: it was Samson's turn now.

'European missions have been spending money all these years, and what is the result—a few stragglers removed from the compact mass of millions not yet Christianised. How do you account for that?'

'Christianity has never yet come to a people without a desperate struggle against manifold opposing forces. Christianity takes time.'

'Well,' said Samson, 'facts speak for themselves. Think of the waste of English money here in Singapore, and think of the miserable results. And what would it all amount to, supposing the results, consisting in a large number of Eastern converts, were much better than they are?'

Tek Chiu replied: 'Missions are not at the present time showing phenomenal results anywhere, it is true, and here in Singapore tangible results are very far from being even in the ordinary sense successful. I admit that. But what are the causes of missionary failure here? It is quite reasonable to concede that here, as elsewhere, the missionaries are not the best possible men. These missionaries themselves are often reminded of this fact. But again the European community here is only nominally, not really, Christian. I am of course speaking of them as a whole. The Europeans here enjoy all the fruits of a Christian civilization in respect of culture and physical comfort. They are justly censurable on two counts: (1) Ingratitude to the source of their civilization; and (2) Contempt, so often ill-concealed, for Eastern races, and for the claim which these races have to enjoy Christianity. For such reasons I respectfully submit that those most responsible for missionary failure are the very people who, as moth victims attracted to the light of cynicism, are themselves absorbed into surrounding heathenism. They are the people who fall victims to this homesick fever, and who grudge Christian missionaries among Eastern peoples their work. The real fact is that a great many of you people yourselves have lost the power of the Christian life, if you ever had it at all. You cannot therefore be expected to sympathise with others who have this power, and who are desirous that Orientals should have it too.'

But Samson and the young Chinaman could not well come to terms either of agreement or of argument. The categories that guided their thought were entirely distinct—this fact neither of the combatants quite recognised; and therefore Samson, taking speech in hand, said many smart things. He took time to blaze and blow on. He repeated his articles in the *Spectator*. He made careful quotations from these articles. Samson's habit was to commit to memory whatever he wrote. At that juncture—the foot of the *Spectator* stairs had been reached in course of the conversation —Samson felt himself to be rich and powerful in resource.

'And then it is utterly absurd,' said Samson, as he resumed for a moment the thread of the historical argument against the opium traffic, 'it is utterly absurd to speak of doing away with the opium revenue, even admitting that the trade is bad. This is one of the many new freaks of Exeter Hall. Anti-opium faddism takes for granted that all nations will act righteously if Britain foregoes her revenue. It is an absurd supposition. Other countries would continue to grow opium.

'And China, even although her Government were to prohibit the trade by law (which is very doubtful), would connive at, or at anyrate would be unable to prevent, wholesale smuggling of opium into the country. In addition to all that, there is moreover the great fact that the Chinese themselves cultivate the poppy more and more from year to year.'

'Those grave difficulties which you enumerate as standing in the way of a complete suppression policy serve but to demonstrate first and before all else the disastrous consequences of the pro-opium policy as hitherto pursued. The anti-opium policy has yet to be put to the test. I should simply remind you that no act of true morality, whether the act of an individual or that of a nation, has as yet been done under the ideal conditions you desiderate as necessary ere Britain can withdraw from the opium traffic. As with a man, so with a nation. Doing any noble act involves incurring a risk of loss caused by others acting ignobly. But for a righteous nation the loss can be but temporary. In the end righteousness is a gain. If Britain desires a guarantee of goodness to be forthcoming from other nations ere she makes amends for what is her own special wrongdoing, then Christian morality is in that direction stifled and destroyed. British morality in the matter of the opium traffic is not Christian morality. Britain, that boasts pre-eminence among Western nations, refuses to claim pre-eminence in the right sense at any point where opium transactions are involved. There she ceases to be the pioneer, and becomes the opponent of that highest morality which advances only as it lives and lives only as it advances, carrying world-wide humanity along with it, to higher and better things.'

It was clear to Tek Chiu that Samson was homeward bound both with respect to Christian missions and opium revenues. Not all Tek Chiu's powers of argument could convince Samson as to Christianity and Christian morality. In vain did Tek Chiu seek to convince this strong one, that if he admitted the truth of Christianity at all, his anti-missionary policy would have excluded Samson from Singapore. Samson and his friends would, by applying the test of his own principle, have been still in Judea, far from his own native land, far from those 'Augæan stables,' as he used to term his favourite slums, probably round about Jerusalem, or in some well-fortified classic spot within the walls of Jericho. Addison might have told Samson this. But Addison's own mind was more occupied with the timetable than with the map of Palestine.

Tek Chiu was evidently on his way to see Mr Addison, and naturally enough Samson was uneasy about it. Might not Addison listen to this presumptuous Asiatic, and weakly rummage the remote pigeon-hole? But Samson, though he hesitated for a moment, walked steadily away from the *Spectator* office. He would think better things of his dear friend and of his own recent achievement.

There were in Singapore other homeward-bound men besides Addison and his great friend Samson.

CHAPTER XXII.

THE OLD AND NEW COVENANT.

YEW LAY did not long survive the worries of witness-bearing. In a little room behind a Chinese mission chapel in Singapore, the habitation of the preacher who belonged to Mrs Watt's Mission, Yew Lay was breathing his last. He had requested Tek Chiu's presence a few hours before the end; but Tek Chiu was engaged in the bustle of his ordinary duties, and did not arrive till late—too late for Yew Lay to be able to speak with him, or even recognise him. The dying man had shown anxiety to speak with the young interpreter. But it was not to be. Yew Lay died. And he was carried upward by the angels to be the companion of Lazarus, at a place a long way off from the rich man's region—that region, the geography and climate of which the young Chinaman had carefully studied and taught. In this way Yew Lay's studies were brought to an end: it cannot be supposed that the citizens of the New Jerusalem, in the perfect activity of their perfect life, continue to think of the hell from which they themselves have escaped. Yew Lay had preached hell from beginning to end of the chapter of his preaching career on earth. Nor was his work vain. Men had trembled at Yew

Lay's message, as the Scottish Queen had trembled at
the tragic thunder-peals of the great Reformer. Overawed by these thunderings of Sinai, men who but for
these louder sounds would have continued to live and
die in their sin, thus compelled to think of life's
meaning and destiny, had come at last, with minds
prepared to hear and love the sweet music of Calvary.
Such men were the trophies of Yew Lay's warfare.
And Yew Lay, as a good and faithful servant, had
earned his Master's 'Well done.' Yew Lay, with all
the faults of his too cleanly cut dogma, had preached
no syrupy Gospel.

Only a fortnight before had news been sent to
friends in China, informing them of his serious illness.
The tone of that letter had presaged his early death.
When the gloomy prophecy was now fulfilled, a second
letter was sent off. It was addressed to Mr Richmond,
sent off by Hok Soan, the Singapore mission preacher.
But ere the second letter reached its destination, Yew
Lay's young wife had left China on her way to
Singapore. Dr and Mrs Sefton, with their two little
children, on the point of leaving Turnabout on their way
home for furlough to England when the earlier of the
two letters arrived, gladly took the benefit of Mrs
Yew Lay's assistance as far as Singapore. The younger
Seftons badly needed a nurse, and Mrs Yew Lay herself, somewhat consistent with traditions attached to a
previous generation of the Pun Kwi family, had not
yet during these years been blessed with a child. Not
without haste and difficulty had Mrs Yew Lay left
Turnabout. But Min Niang was a devoted wife, who
owed a duty to her invalid—haply dying—husband.

Thus, ere the grand and spacious English mail

steamer that carried the Seftons, their children and nurse away from Hong-Kong, reached Singapore, the husband of Min Niang was no more. A few miles out from the city of Singapore, Yew Lay had already been buried. Black Rock, and Three Tree Well, and China would never see him again.

Mrs Watt and the Bible-woman met the young widow at the steamer, and tenderly informed her of her widowhood. Poor Min Niang!

Min Niang would stay with Mrs Watt's Bible-woman until a suitable opportunity would present itself for her return to China. A tender and affectionate letter from Miss Stonebridge, written immediately after the news of Yew Lay's death had reached Turnabout, charged Min Niang to wait with Mrs Watt until Mrs Richmond, who was at that time leaving England, would be passing through Singapore, and then Min Niang would get a favourable return to her fatherland. Min Niang dutifully received the letter. She was glad to sojourn for a time in the land where her dear husband lay buried. And the lady missionary, Mrs Watt, and the Bible-woman, A Kim, were so kind to her!

Poor Min Niang! Even although she stayed in Singapore, she could not raise her dear husband from the dead. Yet for all that she liked the place and the people. A sojourn of six weeks confirmed her in her likings.

Mrs Richmond's steamer had, according to a telegram received, already left Penang. It was a Monday night. The steamer was to arrive in Singapore next morning. Early in the afternoon Min Niang was to leave, along with Mrs Richmond, for China, away from a city of sadness and love. Mrs Watt and A Kim, the Bible-woman, having become very fond of the beautiful and gentle young widow, were very, very sorry to part with her. Yes; A Kim was at that time giving to Min Niang a free expression of her feelings, when Mrs Watt came also in to suggest to Min Niang that a young man who had been a kind friend to her husband might speak with her for a little. He had come with letters, which he wished Mrs Yew Lay to kindly take for him to China. Wu and Tek Chiu had succeeded in making up between them a tolerably respectable packet; and hearing that the young widow was to leave for China next day, they wished to seize the opportunity of communicating with friends in the old country.

'As this young man was very kind to your husband, I'm sure you would like to see him,' said Mrs Watt. 'He has some letters for his folks in China. I'll ask him to come in. It was he,' said Mrs Watt, leaving the room, and intending the last sentence especially for A Kim, 'it was he who took so much trouble in the matter of that Cantonese girl's rescue.'

Tek Chiu, in his dealings with Mrs Watt in that affair of Ah Ho, had avoided through delicacy going into details as to Ah Ho's younger days, and the exact circumstances that had led him to be specially interested in her. And Ah Ho, during all these months of constant fellowship with Mrs Watt and A Kim, had avoided elaborating the circumstances of her ill-advised escape from Black Rock. Ah Ho's remorse, which had made her speak sadly and often about her own past, had invariably caused her to half conceal her story at such times as when she recounted it. And during these weeks of Mrs Yew Lay's sojourn in Singapore, she was never thought of as having aught to do either with the rescued slave-girl or the promoted cooly.

Tek Chiu was unwilling to see any young widow. He wished Mrs Watt to convey to Mrs Yew Lay his greetings, with the hope that God would protect her on her journey back to China.

Mrs Watt—foolish lady, who did not sufficiently appreciate Chinese delicacy—coaxed, and ultimately prevailed upon Tek Chiu to speak with Mrs Yew Lay in person. 'The poor girl would, I am sure, be pleased to see the man who had treated her dying husband with so much kindness. You give her these letters yourself. I won't take them.'

Mrs Watt prevailed with Tek Chiu. But persuasion takes time. In the interval A Kim was making explanations to her friend.

'I have quite neglected to tell you about the interesting release of the girl Ah Ho—a Cantonese girl, who speaks our dialect. Liu Tek Chiu, who comes here now, knew about Ah Ho in China, and he has been the means of saving the girl from her bad life.'

Poor Min Niang! She listened with terrible earnestness to A Kim's remarks, without uttering a word in return. Would she faint? No; she would conceal her bewilderment. There was no time for thought. Tek Chiu entered the room, with his face steeped in crimson blushes, and his eyes turned towards the venetians, as though he felt that the weather outside was tempting.

Love-making and heart-breaking in China and among the Chinese are sorely hemmed in by custom. But are not these clothes of custom only clothes, after all? The romance of love is ubiquitous. Chinese life is human life too.

Poor Min Niang! There was Tek Chiu, the very image of his father, and yet more handsome-looking. Tek Chiu felt awkward in the presence of Yew Lay's widow, just as he would have felt in the presence of any woman. But Min Niang was more self-possessed and more unhappy too. She kept looking steadily at her rejected, exiled lover. How gentle he seemed, and yet how manly!

Min Niang, who sighed for an earthquake, possessed the usual heritage of womankind. She could act her part well. Had Tek Chiu, feeling himself clumsy and in the way, been more critical than he was, he would not have even then been able to see Mrs Yew Lay's heart—so effectively did the young widow conceal her perturbation of mind and soul.

'I cannot thank you enough for your kindness to my poor husband. You had met him in China, I suppose?'

'Yes, I knew your husband in Black Rock. But what I did for him here was very little. I only wish I had met him oftener.'

It was clear to Min Niang that Tek Chiu did not identify her. She could therefore hold out a little longer. Tek Chiu continued to speak.

'I don't suppose you know my friends in China. I have very few near relatives there now. Do you know Black Rock?'

As Tek Chiu was asking a question here, it was necessary—absolutely necessary—for him to look at the lady. A rapid, furtive glance, the first since his father's funeral, years before, and in the process of throwing it somewhere at a point in space on a twelve feet line that sloped downwards and described the lover's angle, Tek Chiu met and recognised the eye of his betrothed wife. It was all the work of an instant. He caught up the letters which he had already laid on the table, and disregarding for the only time in his life the laws of politeness, he rushed headlong out of the room.

Min Niang, as was proper for any woman in the circumstances, fainted. Restoratives having been applied, Mrs Watt, addressing A Kim in Malay, commented on the young man's strange behaviour and on Min Niang's break-down.

Poor Min Niang! A new calamity that came so early in the history of her widowhood! She told A Kim as well as she could her story, the substance of which was communicated by the astonished A Kim to Mrs Watt.

'Chinese customs are peculiar,' said Mrs Watt to herself. 'Yew Lay was doubtless a good husband, but Tek Chiu would have been a better one. But no doubt the girl's highest good was consulted by those managing the matter. Tek Chiu might have turned out bad, but he hasn't. It is a world of surprises. A man who became President of the United States was in his early days disappointed in love, because the lady of his choice didn't think his calling in life sufficiently genteel for her taste. And it seems that Chinese, like American choice, is often misdirected too.'

The heavy sea of Min Niang's distress having somewhat moderated, A Kim recited the story of Ah Ho. And within a few hours of the firing of the gun that would announce the arrival of the P. & O. mail steamer and Mrs Richmond, the young widow heard the tragic story of the dear girl-companion of her childhood.

'And the young interpreter took all that trouble with Ah Ho, did he?' Min Niang ventured to ask.

'Yes; and succeeded at last, at great personal sacrifice,' said A Kim.

'I think you said he was also very kind to my dear husband.'

'Yes. Your husband often told Mrs Watt that the interpreter was the brightest and best and kindest young man in Singapore.'

'My husband was always very extravagant in his language,' said Min Niang. It was time to put on the break. The widow's own heart was driving furiously.

'I must see Ah Ho,' said Min Niang. It was the first practical remark she had made from the depths of her overwhelming bewilderment and perplexity.

Poor Min Niang! Why did she feel, as she lay that night tossing on a sleepless couch, like a ship in a troublous sea, as though she had been hurled into a pit of bottomless perdition? The cause of it all was the acknowledged and undisputed nobility of a character. Min Niang on that night would have slept the sleep of peace had the graduate's son remained undiscovered, or even had he, having been discovered, proved to be as she had once thought him to be—a blackguard. But Tek Chiu was a hero. Hence Min Niang's bitter weeping.

Min Niang's nature was not ignoble. Those who knew her best, among these the two Salisbury ladies, never had doubts as to the beauty and sweetness of her nature. Nor was their judgment wrong. All the same, Min Niang was miserable. Her lover had outlived her rejection, and had excelled and outshone her past habitual estimate of him. And Min Niang blamed no one but herself. She herself had willed to accept a husband, to the violation of her father's ancient covenant, and to the violation, too, of her own best interests, had she only been gifted with sufficient knowledge and wisdom at the seasonable time to know exactly what these interests were. As it was, things had been otherwise ordered. Had not she acted for the best? Had not Tek Chiu remained a heathen while still in China, and was not his reputation ere he left Black Rock a discreditable one? Had not God guided her? Yes, but God's guidance is His own. Although He has guided Min Niang and all the other members of His great family, such guidance is planned not as a cause but as a consequence of his children's short-sightedness. God's plan had surely been fulfilled. And part of that plan which was being fulfilled was to smite Min Niang heavily with the chastisement of distress.

Enticing consolation by falling back on the glorious truth of Divine guidance, Min Niang snatched an hour from the dawning day and slept restlessly. But even then she dreamed of her father's rebuke. In that brief sleep graduate Ming Kuang's look of reproach haunted her. And she saw too a young man with a torch in his hand, that lit up in the darkness his own noble face. Min Niang awoke, frightened at the dream, to find alas! that the dream was real, and that there was therefore no escape from it. For it had actually been made plain to her on the previous night that persistently and at last successfully Tek Chiu, whom she wronged, had entered the dungeon hovel of ruin, and rescued the wayward companion of her childhood. Min Niang had come now to feel that she was unworthy of the man whom she had taught herself to despise.

And what did all this mean? It meant that a six weeks' widow—if the thoughts of her heart could only have been revealed—was guilty of having fallen in love with one who was not her deceased husband. There are those who affirm that a widow's love should be confined to memory. That is a rigid and perhaps right restriction,—a restriction, however, in accordance with which Min Niang's love for Tek Chiu can be justified. Min Niang's heart was now on the rack of distracting duties and sensations. Was not Tek Chiu her real husband? To analyse such thoughts was too much for Min Niang or for any other stronger-minded woman. She had simply to recognise what she felt—that her heart had been humbled and crushed. The experiences of the past evening had turned the tables. Three years before and since that time it had been said that Tek Chiu had lost his bride. The newer and more accurate version, as Min Niang now read it, was that Tek Chiu's bride had lost her bridegroom. All this was rather hard on Yew Lay and his blameless memory. But that young preacher could not well have averted the old wine-party which had taken place before his time. The old covenant had been outraged. But a new covenant was yet to be, and it would fulfil the old.

. . . .

'You have brought the letters back?' said Wu. 'Does the lady not sail? Could not Mrs Watt entrust the foreign missionary lady with them, then?'

Wu was asking many questions. His young friend's silent, dreamy demeanour was puzzling him.

Tek Chiu at last in measured sentences described the incident to Wu.

'She is none other than Min Niang,' he said. 'She is as beautiful as ever, and with the same sparkling diamond look in her eyes. She is just as she was when both of us were very little children together.'

Tek Chiu's knowledge of English and English books had for the moment made him say what he thought; but the blunder was only the blunder of a moment. That reticence as to love and its emotions which the Chinese call modesty had for that very short interval seemed to lose its power over the young Chinaman. And Wu—Wu of all men—tacitly commended this disgraceful outrage on Chinese propriety. The old wine-party was again intoxicating Wu, and making even him insensible to politeness.

There was long silence in the sanctum. Tek Chiu had already spent himself. Either he was ashamed of his own allusion to the diamond eyes or he was still thinking about them. At all events, he was now speechless.

The old oracle spoke again. Wu had something weighty to say. It was as though the old graduate was pronouncing judgment with respect to the quality of American degrees. And the young interpreter gave that respect to the Nestorian dictum which he was accustomed to give to the English Chief Justice, whom he could never sufficiently admire.

'She is a six weeks' widow, but she is your wife.'

Wu had here created an earthquake. Yes, it was a revolution, and conservative Wu was the author of it! About earthquakes Tek Chiu had heard that they often took place in Java. But Singapore was now being visited. Accustomed as Tek Chiu was to hear court sentences, the most thrilling of his past experiences in that connection were as stiff breezes compared with this typhoon. He was too directly concerned in this matter to be otherwise than dumfoundered.

And Wu re-enacted Samson's part by means of another blow.

'She must remain here, let people in China say what they choose. Of course you must not shock society by marrying your wife at once. She can wait a year and bewail her widowhood. In that matter our customs will be duly honoured. But we must have respect unto the old covenant. To-morrow I shall consult with Mrs Watt, and afterwards I shall interview Mrs Richmond.'

Tek Chiu had recovered himself. 'Min Niang must not remain here. Nor must she on any account fulfil our long-since-annulled betrothal if she has no wish to do so. She is but now a widow; and to even mention the matter to her would be the quintessence of scandal.'

Wu had lost his fierceness now, as he looked gently into the young man's face. It seemed for the moment as though Tek Chiu had convinced him. The scandal argument was calculated to have weight with the elder Chinaman.

'Well,' said Wu, who had not quite lost his position, 'supposing Min Niang is herself willing to honour the old covenant, and honour herself too by marrying you —what then?'

Tek Chiu smiled and blushed. Min Niang's diamond eyes were glistening in those of her rejected exile, as Teacher Wu could right well discern.

. . . .

But opposition came from a certain quarter. It was through Cheng Ann. Cheng Ann had returned from following his father. He was again sojourning in Singapore and the neighbourhood. The gambling dens of Johor took him over there occasionally. He could not well go there in the capacity of Carey, gambling being one of the main supports of the state and territory of Johor. Cheng Ann went over to assist the revenue.

And Cheng Ann met Ah Ho as that girl, restored to much of her former beauty, was leisurely driving a perambulator along one of the quiet roads outside of Johor town. He spoke to her, and she answered him first with scorn, then with reproach, and then at last with love. Poor Ah Ho, not long above the waters of ruin! Was not he the father of her only child, a tiny cherub that she had never seen?—for the babe had been carried off she knew not where. Cheng Ann induced her to leave Johor, to live with him as his wife in Singapore. To this big promise Cheng Ann brought himself merely to avert Ah Ho's scorn and feed his own vanity and selfishness. His trump card was a promise to explore Singapore for the lost babe.

The rikisha-puller who was aiding Ah Ho and her captor on the occasion of their elopement from Johor paused at Bukit Timak on the way to Singapore. The cooly had to eat bean-curd and drink a mysterious solution of syrup-water and other chemicals.

At that critical moment a small carriage drawn by a small pony and occupied by two people was passing the rikisha. The occupants of the carriage were Mrs Watt and Min Niang, who were on their way to Johor on a visit to Ah Ho.

Mrs Watt at once recognised Ah Ho; and by this unexpected meeting the latter's journey was wonderfully shortened. The scene was comedy and tragedy in one. Mrs Watt had little difficulty in rescuing Ah Ho once more. Cheng Ann—obliging man that he was—had very seasonably brought the girl thus far on her journey, and Min Niang's desire to meet Ah Ho was all the sooner satisfied.

Beautiful Min Niang addressed Cheng Ann in beautiful Fokien: 'You must claim the girl in a lawful way if you wish to marry her, and you must first prove your sincerity. You are not to be trusted.'

It was Miss Stonebridge and Pun Lun over again. And the words stung and exasperated Cheng Ann.

Mrs Watt too had her innings. 'The Government here give too much protection to the wickedness of you, and such as you. The marriage laws of this place with respect to the Straits-born Chinese are a disgrace to a Christian country. You seem to think that you can ruin a woman at your pleasure. You wouldn't dare do that in China.'

Mrs Watt and Min Niang, who were not to be defrauded of their trip, proceeded to Johor, leading back the runaway with the cords of love.

Cheng Ann, snubbed and sent about his business, began to hate both goodness itself and those who loved it. His conscience was not yet dead, and for this reason chiefly he was either unable or disinclined to answer the reproaches of these two women.

Tek Chiu soon heard the story. His first impulse was to meet Cheng Ann and give him a good sound flogging. Ere long these two companions of tobacco-cultivation met; and Tek Chiu opened his mouth and his mind, denouncing Cheng Ann to his face with alternating scorn and sarcasm.

Cheng Ann—as the Chinese language literally has it —'looked small.' In his heart he vowed vengeance against the independent indigent cooly. Cheng Ann felt with some degree of accuracy that Tek Chiu owed much to him. And instead of being humble and grateful, his attitude towards his benefactor was now that of contempt and scorn.

. . . .

Another year passed by; and then it was that Cheng Ann got his opportunity for revenge. The books of the Great Dragon Lodge of the Ho Seng Society were duly surrendered to Government by Cheng Ann, Executioner, who had been, contrary to usage, custodier also of documents. Lin Tek Chiu, an escaped murderer from China, was known, as Cheng Ann pointed out, to be an active sympathiser with secret societies not registered, and therefore under the ban of the Government. On the eve of his wedding Tek Chiu was arrested and lodged in the civil jail. The qualifying adjective did not lessen the plight.

Levying blackmail on brothels and on street refreshment vendors, training and feeding pick-pockets, stealing watches, subsidising native policemen, paying men to go to jail as substitutes for monied offenders—by such dark things coming to light the Chinese hoeys were proclaimed unlawful, and suppressed. Another Society—the Chinese Advisory Board—constituted by the Government, would take the place of those swarming hoeys, as so much satisfaction to the democratic aspiration. That Board had not yet been formed when Tek Chiu was put under arrest.

Teacher Wu, grief-stricken and anxious at this latest turn of events, yielded to his own urgent counsel and to Min Niang's tears, and interviewed an influential, law-abiding Chinaman who was powerful with the Chinese people and with the Government.

Tek Chiu's bad reputation as an escaped murderer from China had gone against him. In the administration of the Society's Ordinance a man's character rather than his conduct was the principal thing. But Wu at last successfully convinced the great Chinaman that Tek Chiu's life as touching the law had been a beautiful and a blameless one. There was therefore no difficulty with a reasonable Governor, who decreed that Tek Chiu should be neither imprisoned nor deported. And Cheng Ann dutifully left for Penang, whither his father had again called him.

If certain auspices had frowned, others had smiled, on Min Niang's wedding. Miss Eva Stonebridge and Miss Minnie Sand were among those who greatly rejoiced in the good news about Min Niang and in the approved worth of her old betrothed. It was quite enough for these two ladies to be assured of Tek Chiu's worth, and of Min Miang's own sweet will. During that long interval of time Miss Stonebridge had remained with her younger friend in Salisbury. Old and new missionaries went and came, but the energy and devotion of these two ladies, like Lord Tennyson's brook, kept flowing on.

Nothing but the genuine, current coin of Love could purchase love. A bi-metallic theory in Love's kingdom is untenable. In the case of Tek Chiu and Min Niang, Love's true condition had 'clearly been satisfied. And the new covenant in time was ratified in marriage. Teacher Wu presided.

. . . .

The character of a Chinese tale or anything else Chinese requires that the end should be known from the beginning. Pre-determination has been spoken of as a deity that sits enthroned in the heart of the Celestial Empire, ruling and directing the myriads of his worshippers whom he claims as his children. But Pre-determination, designated deity, is a mere abstraction. It is rather an essential attribute of an Eternal Father, who claims the Chinese people as His own, to vouchsafe to them in this age and in coming ages His Liberty and His Love. And, claiming His children, He with whom there is neither beginning nor end of days, claims too that they should learn and know their own past aright. The fault of the Chinese people is not that they look back, but that they don't look back far enough—back along the lengthy line of their own time to a point before that time, back to their Creator and Redeemer Himself, their fathers' Father, and their Father too, with whom is the reconciliation and explanation of all conflicting truths. The two truths of Necessity and Freedom, their true distinction, interdependence, and inter-connection, easily baffle the defining powers of thinking men. The Chinese Christian missionary problem can offer no mean contribution of help towards the removal of one of the most perplexing of philosophic difficulties.

If the Chinese, as the most Calvinistic of peoples, have the vices, they have also the virtues of Calvinism; and that is saying a good deal for China. Every student of the great Chinese problem, everyone that works and prays for the coming of the Redeemer's kingdom among that race which constitutes the half of the hitherto non-Christian world, may reasonably expect that the Chinese Christianity of the future will not belong to the jelly-fish type. It will have backbone. If quality count for anything at all, the last, because the slowest, of the great races of humanity will yet become the first.

.   .   .   .

A widow's marriage is seldom romantic. But the marriage of Min Niang with Tek Chiu was romantic if ever marriage was. On that day when Min Niang gave herself to Tek Chiu, she married, not her second husband, but her first.

THE END.

www.ingramcontent.com/pod-product-compliance
Lightning Source LLC
Chambersburg PA
CBHW022051230426
43672CB00008B/1141